The Rise and Fall
of the
Greek Colonels

The Rise and Fall of the Greek Colonels

C. M. WOODHOUSE

FRANKLIN WATTS
New York 1985

First published in the United Kingdom in 1985 by
Granada Publishing

First United States publication 1985 by Franklin Watts
387 Park Avenue South, New York, NY 10016

ISBN 0–531–09798–6

Dedicated to
PANAYIOTIS KANELLOPOULOS
a great scholar and a great
enemy of all dictatorships

Contents

Acknowledgements   viii
List of Abbreviations   ix
Personalities   x

1   Men of tomorrow   *1963–67*   1
2   Coup d'état or revolution?   *April 1967*   16
3   Resistance and reaction   *April–December 1967*   33
4   The monstrous regiment   *1968*   49
5   Onward, Christian soldiers!   *1969*   63
6   A new era   *1970*   74
7   The American commitment   *1971*   87
8   Towards a home port   *1971–72*   100
9   Turn of the tide   *January–November 1973*   112
10   The students' revolt   *November 1973*   126
11   Down a steep place   *November 1973–July 1974*   142
12   Yesterday's men   *1974–81*   161

Note on sources   174
References   176
Bibliography   185
Index   188

Acknowledgements

I gratefully acknowledge the help of Mrs M. Anastasopoulou, Librarian of Parliament in Athens, who made available to me a number of books which were otherwise unobtainable; of Mr Solon Grigoriadis, who kindly provided me with a copy of his valuable *Istoria tis Diktatorias (History of the Dictatorship)*; and of Mr Peter Thompson, who made available to me the information which he had garnered as Secretary of the European–Atlantic Action Committee on Greece.

For other sources, I am indebted to the Burrows Library at King's College, University of London; the Reference Library of the London School of Economics and Political Science; and the Newspaper Library of the British Museum at Colindale.

C. M. W.

Abbreviations

AEM	Anti-dictatorship Workers' Front
ASPIDA	'Shield' (also an acronym for 'Officers, Save Fatherland, Ideals, Democracy and Meritocracy')
CGS	Chief of the General Staff
CIA	Central Intelligence Agency
DA	Democratic Defence
EAACG	European–Atlantic Action Committee on Greece
EAM	National Liberation Front
EAN	Greek Anti-dictatorship Youth
EDA	Union of the Democratic Left
EDKA	Greek Democratic Movement of Resistance
EEC	European Economic Community
EENA	Union of Young Greek Officers
EK	Centre Union
EOKA	National Organization of Cypriot Combatants
EPOK	National Cultural Movement
ERE	National Radical Union
ESA	National Military Security
IDEA	Sacred League of Greek Officers
JUSMAGG	Joint United States Military Assistance Group in Greece
KET	Armoured Training Centre
KKE	Communist Party of Greece
KNE	Communist Youth of Greece
KYP	Central Service of Information
LOK	Units of Mountain Raiders (Commandos)
ND	New Democracy
PAK	Panhellenic Liberation Movement
PAM	Patriotic Anti-dictatorship Front
UNFICYP	United Nations' Force in Cyprus

Personalities

Angelis, Odysseus: born 1912; commissioned (Army) 1934; CGS 1967–8; Commander-in-Chief of Defence Forces, 1969–73; Vice-President of Republic 1973; sentenced to 20 years imprisonment 1975

Athanasiadis-Novas, George: (1893–1984); entered Parliament 1926; President of Chamber 1964–5; Prime Minister 1965

Averoff-Tositsa, Evangelos: born 1910; entered Parliament 1946; Foreign Minister 1956–61; Minister of Defence 1974–81; Leader of New Democracy 1981–4

Bitsios, Dimitrios: born 1915; entered Foreign Service 1939; Private Secretary to King Constantine 1966–7; Foreign Minister 1974–7

Brillakis, A.: born 1924; entered Parliament 1951; Leader of Communist Party (Interior) during dictatorship

Clerides, Glavkos: born 1919; trained as lawyer in Cyprus and London; President of Cypriot National Assembly 1960–76; Acting President of Republic of Cyprus 1974

Constantine II, King: born 1940; succeeded to Crown 1964; married Princess Anne-Marie of Denmark same year; left Greece 1967; deposed 1973; monarchy abolished by plebiscite 1974

Demirel, Suleiman: born 1924; Prime Minister of Turkey 1965–71, 1975–7, 1979–80

Denktash, Raouf: born 1924; trained as lawyer in Cyprus and London; President of Turkish Communal Chamber, Cyprus, 1960–73; Vice-President of Republic of Cyprus from 1973

Ecevit, Bülent: born 1925; entered Turkish Parliament 1957; Prime Minister 1974, 1977, 1978–9

Fleming, Lady: born (Amalia Koutsouri) 1913; married Sir Alexander Fleming 1953; entered Parliament 1977

Frederika, Queen: (1917–81); married King Paul (as Crown Prince) 1938; Queen of the Hellenes 1947–64

Garouphalias, Petros: (1901–84); entered Parliament 1932; Minister of Defence 1964–5

Grivas, George: (1898–1974); commissioned (Army) 1919; leader of clandestine organizations, 'X' (1943), EOKA (1955–9), EOKA-B (1973–4); Lieutenant-General in Greek Army 1959; commanded Greek and Cypriot armed forces 1964–7

Iliou, Ilias: born 1904; entered Parliament 1951; Leader of left-wing EDA from 1956

Ioannidis, Dimitrios: born 1923; commissioned (Army) 1943; Brigadier commanding ESA 1969; sentenced to life imprisonment 1975

Kanellopoulos, Panayiotis: born 1902; Professor, Athens University 1932; entered Parliament 1935; Vice-Premier and Minister of Defence 1942; Prime Minister 1945, 1967

Karamanlis, Constantine: born 1907; entered Parliament 1935; Prime Minister 1955–63 and 1974–80; President of the Republic 1980

Kollias, Constantine: born 1901; Prosecutor to Supreme Court (Areopagus) 1962–7; Prime Minister 1967

Küchük, Fazil: born 1906; Vice-President of Republic of Cyprus 1960–73

Kyprianou, Spyridon: born 1932; Foreign Minister of Cyprus 1960–72; President of National Assembly 1976–7; President of Republic from 1977

Makarezos, N.: born 1919; commissioned (Army) 1941; Minister of Co-ordination 1967–71; Deputy Prime Minister 1971–3; condemned to death for high treason 1975 (commuted to life imprisonment)

Makarios III, Archbishop of Cyprus: (1913–77); leader of campaign for *enosis* (union with Greece) 1950–59; elected Archbishop 1950; President of Republic of Cyprus 1960–77

Mangakis, George A.: born 1922; entered Parliament 1974; Minister of Justice 1981

Markezinis, Sp.: born 1909; entered Parliament 1946; Minister of Co-ordination 1952–4; Prime Minister 1973

Mavros, George: born 1909; entered Parliament 1946; Foreign Minister 1974; Leader of Centre Union 1974–7

Mercouri, Melina: born 1925; entered Parliament 1977; Minister of Culture and Science 1981; celebrated as film star

Nikolopoulos, Petros: born 1898; commissioned (Army) 1920; Lieutenant-General 1954; CGS 1956–8; first head of Central Service of Information (KYP)

Papadopoulos, George: born 1919; commissioned (Army) 1940; Colonel 1960; staff officer in KYP 1959–64; Minister in Prime Minister's office 1967; Prime Minister 1967–73; Regent 1972–3; President of Republic 1973; condemned to death for high treason 1975 (commuted to life imprisonment)

Papagos, Alexander: (1883–1955); CGS 1936–41; Commander-in-Chief 1949–51; Prime Minister 1952–5; Greece's only non-royal Field-Marshal

Papaligouras, Panayiotis: born 1917; entered Parliament 1946; Minister of Co-ordination 1974–7; Foreign Minister 1977–8

Papandreou, Andreas: born 1919; emigrated to USA 1939–61; returned to Greece and renounced US citizenship; entered Parliament 1964; left Greece again 1968–74; entered Parliament 1974; Prime Minister 1981

Papandreou, George: (1888–1968); entered Parliament 1923; Prime Minister

1944, 1963–5

Paraskevopoulos, Ioannis: (1900–84); Professor, Athens University 1939; Prime Minister 1966–7

Pattakos, Stylianos: born 1912; commissioned (Army) 1937; Brigadier in command of KET 1966; Minister of Interior 1967–73; Deputy Prime Minister 1971–3; condemned to death for high treason 1975 (commuted to life imprisonment)

Paul, King: (1901–64); lived in exile 1923–35 and 1941–6; succeeded his brother George II as King 1947

Pesmazoglou, Ioannis: born 1918; Deputy Governor, Bank of Greece 1960–7; Professor, Athens University, 1967–70; entered Parliament 1974

Pipinelis, Panayiotis: (1899–1970); entered Foreign Service 1922; head of Political Office of King George II 1945; Prime Minister 1963; Foreign Minister 1967–70

Rallis, George: born 1918; entered Parliament 1950; Minister of Public Order 1967; Minister in Prime Minister's office 1974–7; Minister of Co-ordination 1977–8; Foreign Minister 1978–80; Prime Minister 1980–1

Spandidakis, Grigorios: born 1909; commissioned (Army) 1920; CGS 1965; Deputy Prime Minister and Minister of Defence 1967; sentenced to ten years imprisonment 1975

Stasinopoulos, Michael: born 1909; President of Council of State 1966–9; President of the Republic 1974–5

Stephanopoulos, Stephanos: (1898–1983); entered Parliament 1930; Vice-Premier and Foreign Minister 1954–5; Prime Minister 1965–6

Theodorakis, Mikis: born 1925; entered Parliament 1974; celebrated as a popular musician

Tsatsos, Constantine: born 1899; Professor, Athens University, 1932; entered Parliament 1946; President of Republic 1975–80

Tsirimokos, Ilias: (1907–68); entered Parliament 1936; member of central committee of EAM 1942–4; Foreign Minister 1964; Prime Minister 1965

Vlachos, Helen: born 1911; owner and editor of *Kathimerini*; entered Parliament 1974

Xanthopoulos-Palamas, Christos: (1904–77); entered Foreign Service 1935; Ambassador to Washington 1967–70; Under-Secretary, Ministry of Foreign Affairs, 1970–2

Zigdis, Ioannis: born 1913; entered Parliament 1950; Leader of Centre Union from 1977

Zoitakis, G.: born 1910; commissioned (Army) 1932; Lieutenant-General 1965; Under-Secretary for Defence 1967; Regent of Greece 1967–72; sentenced to life imprisonment 1975

Zolotas, Xenophon: (1904–84); Governor of Bank of Greece 1955–67; Minister of Co-ordination 1974

1 Men of tomorrow

1963–67

On 19 May 1963 Constantine Karamanlis, in the eighth year of his first premiership, took a look into the future. The occasion was a conversation with President de Gaulle, who was making a state visit to Greece. The President congratulated him on his country's economic progress. In reply Karamanlis outlined his reasons for anxiety: low national income, lack of capital investment, and 'one of the most aggressive Communist Parties in Europe'. He concluded that 'the next three or four years' would be decisive, for by then 'either stability will be assured or there will be a total collapse'.[1] One month less than four years later, on 21 April 1967, Greece fell under the grip of a dictatorship, imposed not by the Communists but by a group of Colonels and Brigadiers. By then Karamanlis was no longer in Greece: he had been living in self-imposed exile for more than three years.

The crisis which brought about both Karamanlis' exile and the dictatorship of the Colonels was already germinating when de Gaulle and Karamanlis met in 1963. At that date there was another major state visit in prospect: King Paul and Queen Frederika were invited to London in July. But Karamanlis had advised that the visit should be postponed, because he feared that the King and Queen would be subjected to hostile demonstrations in London organized by left-wing supporters of various causes, including nuclear disarmament as well as the release of 'political prisoners' in Greece. There had been a foretaste of such disturbances when the Queen and her daughter, on a private visit to London in April, had been harassed by a small crowd outside Claridges Hotel, led by the English wife of a Greek Communist, Tony Ambatielos. Karamanlis foresaw still graver trouble in July. But the King, and especially the Queen, were reluctant to accept his advice.

The disagreement was temporarily suspended when King Paul had to undergo an operation for appendicitis during de Gaulle's state visit. Although he recovered quickly from the operation, the King was already mortally ill from cancer. Probably he himself sensed that the royal invitation to London in July would be his last chance of such a visit – as indeed it was, for he died in the following February. There were other arguments against a postponement. A state visit to London had been cancelled several years earlier because of the Cyprus dispute; and the visit proposed in 1963 was intended to set the seal on Anglo-Greek reconciliation after the establishment of the Republic of Cyprus in 1960. It was therefore an occasion of public importance, not merely of personal satisfaction. The King and Queen were naturally dismayed at the prospect of another postponement.

No sooner had de Gaulle flown home from Salonika on 20 May than a new complication was added to the crisis. At the end of a political demonstration in Salonika on 22 May, a left-wing Deputy, Grigorios Lambrakis, was run down by a three-wheeled vehicle and fatally injured. Undoubtedly this was no accident but a criminal act. Karamanlis and his government were held to blame not only by the extreme left, represented in Parliament by the Union of the Democratic Left (EDA), but also by the official opposition party, the Centre Union, led by George Papandreou. Karamanlis in fact reacted vigorously and properly, and it was later established in the courts that his government was in no way to blame. But his conviction that the royal visit to London should be postponed was further hardened, since the extreme left now had a fresh outrage to exploit.

After the King returned from a convalescent cruise, the argument about the visit was renewed in the first half of June. The King was concerned with personal relations: Queen Elizabeth would be offended by a postponement. Karamanlis was concerned with political implications: it was a matter on which the King was constitutionally obliged to act on his Ministers' advice. On 17 June, when it was clear that no compromise was possible, Karamanlis resigned. He left Greece for Zürich, saying that he intended to withdraw from political life, though his withdrawal was not yet final.

To ease the King's position, Karamanlis agreed to advise his party, the National Radical Union (ERE), which still held the majority in Parliament, to support a new Prime Minister chosen from the party, provided that the man chosen was one who intended to play no further part in politics. He recommended Panayiotis Pipinelis, a retired Ambassador and former Director of King George II's political office. Pipinelis was sworn in on 18 June, but the undertaking that he would play no further part in politics, if given, was not respected. On 25 June he secured a vote of confidence in Parliament, and on 8 July he accompanied the King and Queen to London. The visit was regarded as successful, but Karamanlis proved right in foreseeing disturbances.

After the state visit the King dissolved Parliament, although it had completed only half of its four-year term. This was generally agreed to be necessary in order to disentangle the political confusion. Moreover, the King felt the need for a change of government in the interests of democracy, after eight years (1955–63) of rule by Karamanlis following three years under Field-Marshal Papagos (1952–5). There was even evidence that the Palace discreetly intervened to promote the prospects of the Centre Union. Undoubtedly the King dreaded the possibility that George Papandreou, who had been preaching for two years a 'relentless struggle' against the alleged corruption of ERE, might abstain from the election altogether if his party seemed likely to lose yet again.

The election took place on 3 November 1963. Karamanlis returned from his temporary exile to lead ERE, but for the first time he was defeated by Papandreou. The margin was narrow: the Centre Union won 138 seats, ERE won 132. The balance of power was held by EDA, commonly regarded as a front for the outlawed Communist Party (KKE), with 28 seats; and the remaining two seats, in a Parliament of 300, were held by the Progressive Party, led by Spyro Markezinis, an old rival of Karamanlis. Since no single party could govern on its own, the King called the party leaders separately for consultation before nominating a Prime Minister.

He had probably decided already to give Papandreou a mandate to form a government, which he did, against Karamanlis' advice. He also gave Papandreou the right to ask for a fresh dissolution if he failed to win a vote of confidence. Karamanlis thereupon left Greece again, declaring that this time his decision was final, in order to avert a constitutional crisis. Papandreou won a vote of confidence on 24 December, but only thanks to the votes of EDA. He immediately asked for a dissolution on the grounds that he would not be dependent on Communist support. The King consented, and a fresh election was held on 16 February 1964.

This time Papandreou won an overall majority, with 171 seats. ERE, led by Panayiotis Kanellopoulos in Karamanlis' place, was reduced to 107 seats. EDA lost six seats to the Centre Union, and the Progressive Party gained six from ERE. King Paul died only a few days after swearing Papandreou into office again. A new era had begun.

Kanellopoulos had a painful task as leader of the Opposition. He was one of Greece's most eminent intellectuals, ill-suited by temperament to the crudity and violence of parliamentary politics. Questions of policy did not separate him from Papandreou so much as the latter's determination to continue the 'relentless struggle' against ERE, which meant damaging the reputation of Karamanlis. Since Karamanlis was married to Kanellopoulos' niece, there were personal as well as political embarrassments in his position.

The results of the 'relentless struggle' proved negligible, and by the summer of 1965 Papandreou was inclined to abandon it, for he had more serious problems to face. Two of the most intractable problems were connected. There was the perennial conflict in Cyprus between the Greek and Turkish communities, which had at least once come near to causing a war between Greece and Turkey. There was also the emergence of clandestine groups, both right-wing and left-wing, within the officer corps of the Army. These two running sores combined to poison the Greek political system for the next ten years.

*   *   *

The problem of Cyprus had not been laid to rest by the settlement of 1959–60, which created a nominally independent, unitary Republic. After living in reasonable harmony under British rule until the outbreak of violence in 1955, the Greek and Turkish communities had been driven into bitter antagonism by the struggle for *enosis* (union with Greece), launched under Colonel George Grivas with the reluctant consent of Archbishop Makarios. Although Grivas' National Organization of Cypriot Combatants (EOKA) had been formally dissolved after the achievement of independence, the struggle was not regarded as finished. A kind of apartheid developed between the Greek and Turkish communities, which looked respectively to Athens and Ankara for political support rather than trying to make the supposedly united Republic function satisfactorily.

The Greek President and Turkish Vice-President, Archbishop Makarios and Dr Küchük, seldom met. By the end of 1963 Makarios was talking of revising the Constitution and even abrogating the treaties which established the Republic. Both Greek and Turkish Cypriots, with help from their respective mainlands, were organizing to settle the future of the island by force. The British, who retained two sovereign base areas, did little to fulfil their obligation under the Treaty of Guarantee, signed with Greece and Turkey, to safeguard the constitution and territorial integrity of the Republic.

According to George Papandreou's son Andreas, Cyprus was the main preoccupation of the Centre Union government during its first nine months of office.[2] A few days before Christmas 1963 fighting had broken out in the island between Greeks and Turks. At first the Greeks had the upper hand, and compelled the leader of the Turkish community, Raouf Denktash, to leave Cyprus under threat of arrest. The fighting was halted with the help of British troops from the base areas. Early in March 1964 the UN Security Council agreed to send a peace-keeping force (UNFICYP), which included a British contingent already on the spot. While the force was being assembled, the Turkish Cypriots established a number of enclaves for their own protection. The government in Ankara even planned to establish a bridgehead on the island, but it was warned off by the US President, Lyndon Johnson, in a strongly worded letter on 5 June to the Turkish Prime Minister.[3]

Johnson also sent a former Secretary of State, Dean Acheson, to devise a plan of settlement. Acheson's plan, published in July 1964, would in effect have given the Greeks most of what they wanted, namely *enosis*, offset by the grant of a sovereign military base for Turkey in the north-east corner, coupled with the cession of Kastellorizo, a small offshore island in the Dodecanese. The Turks appeared willing to accept, but Makarios refused.

That summer was crucial in the history of Cyprus, Greece and Turkey, and of international relations in the eastern Mediterranean. The US government was concerned to achieve a settlement of the Cyprus problem in the interests of security, including that of Israel as well as NATO. There was intense pressure from Washington on George Papandreou, according to his son, to support the Acheson plan.[4] At first the Prime Minister was disposed to accept it, but in view of Makarios' opposition he felt compelled to change his mind. At the same time the problem was becoming more intractable because of Greek and Turkish interventions.

Despite the presence of UNFICYP, fighting broke out again during August 1964. It was again halted, but the long-term prospect was made worse after the cease-fire by the withdrawal of the Greek mainland commander of the Cypriot National Guard, who was replaced by George Grivas, now a Lieutenant-General in the Greek Army. Grivas also had under his command the Greek mainland contingent in Cyprus, which was permitted under the treaties, as was a corresponding Turkish contingent. But both these forces were surreptitiously increased during 1964, far beyond their authorized levels.

Archbishop Makarios was now flanked by dangerous men. There were others besides Grivas. One was Polykarpos Yiorkatzis, Makarios' own Minister of the Interior, who had been a legendary hero of EOKA and was now a compulsive intriguer, sometimes at Makarios' behest and sometimes against him. Others were to be found among the ecclesiastical hierarchy, particularly Bishop Anthimos of Kition, who was bitterly jealous of Makarios' dual eminence as Archbishop and President. These men played significant roles in the troubles which developed between Nicosia and Athens during the next decade.

Grivas, who had influence in Athens as well as Nicosia, was the most troublesome of all. It was he who deliberately exacerbated the second of the running sores in the Greek body politic, which was the habit of military conspiracy. Early in 1965 he sent reports to Athens of what was alleged to be a left-wing conspiracy among Greek Army officers. His was not the only evidence, but it was the most circumstantial.

The secret organization, which was said to have been formed towards the end of 1964, was known as ASPIDA. The word means 'shield', but it was also an acronym standing for 'Officers, Save Fatherland, Ideals, Democracy and Meritocracy'.[5] It was probably no more than a society of radically minded officers, mostly Majors or Captains, to promote their own careers in the frustrating circumstances of the time. But it was represented, not least by Grivas, as something much more sinister. In particular, it was alleged that at least three Ministers in Papandreou's government were associated with ASPIDA. The most prominent of them was his own son, Andreas.

Andreas Papandreou was another controversial personality who was to

5

become celebrated in the next decade and beyond. He had left Greece as a young man in 1939, to escape the dictatorship of General Metaxas (1936–41), and had lived in the United States for twenty years. There he took a postgraduate degree, served in the American Navy, became naturalized, taught economics as a professor at a number of universities, and married an American wife. He returned to Greece in 1959 on a research fellowship. Soon afterwards he decided to resettle in Greece, and obtained an appointment in the Central Bank, with his father's encouragement and Karamanlis' help. He then renounced his American citizenship, and entered politics in the Centre Union. In February 1964, having won a seat in Parliament, he became Minister in the Prime Minister's office. This was an influential post, especially when the Prime Minister was his father.

Andreas' political views, which were always to the left of his father's, moved still further leftwards as his experience of Greece expanded. Once in office, he found confirmation of his belief that Greece had virtually become an American colony. As his antagonism towards the United States grew, his name became anathema to many American officials in Athens, including the Embassy, the Central Intelligence Agency (CIA) and the Joint US Military Assistance Group (JUSMAGG). He also became hostile to the monarchy, which he blamed for Greece's dependence on the USA. These unconcealed antagonisms embarrassed his father, who decided in June 1964 to move him to a less sensitive post, as Deputy Minister of Co-ordination. He was again placed in a key Ministry, but under a more senior Minister.

Still Andreas' abrasive manner brought him under attack, both from the press and from the less radical elements in the Centre Union. In November 1964 he resigned, but he resumed his post in April 1965. It was at this time that the supposed scandal of ASPIDA became the subject of public gossip, with Andreas' name attached to it. By a considerable exaggeration, though probably not without a grain of truth, it was represented as a revolutionary conspiracy, in which Andreas supposedly acted as a political leader. He owed these suspicions to the enemies he had made: to Grivas in Cyprus, to other right-wing officers in the Army, to the more conservative elements in the Centre Union, to the press, and perhaps to some of the Americans in Athens, who had a powerful influence through the CIA on its Greek equivalent, the Central Service of Information (KYP).

Andreas had been concerned, as Minister in the Prime Minister's office, with both Cyprus and the KYP. In Cyprus he had antagonized Grivas by supporting Makarios in the long-running feud between the two Cypriot leaders. Grivas still believed that *enosis* could be achieved by force. Makarios, who enjoyed being a Head of State within the British Commonwealth, would not take risks to achieve *enosis*, although he still aspired to it in principle. Least of all would he cede territory to Turkey as the price of *enosis*.

6

When Makarios rejected the Acheson plan for that reason, Andreas supported him and persuaded his father to do so also. Grivas concluded that both Makarios and the Greek government had renounced *enosis*. Some years later he made this accusation explicit, in a letter published on 6 September 1973 in the Athens newspaper *Acropolis*.[6]

The personality of Makarios was one of several subjects on which George and Andreas Papandreou disagreed. The father found the Archbishop's equivocations as intolerable as Grivas' reckless opportunism. 'We agree on one thing and you do another,' he telegraphed in despair to the pair of them on 8 August 1964; 'and disastrous consequences follow.'[7] Andreas shared his father's view of Grivas, but had a higher opinion of Makarios, whom he found 'an exceedingly intelligent and knowledgeable man'.[8]

In persuading his father to support Makarios' opposition to the Acheson plan, Andreas took an honourable course. But the long-term consequences were indeed disastrous for the Greeks. When the Turks invaded Cyprus ten years later, they seized a much larger foothold on the island than they would have obtained under the Acheson plan. The short-term consequences were also disastrous for Andreas, who made an implacable enemy of Grivas by supporting the Archbishop.

At the same time Andreas was learning disagreeable facts about the KYP, and adding to his enemies there as well. It was later alleged that KYP was financed and controlled by the CIA, independently of the Greek government. The allegation as presented seems incredible: it would have been a constitutional impossibility, and if it were true, Andreas as Minister in the Prime Minister's office would have been able to expose the scandal with concrete evidence, which he never did. But the CIA clearly had a relation of great intimacy with the KYP, which it had helped to set up in the early 1950s. This was the more serious because the relationship entirely excluded the official US Embassy. There was a similar, though less exclusive, relation between JUSMAGG and the Greek General Staff.

Among the enemies whom Andreas made in the Army by his conduct as a Minister in his father's government were two whom he could scarcely have heard of: Colonel George Papadopoulos, who had served in the KYP before the Centre Union came into office; and Colonel Dimitrios Ioannidis, who had served as an intelligence officer with the National Guard in Cyprus. Both already had conspiratorial experience. Some fifteen years earlier Papadopoulos had belonged to a secret group of right-wing officers known as IDEA, an acronym for 'Sacred League of Greek Officers'. Ioannidis, a more secretive character, was said by Makarios (in an interview with an Italian journalist ten years later)[9] to have approached him in 1964 with a plan to eliminate the entire Turkish population of Cyprus once and for all. Makarios, who naturally rejected the plan, eventually became Ioannidis' prime target himself.

Other junior members of IDEA in the early 1950s, all Captains like Papadopoulos and Ioannidis, were unknown outside their own circle. Among them were C. Aslanidis, I. Ladas, N. Makarezos, A. Mexis, M. Rouphogalis. Ioannidis and Ladas were infantry officers; Papadopoulos, Makarezos and Rouphogalis were in the artillery, a *corps d'élite*. The last three had all served as instructors in the School of Artillery in 1951, under Colonel Odysseus Angelis, who had become a Lieutenant-General and Deputy Chief of the General Staff by 1967. Another officer at the School of Artillery in 1951, by coincidence, was Major A. Papaterpos, who was to be named in 1965 as the ringleader of the left-wing conspiracy, ASPIDA.

The conspirators who gravitated round Papadopoulos were far from negligible men, though their political ideas were crude and naïve. As in other developing countries, the Army was a *carrière ouverte aux talents* for young men from the provinces without social or financial advantages. The officer corps led a strictly regulated and almost segregated life. Patriotism was instilled into them from the first. Even this was unusual, for although the word *patriotis* is much used it normally means loyalty to a narrower community than the nation.

The Army taught its officers to take a wider view of their patriotic duty, and to regard themselves as protectors of the nation in every sense. Army officers had often felt obliged to take over power from the politicians, though usually not for long. The other services were less active politically, and they provided Papadopoulos with few adherents. In the Air Force one officer of equivalent rank to the Colonels was a member of the conspiracy, though not a leading one;[10] and the Chief of the Air Staff, Air-Marshal Antonakos, was believed to be sympathetic.[11] In the Navy there were no adherents, though unfortunately one destroyer was later to be used as a prison, and three of its senior officers and three petty officers were convicted of torture.[12] With a few such minor exceptions, the dictatorship was to be wholly an affair of the Army.

Competition for promotion in the Army was strong, and only the best reached the top. Makarezos and Papadopoulos had graduated respectively second and fourth from the Officers' School in 1940. (The first in their class was Dimitrios Opropoulos, who became one of their most determined opponents after they seized power.) Makarezos held a degree in economics, and had served as an instructor at the Staff College. He had also been Military Attaché at the Embassy in Bonn. But in general it was a weakness of Papadopoulos' group that none of them had much experience abroad.

The secret society of IDEA, which had been formed among the Greek forces of the Middle East in 1944, was formally dissolved in 1952. In that year

Field-Marshal Papagos became Prime Minister, so the purposes of IDEA could be regarded as fulfilled. But Papadopoulos kept his personal group in being. Kanellopoulos, as Minister of Defence between 1952 and 1954, noted 'certain vague indications' of the continued existence of IDEA, but found no proof that would justify action against particular officers.[13] This is surprising, since there was so little secrecy about Papadopoulos' activities that he came to be nicknamed 'Nasser'. He made unconcealed attempts to recruit other officers, many of whom refused. The most contemptuous rebuff came from Papaterpos, his left-wing colleague in the School of Artillery.[14] But Papadopoulos successfully recruited two officers senior to himself – Ioannidis from the Infantry and Stylianos Pattakos from the Armoured Corps. All of them were well placed in key positions when the time for action came.

Papadopoulos' intrigues did not escape the high command. In the late 1950s, when the Minister for War asked the Chief of the General Staff, Petros Nikolopoulos, if he knew what a certain Major G. Papadopoulos was up to, the General simply replied: 'Conspiring [*synomotei*]!' In 1958, when Nikolopoulos was about to retire, he asked Kanellopoulos, who was not then in office, to use his influence with Karamanlis to extend his appointment for a year in order to complete his investigation of Papadopoulos, with a view to forcing him to retire. But the Supreme Military Council, comprising all the senior Generals, did not endorse Nikolopoulos' suspicions, and Kanellopoulos felt unable to act.[15]

Subsequently, as a staff officer of the KYP in 1961, Papadopoulos helped the CGS of the day, General Kardamakis, in preparing the 'Pericles Plan', which was alleged by Papandreou to have been used by Karamanlis' government to ensure the electoral victory of ERE. This accusation formed the basis of Papandreou's 'relentless struggle' for the next five years. Although the accusation was circumstantially repudiated both by Karamanlis and by Kardamakis, it continued to be asserted by Andreas Papandreou a decade later.[16] The fact that Papadopoulos had been associated with the Pericles Plan naturally gave the accusation some credibility, though the plan had no relevance to an electoral situation. It envisaged an internal emergency, which never in fact occurred; and the plan was simply kept on file in the Ministry of Defence.

According to an unnamed source quoted by Andreas Papandreou, Papadopoulos' group took organized form in 1965, after several years of informal existence, as the Union of Young Greek Officers (EENA). The source noted that many of its members had risen from the non-commissioned ranks, which supported their claim to be true representatives of the people. He added that Papadopoulos had been trained in the USA 'under the auspices of the CIA', and became the leading agent of the CIA in Greece. This story is doubtful, but it is still generally believed in Greece. Andreas Papandreou himself expressed scepticism about some of the facts alleged in his source's

9

report, without specifying which. But the source was certainly well placed, being described (in 1969) as 'a disaffected member of Papadopoulos' junta, now living abroad'.[17]

If Papadopoulos were really a CIA agent, his unconcealed plotting in the 1960s cannot have been welcome to his employers. As if to make sure that he was not overlooked, he drew attention to himself in June 1965, when serving in Thrace, by making a sensational claim to have uncovered a Communist conspiracy in the Army. It was not, he alleged, localized in the north-east; its tentacles spread even to Athens. Naturally the story became linked with the current investigation of ASPIDA. On investigation, however, it proved to be entirely fictitious. Papadopoulos was criticized by name in Parliament on 23 June by the leader of EDA, Ilias Iliou, who uttered the prophetic words that if such accusations were to be repeated, thousands of citizens could be imperilled, and then: 'Behold, the *coup d'état* is prepared!'[18]

The sequel was a strange one. The head of the Army legal directorate was considering disciplinary action against Papadopoulos, when the case against him was dropped on higher orders. It was said that the Prime Minister intervened to protect him because they both came from Achaia, and Papandreou was a friend of Papadopoulos' father. The story rests only on the authority of a former Minister in Papandreou's government (P. Garouphalias) who had a grievance against him because he had been dismissed.[19] But it may still be true, for such was the system of patronage by which Greek politics functioned.

By mid-1965 George Papandreou was in deep trouble over the affair of ASPIDA. When he first came to power, he had the benevolent support of the Palace. But after the death of King Paul and the accession of his son as Constantine II, the atmosphere changed. The young King was influenced by his mother, who had not much respect for the Greek politicians. He was also surrounded by Palace officials who had been appointed during the previous twelve years of conservative rule. It was perhaps in deference to the Palace that Papandreou had appointed Garouphalias, a wealthy industrialist and intimate of the royal family, as Minister of Defence.

But this appointment became an embarrassment during the next year. The Ministry of Defence was investigating the ASPIDA affair, and the Prime Minister's son was said to be implicated in it. Andreas assured his father that he had no connection with ASPIDA, and had never even heard of it before May 1965.[20] He recognized that it 'obviously had a grain of truth in it', but insisted that so far as he himself was concerned, it was a 'frame-up'.[21] George Papandreou accepted his son's assurances, but the investigation had to continue. At the same time he was concerned by the problem of establishing officers loyal to himself in the highest ranks of the armed services. This was a problem for all new Prime Ministers, especially after a long period of government by the opposite party.

Papandreou became convinced that his efforts to bring officers in whom he had confidence to the fore were being frustrated by Garouphalias, and even by Constantine. In July 1965 he decided to dismiss Garouphalias and take charge of the Ministry of Defence himself. The King agreed to the dismissal of Garouphalias, but not to the appointment of the Prime Minister simultaneously as Minister of Defence while his son was under investigation. So far the King's action was constitutionally correct, but his next step was not.

Papandreou reacted impetuously. He was already exasperated by an acrimonious correspondence with the King, in which Constantine complained that he was not kept properly informed of the government's business, and even that the KYP was helping to create a conspiracy in the armed forces against the constitution.[22] The argument over the Ministry of Defence was the last straw for Papandreou. On 15 July he offered his resignation, assuming that since he still had a majority in Parliament, the King would be obliged either to yield or to grant him a dissolution. But the King did neither. He already had an alternative Prime Minister standing by it was said, in the next room at the Palace – who was immediately sworn in.

The new Prime Minister, George Athanasiadis-Novas, had previously been President of the Chamber. He failed to win a vote of confidence and resigned on 8 August. But during his brief tenure he made a major change in the control of the KYP, replacing its director with a new officer more acceptable to the King. The King next appointed another Prime Minister from the Centre Union, Ilias Tsirimokos, a Socialist who had been a member of the National Liberation Front (EAM) during the German occupation. He also failed, on 28 August, to win a vote of confidence, and resigned.

The King's next choice was Stephanos Stephanopoulos, who had been Karamanlis' rival for the premiership in 1955, and had later transferred his loyalty to the Centre Union. He formed a government with Tsirimokos as his Deputy and Foreign Minister. With the support of ERE and forty-five renegades from the Centre Union, who became known as 'the Apostates', he won a narrow vote of confidence on 24 September. He then took another step which earned the King's approval. In October he appointed a new Chief of the General Staff, Grigorios Spandidakis, who was later to betray both his King and the constitution.

Whether deliberately or not, Spandidakis made a number of transfers which assisted Papadopoulos' plans. Papadopoulos himself was recalled from distant Thrace, first to the First Army HQ at Larisa and then to the General Staff in Athens, housed in the building known on the American model as the Pentagon. His accomplices, Makarezos and Pattakos, were also appointed to key posts in Athens. According to Major-General Panouryias, a loyal officer who kept in touch with Karamanlis in Paris, Spandidakis had a close relationship with both Papadopoulos and Pattakos, though he was probably not privy to their plans in advance.[23]

The conspirators soon made themselves noticed again. On 23 January 1966 an open letter addressed to the King was published in a northern newspaper, ostensibly from a group of officers in 22 Division but actually composed by Pattakos. It warned the King of 'the fatal period of Rasputin–Kerenskyism' – a phrase which would have been instantly recognizable to later connoisseurs of Pattakos' prose. An investigation into the authorship was ordered by the commander of III Corps in northern Greece, of which 22 Division formed part; but he was ordered by Spandidakis from Athens to discontinue it.[24]

Papadopoulos had a more natural cover for his intrigues than Pattakos, since he was assigned by Spandidakis to revise the so-called 'Prometheus Plan'. This was not, as the Pericles Plan had been, a purely internal affair. It was closely connected with NATO planning for a contingency of war. If it were to be activated, it would imply the collective co-operation of the allies in an international crisis. This implication gave the Prometheus Plan a weight and respectability which Papadopoulos was ready to exploit when the time came.

Neither the public nor the government gave much attention to the Army during the early months of 1966. Stephanopoulos survived by doing very little. Kanellopoulos advised his colleagues in ERE to continue supporting the government *faute de mieux*. But he was aware of the disquiet in the Army, as his letters to Karamanlis showed. There were also related causes of disquiet in Cyprus, as was inevitable so long as Grivas held his command there.

Stephanopoulos made a fresh attempt to solve the problem of Cyprus by direct negotiation with the Turkish government.[25] It proved impossible to formulate concessions which would satisfy the Turks without dissatisfying Makarios, but at least communications were kept open and reasonably friendly. More serious than Greco-Turkish relations over Cyprus were relations between Makarios and Grivas. In April 1966 Makarios asked the Greek government to confine Grivas' command to the Greek mainland forces in the island. Tsirimokos, the Foreign Minister, supported his request, but Stephanopoulos rejected it. Tsirimokos thereupon resigned, but the government did not fall.[26] There seemed to be no reason why Stephanopoulos should not hold office until the next election, which could be delayed until early 1968.

The calm was broken in October 1966, when the preliminary investigation into ASPIDA was published.[27] The ringleader was said to be Colonel A. Papaterpos, the former colleague of Papadopoulos in the School of Artillery. He and twenty-seven other officers were committed for trial. The Public

Prosecutor, Constantine Kollias (who was to become more notorious six months later), announced that civilians might also be included in the indictment; and if they were Deputies, he would request that their parliamentary immunity should be lifted. The allusion to Andreas Papandreou and one or two of his colleagues was unmistakable.

At the same time there were persistent rumours of an impending military coup. Stephanopoulos declared that such an action could not possibly succeed, but his confidence reassured nobody. There was a general feeling, shared by the King, that confidence could be restored only by the return of Karamanlis; but he showed no inclination to return. He wrote regularly to his friends from Paris criticizing everybody, but especially George and Andreas Papandreou, for the unstable state of Greece.[28]

George Papandreou, however, was beginning to have a change of heart. He dreaded Communism and revolution, he was alarmed by his son's extremist associations, and he was feeling his age. The only way for him to recover power was to overthrow Stephanopoulos and force an early election. To do that, he needed the co-operation of Kanellopoulos; and he no doubt reasoned that Kanellopoulos could also secure Andreas' immunity from arrest in the electoral period.

He chose an indirect approach to Kanellopoulos, through the Palace. With the help of the King and the Director of his political office, Dimitrios Bitsios, two secret meetings were held between Papandreou and Kanellopoulos, which resulted in a wide-ranging agreement. In anticipation of an election, Papandreou undertook unilaterally that if he failed to win an overall majority, he would enter a coalition with Kanellopoulos.[29] On 20 December Kanellopoulos withdrew the support of ERE from Stephanopoulos' government, which resigned next day. A 'service' government was appointed under a retired banker, I. Paraskevopoulos, to supervise the coming election. But Parliament was not immediately dissolved, for it was necessary first to pass legislation establishing the electoral procedure.

The question remained whether Andreas Papandreou could be protected from arrest during the electoral period, when he would no longer have immunity as a Deputy. On 24 February 1967 the Public Prosecutor, Constantine Kollias, made a formal request that his immunity, together with that of one other Deputy, should be lifted. The parliamentary legal committee voted by eleven votes to eight on 15 March to reject the request. The next day, fifteen of the twenty-eight officers on trial in the ASPIDA case were convicted and sentenced to terms of imprisonment; the rest were acquitted, but new charges were laid against some of them.

These were the circumstances in which the 'service' government had to introduce its draft electoral law. The draft included a provision for simple proportional representation in place of the 'reinforced PR' previously in force. It contained no clause relating to parliamentary immunity. The draft was passed in principle (the equivalent of 'second reading') on 22 March, and consideration clause by clause (the 'committee stage') began at once in the full Chamber. By 28 March all twelve clauses had been passed, but the Centre Union then gave notice of its intention to present a new clause extending parliamentary immunity for forty-five days, to cover the election period.

Andreas' supporters maintained that it had been agreed in principle that the new clause would not be a party issue. But when the debate took place on 29 March, Kanellopoulos argued that it was unconstitutional, and claimed that this had been publicly stated by the Minister of the Interior in the Paraskevopoulos government.[30] Since both sides were adamant, Paraskevopoulos recognized that he could not continue in office, and resigned on 30 March. The results were far-reaching. Parliament, though not yet dissolved, did not meet again. The draft electoral law therefore lapsed, so that the coming election would have to take place under the previous system. More seriously, Andreas' immunity from arrest was not extended.

Since almost every possible form of administration in the existing Parliament had been exhausted, the King now gave the mandate to Kanellopoulos, with a right to dissolve Parliament when he thought fit, if necessary without seeking a vote of confidence. George Papandreou was angry with Kanellopoulos over this outcome, and Andreas was angry both with Kanellopoulos and with his father over their secret agreement, which was already common knowledge.[31] Since Kanellopoulos had little chance of winning a vote of confidence, he requested a dissolution on 15 April. Andreas believed that he did so because he learned that the King had changed his mind again, and had decided to appoint a new 'service' government under the President of the Council of State; but of that there is no independent confirmation.[32]

May 27 was fixed as the date of the election. There was no danger that it would be corruptly conducted under Kanellopoulos, who only wanted a stable and representative Parliament. He liked George Papandreou personally; and although he found Andreas exasperating, he would do his best to save him from being arrested.[33] But Andreas was unrepentant. He criticized his father and openly attacked the Palace and the Americans. On 1 March he made a speech to the Foreign Press Association in which he abused the US government so offensively that two American diplomats walked out. He believed that both the Palace and the US Embassy were still seeking to have the elections postponed.[34]

The motive for so much anxiety in Athens was the fear that the Centre Union would win the election, and that a new government under George Papandreou would become over-dependent on Communist support. The next step, it was supposed, would be what was called a 'deviation' (*ektropi*), the current euphemism for a *coup d'état*, whether from the left or the right. So general was the fear that at one stage, in September 1966, the King had sent a startling message to Karamanlis, through Bitsios, that if he would return to office the King would, in certain circumstances, authorize a 'deviation' of his own.[35]

By early March 1967, according to a letter from Kanellopoulos to Karamanlis, those who desired a 'deviation' were systematically terrifying the King with warnings of 'an imminent St Bartholomew's Eve', and no one except Kanellopoulos himself was trying to counteract their propaganda.[36] Such was the feverish atmosphere that it is not surprising to find Karamanlis writing to a former colleague on 10 April: 'I hear you have all gone mad!'[37]

2 Coup d'état or revolution?
April 1967

Early in 1967, while rumours of conspiracies in the Army were flying round Athens, a close friend of the King felt emboldened to warn him that his name was being associated with them, and to express the hope that there was no truth in the rumours. He replied: 'Do you imagine I don't know that *any* dictatorship would be certain to get rid of me?' In the confusion of those tense weeks, one thing at least is certain: the King was not involved in any unconstitutional movement whatever. But that did not prevent the allegations against him from being commonly believed.[1]

Rumour spoke of at least three distinct plots: a Generals' plot, commonly known as the senior, or greater, junta; a Colonels' plot, known as the junior, or lesser, junta; and even a Captains' plot. But the last of the three plots can be dismissed as insignificant. It simply consisted of a group of junior officers who were worried about their prospects of promotion. There were some 2,000 Captains in the Army, of whom fewer than 150 could be promoted annually.[2]

The so-called Generals' plot was also an almost total fiction. After the downfall of the military dictatorship, three Lieutenant-Generals – Spandidakis, Angelis and Zoitakis – were put on trial among the principal defendants in 1975. They were all convicted. But although it was clear that each of them had been in collusion to some degree with one or other of the conspiring Colonels, there was no evidence that they had conspired with each other; nor that they had even discussed the possibility of a military intervention with each other until the day before the Colonels' coup, and then only in the presence of other Generals who firmly repudiated any suggestion of unconstitutional action.

That all three had separate links with the Colonels is beyond doubt. Spandidakis had placed half a dozen of the conspirators in key positions, and was particularly intimate with Papadopoulos.[3] He was said to have discussed plans for a military intervention with Papadopoulos and Pattakos; and he did so also with an officer (Major-General P. Panouryias) who would have no part in any conspiracy and gave evidence for the prosecution in 1975.[4] Angelis was equally intimate with Papadopoulos, and admitted at his trial that 'I believed a revolution ought to take place through the military leadership.'[5] Zoitakis' close relationship with Makarezos was proved at his trial to have played a crucial role in the coup of 21 April.[6]

16

All three Generals denied at their trial in 1975 that they had been involved in any conspiracy with Papadopoulos' group.[7] The court disbelieved all three on this point. But no evidence pointed to any conspiracy between themselves. In other words, there was no 'senior junta' or Generals' plot. That this had never existed was apparent from the evidence of three other Lieutenant-Generals – Kollias, Manettas and Papadatos – who remained loyal to the King and constitution, and gave evidence for the prosecution in 1975. Papadatos, a wholly reliable witness, said explicitly that 'there was no senior junta led by Spandidakis'.[8] That this was the correct view emerges clearly from the dispassionate account reconstructed in court in 1975 of the events of Thursday 20 April 1967, the eve of the Colonels' coup.

April 20 was the last day of a routine conference of the Supreme Military Council at GHQ (the Pentagon). The Council comprised the ten Lieutenant-Generals of the Army, under the chairmanship of Spandidakis as CGS. The day had begun with a mysterious incident in the early morning, which was never satisfactorily explained. The wife of a senior staff officer at GI IQ, Major-General I. Laskaris, who had no involvement in any clandestine activity, received an anonymous telephone call from a male voice, which declared without elaboration that: 'They will strike tonight!' Laskaris reported the incident to his colleague, Panouryias, who reported it to Spandidakis between 08.30 and 09.00.[9]

Spandidakis told Panouryias to discuss the message with Pattakos. He himself summoned Papadopoulos to discuss it.[10] It was remarkable, to say the least, that Spandidakis chose as the first officers to be informed of the incident two men who were to emerge as the arch-conspirators within twenty-four hours.

Neither Laskaris nor Panouryias attached much significance to the anonymous call. They thought it was either a hoax or part of a 'war of nerves'. But Pattakos and Papadopoulos were more seriously perturbed. Pattakos assumed that the plot had been betrayed, but behaved coolly in front of Panouryias. When Pattakos and Papadopoulos discussed it alone, the latter guessed the identity of the anonymous caller (which was never revealed), and telephoned to him to say that the coup had been postponed.[11] No further action was taken by any of those who knew about the mysterious message.

The last session of the Supreme Military Council then began. There was not, and had not previously been, any reference to the possibility of an emergency during the electoral period. But during an interval in the middle of the morning, Angelis approached Spandidakis to suggest that there ought to be some discussion of the supposedly impending crisis, which was linked with the opening of Papandreou's electoral campaign two days later in Salonika. Spandidakis agreed, and asked Angelis to convene a group of his

17

colleagues for an informal exchange of views after the closing session of the Council.[12]

Angelis passed the invitation to four only of his colleagues – Zoitakis, Kollias, Manettas and Papadatos – later in the morning. Thus in the early afternoon only six of the most senior Generals met in Spandidakis' office. They were the occupants of crucial posts: Chief of the General Staff (Spandidakis); Deputy Chief of the Defence Staff (Angelis); Commander of III Corps at Salonika (Zoitakis); Commander of the First Army (Kollias); Commander of II Corps at Verria (Manettas); Garrison Commander of Attica and the Islands (Papadatos).

Angelis was unable to explain at his trial in 1975 why he, the most junior of the six, had taken this initiative; nor why the remaining four Lieutenant-Generals were not included.[13] It was disputed whether they were deliberately excluded, as being unreliable from Spandidakis' point of view, or by the accident of being unavailable: Papadatos thought the former, Spandidakis claimed the latter.[14] But if the choice of those invited was deliberate, it was a bad choice for Spandidakis, since three out of the six would have nothing to do with any unconstitutional action. Once again it is clear that there was no 'senior junta'.

It is beyond doubt that this was the first occasion when any group of senior Generals met to discuss emergency action. At his trial in 1975, Spandidakis said, without contradiction, that there had been no discussion of the subject before Angelis approached him that morning.[15] This was confirmed by the loyal Generals' testimony. Kollias said that the meeting on 20 April was 'entirely unexpected'.[16] Manettas said that, when the idea of intervention by the Army was mooted by Spandidakis, he had pointed out that no plan of any kind existed.[17] Papadatos said that there had been no discussion of the subject among the six Generals prior to that day.[18] Since these were the three who never deviated from their duty, and they were giving evidence for the prosecution in 1975, the court accepted their statements as conclusive. It is equally certain, a fortiori, that there had been no discussion of a military intervention with the King, who never authorized Spandidakis or any other officer of whatever rank to consider or plan any such action.

When Spandidakis invited his colleagues to express an opinion on the need for emergency action, the division between them was clear-cut. He himself, with Angelis and Zoitakis, favoured action; Kollias, Manettas and Papadatos opposed it, unless clearance were first obtained from the King.[19] Spandidakis then invited their views on an approach to the King. Only Zoitakis favoured action without the King's consent. With the support of the majority, Spandidakis then undertook to seek an audience with the King; but as he had to go to Crete the next day (Friday), he said that the audience would not be possible before Saturday or even Monday.[20]

His colleagues, both the loyal and the disloyal, were not convinced that he appreciated the gravity of what was at issue. Kollias suggested that the approach to the King should be made not by Spandidakis alone but by the Chief of the Defence Staff (an inter-service post) or by the Chiefs of Staff of the three services collectively. Spandidakis evasively replied that 'something like that will be done'.[21] Zoitakis pointed out that his position in Salonika could become embarrassing if trouble broke out over the weekend because of Papandreou's visit. He claimed in his evidence to the court in 1975 that he had suggested to Spandidakis that he should consult the Prime Minister, Kanellopoulos.[22] Spandidakis brushed the suggestion aside, if it was indeed made. He called on his colleagues to swear on their word of honour that they would maintain absolute secrecy, and adjourned the meeting until Monday 24 April.

Spandidakis told the court in 1975 that he had intended to be accompanied at his audience with the King by his Navy and Air Force colleagues; but although he dined with Air-Marshal Antonakos, the Chief of the Air Staff, that night, he did not broach the subject with him.[23] When he was asked why he had not included the other Chiefs of Staff in the original discussion, he replied that he already knew their views; nor had he thought it necessary to consult the Minister of Defence, Papaligouras, because the latter knew his views.[24] It appears that Zoitakis, on his own testimony, was the only General who thought that the matter had anything to do with civilian Ministers; but his testimony was not reliable.

Zoitakis was naturally concerned to exculpate himself, since he stood accused of communicating the substance of the Generals' discussion to the revolutionary group of the Colonels. Although he denied having done so, there was strong evidence against him in the form of recorded interviews given by Pattakos to two journalists in the latter part of 1974.[25] Since almost all the Colonels refused to plead or to give evidence at their trial in 1975, Pattakos' interviews constitute almost the only authoritative account of the critical days in which the Colonels' conspiracy came to its climax. The narrative which emerges from them is clear and convincing, and was accepted by the court.

Of all the rumours current in April 1967, the Colonels' plot is the only reality. There was no Generals' plot, although three Lieutenant-Generals had individual links with the conspirators. The King was wholly innocent of any complicity whatever. There was also no Communist plot, although the Colonels believed, no doubt sincerely, that there was. One fact exposes the unreality of their claim on this point. Although scores of trials were held under the military dictatorship between 1967 and 1974, not one person was ever brought to trial, let alone convicted, on any charge of subversion committed or contemplated before the day of the Colonels' coup. Every so-called crime was committed against the dictatorship itself.

Almost certainly there was no CIA plot either, though Greek mythology still insists that there was. It was popularly believed that the CIA, and possibly JUSMAGG also, were implicated in the Colonels' plot. Papadopoulos was alleged to have been trained by the CIA and to have acted as the Agency's principal point of liaison in Athens, but no serious evidence was ever presented to support the allegation. At the second of the major trials of 1975 (the Polytechnic trial) Papadopoulos said that he had never been trained or employed by the CIA, and that he knew the USA 'only from TV and the cinema'.[26] His claim was not rebutted. It was even corroborated by the evidence of later investigations conducted by members of the US Congress hostile to both the dictatorship and the CIA.[27]

This is not to say that American intelligence was totally unaware of the conspiracy. Both the CIA and JUSMAGG would have been failing in their duty if they had no contact with dissident Greek officers. A journalist who interviewed many of the conspirators in later years wrote that 'all of them accepted that the Americans knew of the existence of both the Generals' junta and the junior officers' junta'.[28] However exaggerated the claim may be, even if it is taken at face value it clearly does not substantiate the myth that American agents promoted or encouraged the conspiracy. At most they knew that something sinister was going on.

The Greeks are inclined to believe that everything which happens to them is due to foreign influences. But the Colonels needed no such external stimulus. They saw themselves as divinely chosen saviours of the nation. After years of conspiring and experimenting, they took the dissolution of Parliament on 15 April as the signal for action. In anticipation of Papandreou's trip to Salonika on 22 April, the chief conspirators held a decisive meeting at Pattakos' house on Tuesday 18 April.[29]

It was only at this meeting that Papadopoulos' leadership was formally confirmed. He stood at the head of a small pyramid on a wider base. At the top was the triumvirate of Papadopoulos, Pattakos and Makarezos. At the base was a so-called Revolutionary Council, whose exact number was never established. Indeed, its very existence is questionable, for Papadopoulos considered it unnecessary and persistently avoided convening it.[30] Between the apex and the base there was an inner executive circle, known as the 'revolutionary group', which was to control the operation. This group numbered about fifteen, mostly Colonels, and included the triumvirate at the top.

It was the revolutionary group which met at Pattakos' house on 18 April. Between them they held many key positions, thanks to Spandidakis' connivance or toleration. Papadopoulos was on the General Staff at the Pentagon, armed with his exact knowledge of the Prometheus Plan. Makarezos and Rouphogalis were in the KYP. Stamatelopoulos (who later defected from the junta) was in the equivalent of the Adjutant-General's branch in the Pentagon, responsible for the posting of officers. Pattakos, a Brigadier and the most senior of the conspirators, was in command of the Armoured Training Centre (KET). Ladas was in command of the Military Security Police (ESA), and Aslanidis of the élite Commando units (LOK). Ioannidis was battalion commander at the Officer Cadets' School, with a loyal following among the young officers of the future. Although some of them later made fools of themselves by their public utterances, they were able officers, all burning with their own brand of patriotic idealism. Ioannidis was the subtlest, the most sinister, and perhaps the most underestimated.

After confirming Papadopoulos as the leader, the meeting on 18 April took the decision to launch the coup on the night of 20–21 April. This is the most probable account, though an alternative version suggests that they originally planned to act on the 22nd, but advanced the date because of two disturbing events on 20 April. The first of the disturbing events was the anonymous telephone call in the early morning to General Laskaris' wife, which alarmed Pattakos and Papadopoulos. The second was the outcome of the Generals' conference that afternoon, the news of which reached the Colonels while they were holding a final meeting during the same evening.[31]

There is no doubt that Zoitakis was responsible for betraying the Generals' discussion to the Colonels. He denied it at his trial in 1975, claiming that he knew 'nothing of the role of the Colonels'[32] and that Pattakos' tape-recorded account was 'fabricated'.[33] But the court accepted Pattakos' story that Zoitakis, on leaving the Pentagon about 17.00, had gone to look for Makarezos at his home. Makarezos was absent, at the Colonels' final meeting, so Zoitakis telephoned to their meeting-place (the home of another of the Colonels) and asked Makarezos to come home and hear some important information.

What passed between the two when they met was never disclosed, but it was apparently not that Zoitakis urged the conspirators to hasten their plans. When Makarezos returned to the meeting, he said that Zoitakis was 'again backing water'.[34] Evidently this meant that he was urging the Colonels to postpone action, perhaps because he was breaking his word of honour to Spandidakis by forewarning them. It was disturbing advice, because Zoitakis' co-operation was essential to the Colonels. They could hardly succeed without the support of his III Corps, since this, as Spandidakis later put it, 'was almost the whole of the Army'.[35] Papadopoulos therefore decided to tell Zoitakis that the operation was postponed, but to carry it out that night as planned; and in order to protect Zoitakis' 'word of honour', he was to be arrested along with other Generals during the night.[36] Pattakos claimed that it was he himself who persuaded the revolutionary group not to follow Zoitakis' advice.[37]

Zoitakis' motives were obscure, but at least his conduct showed that there were deep divisions among the Generals. So there were also among the Colonels. One of their least-known but most forceful henchmen, Major Steiakakis (later nicknamed 'Gaddafi', as Papadopoulos was 'Nasser'), told a journalist that 'the origins of the fall of Papadopoulos and the failure of the revolution' could be traced to the day after it occurred: 'instead of looking to the future, they looked to see how they could destroy each other'.[38] There were examples of their divisions from the earliest days.

In the first instance, they could not decide what to do with the King. Ioannidis later admitted to a royalist General that he had favoured eliminating and even executing the King at once.[39] Pattakos, however, more than once acknowledged that without the King's name, the coup had no chance of success. The view of the majority was that the issue of a forged 'royal decree' was essential, whatever fate might later be decided for the monarchy.[40] Of the Generals, perhaps only Zoitakis would have supported such a cynical exploitation of the King.

The Colonels were also uncertain how they would use power once they had achieved it. Even during their final conference on 20 April, they were still debating the allocation of responsibilities in the government. It was eventually agreed that Papadopoulos should be Minister in the office of the still undesignated Prime Minister, Pattakos should be Minister of the Interior, and Makarezos, as an economist, should be Minister of Co-ordination. But all the other Ministers were still to be chosen. It was agreed that they should be civilians, but the Revolutionary Council was to exercise a monitoring role over them. Even this decision was ambiguous, since Papadopoulos himself preferred that there should be no Revolutionary Council at all.

These naïve theories of revolution were certain to be modified by experience of office and internal rivalries. Papadopoulos had to contend both with the other two members of the triumvirate and with others in the revolutionary group, particularly the hard-liners, Ladas and Aslanidis. Another rival, less conspicuous at first, was Ioannidis, who eventually brought about Papadopoulos' downfall. There were also dissidents on the moderate wing of the conspiracy, two or three of whom later defected. One was the anonymous informant of Andreas Papandreou;[41] another was Colonel D. Stamatelopoulos, who was to become a penetrating critic. Not surprisingly, the aims of the coup were variously interpreted by its organizers.

The operational planning, however, was highly skilled.[42] Only a small number of units in and around Athens were needed to control the capital, since the bulk of the army was in the north, concentrated near the Turkish frontier in view of the perennial threat of hostilities over Cyprus or the Aegean. Four powerful divisions (including the only Armoured Division) were under the command of Zoitakis' III Corps in the north-east. At Zoitakis' HQ there were also secret members of the revolutionary group, who could ensure that undesirable orders did not reach the northern units.

Zero hour for the military action was 02.00 on 21 April. No one outside the conspiracy seems to have had an inkling of the threat. The King had gone to bed late in his country house at Tatoi. The American Ambassador, Phillips Talbot, was asleep at home. Senior officers of the CIA and JUSMAGG appear to have suspected nothing out of the ordinary. The Greek Council of Ministers had met in the evening of the 20th, after which Kanellopoulos went back to his flat on the lower slopes of Lykavittos (Lycabettus). Andreas Papandreou spoke at a meeting of Democratic Clubs that evening, and returned to his house in the suburb of Psychiko – somewhat unusually, because he lived in fear of attack and frequently slept at the homes of various friends. General Papadatos, who commanded all the troops in Athens and Attica, had other engagements after Spandidakis' conference. Returning home on foot in the early hours of Friday morning, he was amazed to see tanks moving through the streets, without any orders known to himself.

The movement had started exactly on time. After a last-minute gathering at Ioannidis' house, Pattakos had gone home and telephoned his deputy commander of the Armoured Training Centre (KET) to meet him there at 22.30. He put on his uniform and told his wife that a 'practice alert' was to take place, which was a normal exercise. At the KET he told his deputy commander the same. When all units were reported ready, he summoned his officers and regular NCOs to an assembly at 00.30. He then told them what was really intended.

By his own account, they all applauded – a response contrary to all military convention.[43] Thus reassured, he next offered them the chance to dissent or withdraw, but none did so. Returning to his office, he telephoned Papadopoulos to report that everything was ready. Papadopoulos and Makarezos then came to join him at the KET. Meanwhile units of infantry and artillery, which had been similarly notified, were also concentrating there. At 02.00 the force moved out from three gates of the camp. All were on the streets by 02.45, where Papadatos had his disturbing encounter with them.

At the same time a unit of light tanks was sent to surround the King's country house at Tatoi. Other units were sent to take over the central telephone-exchange and the radio-station; others to arrest the political leaders – Kanellopoulos and his colleagues Papaligouras and George Rallis; George and Andreas Papandreou and their colleague Costa Mitsotakis; and Iliou, the leader of EDA. Many loyal senior officers were arrested at home; but

Papadatos, warned by his son not to go home, escaped by spending the night at his own headquarters.

A few well-known figures of the left escaped arrest at first, including the Communist leader, Brillakis, and the popular musician, Mikis Theodorakis. The King's private secretary and confidant, Major Arnaoutis, was arrested, though the Director of his political office, D. Bitsios, was not. But the King's entourage also included a number of members of the conspiracy. Like General Papadatos, the King was clearly ignorant of the disloyalty around him.

Among the first to be conveyed forcibly to the Pentagon were the Chiefs of Staff of the three services: General Spandidakis, Admiral Engolphopoulos, and Air-Marshal Antonakos. The Admiral would have nothing to do with the revolutionaries. The Air-Marshal was initially less determined in his opposition. Spandidakis, according to Pattakos' account, began by protesting at the betrayal of his confidence, no doubt to establish that he was innocent of collusion. But Pattakos replied: 'General, forgive me, but the nation comes first!'[44] He then offered Spandidakis the opportunity to join the revolution. Spandidakis agreed – reluctantly, by his own account. This was a turning-point for the Colonels.

Several attempts to recover legitimate control were made that night: by the King, by the Navy, by Kanellopoulos, and by George Rallis, his Minister of Public Order. The first to react was Kanellopoulos, who was the first to be seized. When troops broke into his flat at 02.10 on Friday morning, he gained time by protesting vigorously while his wife, in the next room, telephoned to his nephew, Dionysios Livanos, with a hurried warning. A few minutes later Bitsios, the King's political adviser, rang to ask Kanellopoulos what was happening. He had been alerted by his secretary, whose husband (a Brigadier) was one of the first to be arrested.[45] But almost at once telephone communication was cut off, and Kanellopoulos was carried off to the Pentagon.

Bitsios, however, had warned the King; Livanos was hurrying to the US Ambassador's house; and Livanos' wife was on her way to warn Admiral Spanidis, who was Secretary-General of Kanellopoulos' party, ERE. Spanidis, though retired, was still influential in the Navy. He hurried by car to the naval base at Skaramanga, but found that the senior Admirals were not available: Engolphopoulos was already a prisoner, and others were absent with their squadrons. The senior Commodore at Skaramanga put his ships on alert, and managed to telephone to the King on a secret line independent of the central exchange. He proposed that Spanidis should assume command in the absence of his own Admiral, but the King disagreed and told him to stand by for further orders. By 05.00 the ships at Skaramanga were ready to sail. A jeep had been sent for the commander of the Skaramanga base, Admiral Rozakis, who arrived in the early morning. But in the meantime the conspirators had become aware of the secret line from the naval base to Tatoi. It was quickly cut, and the Navy was left without orders from the King.

There was another secret line to Tatoi, from the Police Emergency Centre in the suburb of Maroussi. It was known to George Rallis in his capacity as Minister of Public Order. About 04.00 he too succeeded in making contact with the King by this line. He described the situation in Athens, and pointed out the importance of controlling the northern forces. His first thought was to fly to Salonika himself, where he was sure that the Chief of Staff of III Corps, Brigadier O. Vidalis, would remain loyal. But on sending a police patrol-car to the small aerodrome at Tatoi, Rallis found it already in revolutionary hands.

There remained the wireless, through which Rallis could send a message to the police headquarters at Salonika, for transmission to Vidalis. He drafted a directive in the King's name, which he read over the telephone to the King, instructing III Corps to move on Athens.[46] Although the King approved it, and Rallis despatched it, the directive never reached the Brigadier. Years later it was learned that two staff officers who were members of the conspiracy had intercepted and suppressed it.[47]

Soon afterwards Spandidakis, having allied himself with the conspirators, decided to issue an order to III Corps putting the Prometheus Plan into operation. It is possible that his order had already been anticipated by Zoitakis, as Brigadier Vidalis maintained during the trial in 1975, rebutting the denials of Zoitakis.[48] In any case, the order was received at latest by 06.00, and probably earlier. The plan required all units to stand fast in their positions, so that the powerful force in the north never moved. About dawn Rallis telephoned the King again to tell him despondently that he had no reaction from III Corps.

By that time the King already knew the identity of the triumvirate. He told Rallis their names, and added that they were reported to be already on their way to Tatoi. According to his principal ADC, they arrived soon after 06.30.[49] Rallis could do no more, for it was not long before he himself was under arrest. The King was left alone to face the triumphant revolutionaries.

Athens at dawn was quiet but terrified. Two girls and a boy had been killed by trigger-happy soldiers, but otherwise hardly a shot had been fired. Tanks were at every crossroad in the centre. The police, who had quickly capitulated, were patrolling the streets. No other vehicles were allowed to circulate; no telephone calls were possible. A few newspapers reached the streets, even carrying brief reports of the coup. Banks and the Stock Exchange were ordered to remain closed. The only source of information was the radio, which broadcast soon after 06.00 a decree supposedly in the King's name, suspending eleven articles of the constitution.[50] It was said to be signed by 'the

President and Members of the Council of Ministers', none of whom was named. This broadcast was the first news the King had of the decree forged in his name.

The next blow was Spandidakis' letter, carried by the triumvirate, which confirmed that he supported the coup. After reading it, the King demanded to see Spandidakis. The three left to convey his order to the CGS, thus confirming that they still respected the King's authority, at least nominally. Spandidakis arrived at Tatoi about 08.30. Their conversation was bitter on the King's side and feebly apologetic from Spandidakis. He told the King, according to his later account, that 'what is done has been done for the throne and the country'.[51] The King then decided to go personally to the Pentagon, driving himself with Spandidakis and an ADC in his car.

He put on full uniform and carried his Field-Marshal's baton for the occasion. On the way he called for a few minutes at his mother's house in Psychiko, in order to reassure her. In the car he discussed with Spandidakis what was to be done. According to the latter, the King proposed that he should become Prime Minister; but Spandidakis declined, and proposed instead the name of Constantine Kollias, Chief Prosecutor at the Supreme Court (the Areopagus).[52] On arrival at the Pentagon, the King was cheered and clapped. All the officers there were in a state of feverish excitement, certain of the immediate outcome but uncertain of the consequences.

The triumvirate was back at the Pentagon, trying to impose order on the confusion, but also in an exuberant mood. The King's first demand was for the release of his trusted friend Major Arnaoutis, which was granted with some reluctance after several hours of confinement and rough treatment. He was then allowed to talk to all the Generals present at the Pentagon, both collectively and individually. According to his ADC, giving evidence at the trial in 1975, only one of the Generals advised him against submission.[53]

The King nevertheless tried to persuade the triumvirate to end their mutinous action and return to duty. He pointed out the disastrous impression which their action would make on Greece's allies. Pattakos characteristically replied that if they had to take account of the reactions of foreigners, then Greece would not be a free country.[54] He thought the allies would not intervene, and his judgement proved correct. Clearly the three men were in no mood to withdraw.

As a last recourse, the King asked to talk in private with his Prime Minister, whom he knew to be held in the Pentagon. The request was granted – a sign that the revolutionaries were still striving for legitimacy but confident of success. It is hardly surprising that in the stress of the moment the King and Kanellopoulos retained slightly different recollections of the conversation which followed, but the outcome is not in dispute.[55] The King decided that to call on the armed forces to resist the coup would lead to useless bloodshed. He must therefore compromise with the conspirators. Kanellopoulos said that in that case he would cease to be King.

When the King, thinking aloud, made the suggestion of forming a government under Kollias, evidently with the thought that this would ensure the support of Spandidakis, Kanellopoulos replied that he had no further comment. In effect he regarded himself as having resigned from that moment. The King then proceeded to renew the argument with the triumvirate, which lasted another two hours. Pattakos was becoming impatient, because the radio was broadcasting at intervals that the new government would be announced shortly, and none was ready. The main point was whether the Prime Minister should be a General or a civilian. The conspirators wanted Spandidakis, now that they had him on their side. The King insisted on Kollias.

Finally it was agreed that Kollias should become Prime Minister, with Spandidakis as his Deputy. The latter was also to be Minister of Defence. Papadopoulos, Pattakos and Makarezos were to take the three Ministries which they had chosen in advance. It was announced on the radio that the government would be sworn in at 16.00, but the ceremony was in fact postponed till 17.15. It was to be conducted by the Archimandrite Ieronymos, the King's personal chaplain, because the Archbishop Chrysostomos was old, sick, and anxious to be excused.

A car was sent for Kollias, who had not even been consulted. He arrived at the Pentagon as the King was leaving, to be told of his appointment with no option of refusal.[56] The King then hurried to his residence in Athens, where he received the American Ambassador, Phillips Talbot, and asked his advice. Talbot was unable to give an answer without consulting Washington. He may have suspected that there was truth in the rumours about the CIA's complicity in the coup, but the probability is that the CIA station in Athens was as much taken by surprise as he was.[57] The most that can reasonably be argued, as Andreas Papandreou believed, is that the CIA quickly decided to support the Colonels once they were clearly in control.[58]

One of the few relevant documents published later is a State Department memorandum dated 6 February 1967, which summarized CIA reports from 19 June 1965 to 23 January 1967.[59] The memorandum spoke of a 'rightist military conspiratorial group' in Greece, of which about twenty names were known. Prominent among them were said to be a Lieutenant-Colonel D. Papadopoulos and a Lieutenant-Colonel Stamatelopoulos. Papadopoulos' initial was incorrect, and the importance of Stamatelopoulos (later a defector) was exaggerated. Since Papadopoulos' activities had become public knowledge in June 1965, there is nothing remarkable about the report. Although the State Department requested further information early in 1967, none seems to have been forthcoming. It is hard to accept the fanciful theory that the CIA was simply covering up the activities of an agent of its own. The result was to give a lamentable impression of inefficiency in its primary task of providing intelligence.

There is some evidence, however, that Talbot had been given the opportunity in advance to consider the right reaction to events if they became out of control. The sources of this evidence have not been named, but they seem to have been well placed.[60] Early in 1967 Talbot had been persuaded to recommend that the CIA 'be directed to undertake political action to head off a Papandreou victory', but the proposal was vetoed by a committee of the National Security Council in Washington. During March, however, Talbot was again asked for advice on an 'extra-parliamentary solution' to the problem if Papandreou won the election. (It was said that the request came from the King, but this is certainly untrue.) Talbot drafted a feeble response, that the US reaction 'would depend on circumstances'. A stronger draft was in preparation when it was overtaken by the coup on 21 April. The only reasonable conclusion is that Talbot had been obliged to give thought to the problems which might arise, but neither he nor the CIA had any role in precipitating them.

Talbot was therefore bound to be cautious when the King appealed to him on 21 April. He could hardly commit the United States to any kind of forcible intervention. While he sought instructions from Washington, there was only one sensible initiative which he could take on his own authority. He knew that a shipment of American weapons, including tanks, was approaching Piraeus. Since it would be taken as a sign of US approval for the coup if these were to be seen being unloaded in the next few days, Talbot proposed, with the agreement of the General commanding JUSMAGG, that the ship should be diverted. Ironically, its new destination was to be Turkey. This was the first, almost accidental, step towards a ban on the delivery of heavy weapons to Greece.[61] Apart from this, the United States' first reaction to the coup was a stunned silence.

Andreas Papandreou was convinced, however, that the US Embassy advised the King to accept the *fait accompli*, and that the British Embassy did the same. He thought that the US Embassy favoured the Colonels' plot because the British Embassy favoured the Generals' plot, but that was pure speculation.[62] In any case the King felt that he had no alternative, in default of any reaction by his major allies. In desperation, he even turned to the Soviet bloc for advice. Knowing that the Soviet and Yugoslav Embassies were under armed surveillance, he sent an emissary to the Czechoslovak Embassy. There too the response was extremely reserved. The Czech Ambassador was said to have blamed the CIA for the coup, and to have warned of international disapproval if Greece's new rulers resorted to political persecution.[63] None of this gave the King any help.

It is inconceivable that any Ambassador could have advised the King to accept the *fait accompli*. The coup had no claim to legitimacy except under Article 91 of the Constitution, which empowered the King to suspend a number of articles under certain conditions. But the specified conditions included a recommendation by the Council of Ministers (which meant Kanellopoulos' government), either in case of war or of a grave threat to public order. None of these conditions had in fact occurred.

Even after a decree of suspension under Article 91, the legitimacy of the existing government would not be in question, and the decree would have to be submitted to Parliament for approval. All of these provisions were illegally overridden by the coup. The King's acquiescence was therefore even more questionable than that of his uncle, George II, towards the dictatorship of General Metaxas in 1936; for Metaxas was at least himself the Prime Minister who recommended the partial suspension of the constitution. No foreign Ambassador could in good conscience have advised Constantine to acquiesce in a still more unconstitutional action. The US and British Ambassadors certainly did not do so.

The King's dilemma was poignantly revealed during the evening of 21 April, when telephone services were restored. Helen Vlachos, the proprietor of the conservative newspaper *Kathimerini*, rang the Palace and asked to speak to the King's private secretary.[64] She recognized the voice which replied as that of the King himself. Immediately she asked if it was true that he had sworn in the government under Kollias. He replied that he had had no alternative. 'I have found myself completely isolated,' he said, 'completely alone ...' After a further brief conversation, she advised him to keep his distance from the Colonels and to avoid being photographed with them. She thought he agreed, but less than a week passed before a photograph was published of the King in the midst of his new government.

Once the government was sworn in, it could issue genuine decrees in the name of the King. The first was broadcast on the day of the coup. Based on the suspension of the constitutional articles safeguarding human rights, although that had been promulgated illegally without the King's consent, it authorized arrest and preventive detention without time limit; it precluded bail in the case of political offences; it established trial by extraordinary tribunals or courts-martial; it forbade public or private assemblies; it abolished trade unions and declared strikes illegal; it authorized searches in private houses or public buildings, by day or night, without restriction; it established censorship of broadcasts by radio or television; it authorized the opening of correspondence; it gave power to courts-martial to try all types of crime, including political offences and offences by the press, whether or not they were directed against the military authorities. The last clause, for good measure, was stated twice over in different words.[65]

On the same day the new Prime Minister broadcast a message to the people.[66] He spoke of the corruption of the political system, using for the first time the word *phavlokratia* ('corruptocracy') which became a standard term of abuse under the dictatorship. He contrasted it with the new spirit of 'brotherhood', and emphasized the plebeian origins of the country's saviours: 'we belong to the working class'. He defined the government's purpose merely as 'to restore the health of public life' – a phrase which had often been used by Karamanlis ten years earlier. There was no mention as yet of saving Greece from Communism.

There was even a passing tribute in the Prime Minister's broadcast to the principle of democracy. He spoke of establishing 'a healthy basis for the return to a truly orthodox parliamentary life'. He promised that, once the government had created suitable conditions, as quickly as possible, 'the country will return to parliamentarism on a healthy basis'. Health was a constantly recurring metaphor of the dictatorship. In Papadopoulos' case its vocabulary was drawn from surgery, and he often referred to the need to keep Greece's fractured limbs encased in plaster.

The coup met with little resistance in the major cities. Demonstrations at the University of Ioannina and at Iraklion in Crete were quickly suppressed, and their leaders put on trial. With very few exceptions, loyal officers in the armed services found themselves impotent to react, though some turned their minds immediately to resistance: among them, Brigadier Vidalis at III Corps HQ, and Colonel Opropoulos, who had been the successful rival of Papadopoulos and Makarezos earlier in their careers. A number of Generals also planned active resistance, but most of them had to do so from retirement, since there were inevitably immediate changes in the high command.

General Angelis, the trusted superior of Papadopoulos in the artillery, succeeded Spandidakis as Chief of the General Staff. The Naval Chief of Staff, Admiral Engolphopoulos, would stay at his post only if he were assured that there would be no enforced changes under his command. That assurance was refused, and he was retired at once. He was succeeded by Admiral Dedes, who was equally loyal to the King and believed he could serve his country best by remaining at his post. The Chief of the Air Staff, Air-Marshal Antonakos, took the same view and retained his post. Both officers put themselves unreservedly at the King's disposal eight months later, when he tried to overthrow the Colonels. Angelis naturally did not. Such disloyalty and treachery were confined to a small minority of the Army alone: Spandidakis, Zoitakis and Angelis being the chief examples.

On the day after the coup, fourteen more Ministers were appointed. The most significant newcomers were three: Zoitakis as Deputy Minister of

Defence; a professional diplomat, P. Oikonomou-Gouras, as Foreign Minister, to humour a wish of the King; and P. Totomis, an employee of the Greek–American millionaire, Tom Pappas, as Minister of Public Order. These appointments clearly reflected the attitude of the Colonels in public policy: a second General to strengthen the military control of administration; an ex-Ambassador to show that foreign policy was to be a matter of window-dressing; and the nominee of a business tycoon who was expected to be influential with the Americans. In the event, Tom Pappas was to prove even more useful to the Colonels under the subsequent US administration, after 1968.

Four more Ministers were added on 26 April, making a total of twenty-three. The full Council of Ministers was presented to the King on that day. Kollias again took the opportunity to speak of a future return to parliamentary government; so did the King. He also urged his Ministers to be 'modest and popular' in their conduct.[67] If they did so, they would have his co-operation. No comment was made in reply, but what the King or Kollias might say was of no consequence to the successful conspirators. Nor did they take any notice of a statement issued by Karamanlis in Paris on the 23rd. Karamanlis claimed, gloomily but rightly, to have foreseen the catastrophe and to have tried to save Greece's 'unstable democracy', until he saw that he was wasting his time.[68] After that he held his peace for seven months. Naturally his statement was suppressed in Athens, and ignored by the Colonels.

The nature and structure of what came to be known as the 'junta' are not easily defined. The name, with its Latin American connotations, had an agreeably contemptuous ring on the lips of its enemies, especially in its Greek transliteration as *khounta*; but what did it describe? Obviously not the Council of Ministers, with its majority of insignificant civilians. Of the three concentric circles of the Colonels – the triumvirate, the inner revolutionary group, and the outer Revolutionary Council – it can hardly describe the last, which perhaps never met and in any case soon withered away. It would be too narrow a term to apply only to the triumvirate, so the intermediate revolutionary group is best identified as the junta. Most of the fifteen or so members of this group held office either as Ministers or as Secretaries-General of Ministries at one time or another. They called themselves collectively 'the Revolution'.

They did so at first with no clear conception of an ideology. A perceptive analysis of the junta's putative ideology, written while it was still in power, wittily exposed its primitive thinking.[69] Pattakos, for example, claimed that the task of the Revolution was 'to fashion a New Man', and this New Man 'must have the strength to do Absolute Good'. Papadopoulos regularly insisted on the inherent superiority of 'Helleno-Christian civilization', which must make Greece 'a pole of ideological spiritual attraction'. Ladas claimed that 'Greece is a mission, and this mission consists of civilization'. The world was therefore destined to be led into a new Golden Age by the Greeks, with their Revolution in the van.

Most of this verbiage was meaningless. Perhaps the nearest that Papadopoulos came to a significant statement of ideology was in a speech at Salonika on 28 August 1971, when he tried to define what he meant by democracy:

> Responsible democracy ... cannot be merely that democracy which is expressed by the casting and canvassing of votes ... There is no possibility of democracy as practised in the past ever returning to Greece ... Democracy means the exercise of responsible authority on the part of the representatives of the people for the satisfaction of the public interest.[70]

This definition begged many questions, including one which probably never occurred to him: *sed quis custodiet ipsos custodes?* There was no one to whom the junta was responsible except itself. There was no one whom it represented except itself. Satisfaction and public interest were both determined and defined by itself. All this circular argumentation merely echoed Metaxas and Mussolini. The task of rationalizing it was committed to a few hireling pseudo-intellectuals, some of them ex-Communists. It was one of these, G. Yiorgalas, who first formulated the claim that the action of 21 April was not a *coup d'état* (which implied a minority seizing power for its own ends) but a revolution embodying 'the aspirations of the race'.[71]

The Revolution, however, is a term which must be discarded, because it has a legal connotation in Greece, where there have been many revolutions. A revolution, once it has prevailed, is deemed to become legitimate and to create its own law. A *coup d'état* is an illegal act, whose decrees are invalid. By a vote of the restored Parliament in 1975, it was declared that the Colonels had perpetrated not a revolution but a *coup d'état*. This was the basis on which they were tried and convicted of high treason.

So their own description of themselves will not do. It would be useful if the English language had an equivalent for the Greek *praxikopimaties*, or 'perpetrators of a *coup d'état*'. Since that is lacking, they can best be described collectively as the junta, or individually as the Colonels, as may be convenient. The ambiguity reflects the absence of any firm, classifiable structure of government. Like every other junta, they were an unstable alliance of diverse and ambitious rivals. It soon became clear that Papadopoulos was the dominant figure, but his leadership was never entirely unchallenged.

3 Resistance and reaction
April–December 1967

Papadopoulos made his first public appearance at an international press conference on 27 April. He spoke calmly, but with none of the moderation of Kollias. He justified the Army's intervention by the threat of anarchy. In his own variant of the medical metaphor, he asked his audience to remember that

> we have here a sick man, whom we have on the operating table, and if the surgeon does not strap him down for the duration of the operation on the operating table, there is a possibility instead of the operation giving him the restoration of his health, it may lead to his death.[1]

It was the first time that the world had encountered the peculiarities of Papadopoulos' vocabulary, and the first time also that it had the opportunity to assess the truth of his accusations. He told the journalists that in the offices of EDA there had been found a quantity of documents which required 'seventy three-ton lorries to carry them away'. Yet not a single Communist or other member of EDA was ever convicted on evidence found in those documents. In later statements Papadopoulos undermined his own argument by boasting that the Communists were a negligible danger in Greece.[2]

On the day after his press conference, a decree was published dissolving all political parties. But simultaneously, representatives of the international press were allowed to see some of the political detainees, including Andreas Papandreou and three retired Generals, to show that they had not been maltreated. No such consideration was given to known or suspected Communists. Ilias Iliou, the leader of EDA, was brutally treated, and at least one member of the KKE died in police custody during the early days. A lawyer who had appeared for the defence in the ASPIDA case was found drowned in May on a beach in Rhodes. Most of the left-wing detainees were deported to remote islands of the Aegean: at first Leros and later Gyaros (Gioura or Yioura). Both had been used as prison-camps in the civil war of 1946–9, and were now brought into service again.

Better-known figures were handled variously, but more cautiously. George Papandreou was held in a military hospital, Andreas in the Averoff prison, Kanellopoulos under house arrest. It was reported that George and Andreas Papandreou were to be tried for treason. A letter allegedly sent by George Papandreou, while he was Prime Minister, to Papaterpos, the supposed ringleader of ASPIDA, was published on 6 May in the pro-junta

33

newspaper *Elevtheros Kosmos*, as part of the case against father and son. But it was at once denounced as a forgery, and quickly forgotten even by the Colonels.[3]

On 9 May George Papandreou was released on grounds of health. Andreas was held without trial for eight months. Restrictions on Kanellopoulos' freedom were quietly lifted by stages. Few senior officers were detained after the first few days, but those who would not co-operate with the junta were compelled to retire and kept under surveillance. Among them were seven Lieutenant-Generals and two Admirals, as well as hundreds of other officers between the ranks of Lieutenant-Colonel and Major-General.

These compulsory retirements opened the way for the promotion of officers loyal to the junta. In addition 800 new posts were created to satisfy officers who were feeling frustrated in the lower ranks. These appointments were monitored by committees of junior officers responsible to the revolutionary group. Once these precautions were taken, the junta assumed (although mistakenly) that the officer corps could be regarded as trustworthy. They gave no thought to the effect on the armed forces' capacity for external defence.

A more ruthless purge was carried out among state employees in the civil sector. This affected particularly government offices, education and the judicial system. Civil servants were deprived of their security of tenure by decree (under the authority of the initial suspension of parts of the constitution, which was itself illegal). The educational service was decimated, especially at the higher levels: for example, nearly sixty professors and associate professors were dismissed under the dictatorship. Officers loyal to the junta were infiltrated into government departments with the rank of Secretary-General, and retired officers were appointed as Commissioners (*epitropoi*) in every institute of higher education.

The function of the Commissioners was to keep watch on what was taught, and to report on the character, political views and conduct of both teachers and students. In the judicial service, uncompliant judges and prosecutors were dismissed. Even the Church was kept under control, so that a year later Papadopoulos could launch his famous slogan: 'Greece of the Christian Greeks'.[4] Archbishop Chrysostomos was forced to resign and replaced by the King's chaplain, the Archimandrite Ieronymos, who carried out an ecclesiastical purge of his own. The King was deeply pained by his disloyalty, for Ieronymos had been his confessor.

In other respects, the junta was careful not to humiliate the King unnecessarily. Pattakos several times expressed in public his loyalty to the monarchy. On the birth of Constantine's heir on 20 May, followed by his name-day on the 21st, the whole government assembled to attend a celebration in the Cathedral. The King was also allowed considerable freedom of movement.

He travelled twice to northern Greece in June, which enabled him to renew contact with loyal officers. At an Army lunch in Salonika on 25 June he spoke of the need for 'the strongest possible guarantee of democratic life'.[5] His words were not reproved.

In September 1967 the King was even allowed to fly to Canada, for the centenary of the Federation. He went on to Washington, where he lunched with President Lyndon Johnson at the White House. During this visit he also met the Senate Foreign Relations Committee, and made a much publicized retort to a Senator who spoke of 'your government': 'It is not my government!'

Although the King thus retained a shred of independence, he was also useful to the junta as the mouthpiece of their policies, however much he disliked them. It was he who had to announce on 23 May that a new Constitution was to be introduced. A Constitutional Commission of twenty experts was appointed a week later, and met for the first time on 16 June. The King had authorized, willy-nilly, his own first step down from the throne, as Kanellopoulos had foreseen on the fatal 21 April.

The monarchy presented the junta with a problem from the first. Some of them regarded it as expendable, others regarded it with reluctant awe. Most of them regarded the actual incumbent of the throne with contempt, tinged in some cases with amusement and in others with jealousy. On balance, they were in no hurry to dispose of the monarchy permanently, for several reasons. It was useful to them so long as the King was docile; it had a residual popularity in the armed forces, particularly the Navy; it was strongly supported in some provincial areas, particularly the Peloponnese, from which Papadopoulos himself came; and in any case they could not decide how to replace it.

Apart from the monarchy, the junta had no reason to show tenderness to other institutions of Greek society. Trade unions were dissolved and their assets confiscated. The General Federation of Trade Unions (GSEE) was an innocuous body, already under right-wing control: it even sent a message of congratulation to the King on the coup. But naturally there were Communists among the rank and file, not all of whom were rooted out.

Other societies were compulsorily closed by the hundred. Young people were ordered to cut their hair, to dress decently, and to go to Church. Offences against martial law were rigorously punished, even to the point of briefly imprisoning Evangelos Averoff, a former Foreign Minister, for inviting a group of more than five people to his flat. The music of Mikis Theodorakis was banned because he was, or had been, a Communist; so too was Russian caviare. An index of 760 forbidden books by over 200 Greek and foreign authors (including Sophocles, Aristophanes and Shakespeare) was published. Such was Papadopoulos' notion of surgery.

Censorship of the press was naturally total. Everything to be published had to be submitted in advance, so that the censors could prevent publication by mere delay. Newspapers were also compelled to publish certain items, including commentaries on the government and its work. Offences were severely punished: six newspapers were banned in May 1967. One paper, Mrs Vlachos' *Kathimerini* (with its evening partner *Mesimvrini*), refused to publish at all under these conditions, despite strong pressure from the junta.[6]

Mrs Vlachos was put under house arrest, but escaped from Greece in disguise at Christmas 1967. Many other journalists also escaped. But those who stayed found a curious loophole in the censorship: it did not apply to the foreign correspondents. They could report what they liked, and foreign newspapers could be sold in Greece and even quoted in the Greek press. There still remained, however, the power to deport the correspondents or confiscate their papers if they went too far.

The reaction to this oppression was predictable. There was resistance, both active and passive. The chief weapon of passive resistance was ridicule, at which Athenians were adept. There was much indignant talk, and strong statements of opposition on occasion, from former politicians. As a general rule, the junta did not mind hostile talk, so long as it did not go beyond words. In the early days there was little opportunity for action, apart from a few symbolic gestures, for the Colonels' one unquestioned talent lay in crushing conspiracies.

The roots of clandestine opposition were not deep. Although sources outside Greece identified a proliferation of organizations by their initials, the very number of them showed their fragmentary state.[7] Most of them were quickly known by the junta. The former political leaders were all under restraint or surveillance. They could give moral support to the resistance by public statements, and Kanellopoulos in particular often did so. His first major attack on the junta took place at an improvised press conference in his flat on 27 September, and made a great impact at home and abroad.[8] But where was the resistance for such an attack to support?

The only Greeks who possessed what they called 'conspiratorial experience' were the Communists, but the KKE was itself divided. It had split several times in recent years: over its failure in the civil war of 1946–9, over the campaign against Stalinism, over the Soviet disputes with Yugoslavia, China and Albania. After 1967 the split became wider still. What was called the 'Interior Office' of the KKE in Greece, headed by A. Brillakis, undertook the struggle against the junta, but the Secretary-General in exile, K. Koliyiannis, insisted on following the Moscow line, whatever it might be. At a meeting held in Bucharest in February 1968, in preparation for the 12th Plenum of the party, the split became absolute.

A minority led by D. Partsalidis, a veteran of the wartime resistance and the civil war, was then defeated and removed from office. The majority, led by Koliyiannis, declared the Interior Office abolished because it had backed the minority. After the invasion of Czechoslovakia by the Red Army in August 1968, the split was further aggravated. The Interior Office refused to accept dissolution. In 1969 it reconstituted itself formally as the KKE (Interior), and thereafter referred to Koliyiannis' faction as the KKE (Exterior). The latter, however, repudiated the designation because it was the only KKE recognized by Moscow. Paradoxically, but understandably, the meeting which established the KKE (Interior) was held outside Greece, in Italy. All these ideological squabbles gravely undermined the effectiveness of what should have been the strongest force of resistance to the junta.

The formal division between the two KKEs did not exhaust the splits in the Communist front. There were also maverick Communists who would follow no party line but their own, such as the musician Theodorakis, whose banned songs became anthems of the resistance, and Manoli Glezos, who had won glory as a boy under the German occupation by climbing the wall of the Acropolis at night to tear down the Nazi flag. Both of these men were too well known to escape arrest. Glezos was caught on the day of the coup; Theodorakis immediately went underground, but was caught four months later.

Finally, there were the renegade Communists who served the junta. Theodore Papakonstantinou, a wartime member of the KKE, wrote a pamphlet for the junta called *Political Education*; George Yiorgalas, who had been condemned to death *in absentia* during the civil war for broadcasting Communist propaganda from Budapest, wrote *The Ideology of the Revolution*; and Savvas Konstantopoulos edited the pro-junta *Elevtheros Kosmos*. Probably all three contributed to the seven volumes of mumbo-jumbo published under the name of Papadopoulos as *Our Creed (To Pistevo mas)*.[9]

Despite their handicaps, the Communists did manage to keep some resistance in being. At first they had to operate from outside Greece, but from 1971 onwards several leading members were clandestinely infiltrated at great risk. They had no prospect of overthrowing the junta themselves, but they were quick to seize opportunities which fortuitously presented themselves – for example, student protests. The students themselves put up a strenuous but intermittent resistance. They lacked only the conspiratorial experience which the Communists could supply.

Resistance in 1967 was unavoidably sporadic. Apart from the early demonstrations in Ioannina and Iraklion, the first open sign of resistance was the distribution of leaflets by a short-lived organization called the Greek Democratic Movement of Resistance (EDKA). It was active only from April to July 1967, when its leaders – all supporters of Andreas Papandreou – were arrested and given long prison sentences. Other organizations soon followed.

The Patriotic Anti-dictatorship Front (PAM) was founded in May by the KKE, EDA and other left-wing groups. Democratic Defence (DA) was founded by members of the Centre Union some ten days later. In August an Anti-dictatorship Workers' Front (AEM) was founded by Tasos Dimou, one of the few left-wing trade unionists who escaped arrest throughout. But the capabilities of these organizations were severely restricted. Leaflets and illegal newspapers might sustain morale but did little to undermine the junta. When bombs began to explode, they proved two-edged weapons. The first recorded case, outside an American PX shop on 17 October, had a merely symbolic significance. But on 30 November another bomb killed an innocent passer-by in the centre of Athens.

The junta's security services quickly proved their strength and brutality. PAM, the most active organization, was soon crippled. At the end of August 1967, fourteen of its members were arrested and tried in Salonika for publishing an illegal newspaper. In mid-November thirty-one more, including Theodorakis, were convicted in Athens. In the same month, to crush even passive resistance, a man was sent to prison simply for selling Theodorakis' records. Many other trivial offences were similarly punished.

In these conditions the early impact of resistance was slight. Many Greeks, particularly businessmen, showed little inclination to oppose the junta: their attitudes varied only from sullen acquiescence to warm approval. The intellectual community was by no means wholehearted in its opposition. Members of the Academy of Athens were criticized for their tolerance, and their retrospective defence after the fall of the dictatorship was not impressive.[10] Only Kanellopoulos, the most courageous of the Academicians, significantly refused to attend any meetings during the dictatorship – a gesture that amounted to a tacit criticism of his colleagues.

In most sectors of the community, it was individuals rather than organizations who took the risks. Among the professions, this was true of the lawyers, journalists, writers, artists, actors, teachers, priests. The cases of the musician, Theodorakis, the actress, Melina Mercouri, the lawyer, George B. Mangakis, who defended many victims in court, and his cousin Professor George A. Mangakis, attracted world-wide notice. Not the least courageous were a minority among the armed services, for these had the most to gain from the junta and were the easiest to detect and discipline. The main agencies of repression were themselves drawn from the armed services: the Central Service of Information (KYP), the National Security Service (Asphaleia), the National Military Security (ESA); and they were supported by élite units such as the Marines (founded by Papadopoulos' brother, Constantine), the Commandos, and even the Officers' School.

*　　　*　　　*

It drew little attention at first that internal security was bought at the cost of external defence. The Colonels no doubt reasoned that because Greece was indispensable to the western alliance, their allies would protect them against any external threat. The demoralization of the armed services therefore passed undetected for seven years. When the final catastrophe came in 1974, Greece's allies failed them. But in the early days of the dictatorship, external relations caused them little inconvenience.

Since the King had sworn them in, no problem arose at first of diplomatic recognition. Neither in the west nor in the east was there any decisive opposition. The Soviet government contented itself with an unfriendly warning and a demonstration outside the Greek Embassy in Moscow. The US Secretary of State, Dean Rusk, waited a week before issuing a statement on 28 April. He then expressed a cautious toleration of the junta, provided that it remained loyal to NATO, refrained from maltreating prisoners, and moved towards democracy.[11] The junta systematically flouted the last two conditions, but suffered few penalties.

At the beginning of August the junta shrewdly appointed as its new Ambassador in Washington a professional diplomat of impeccable respectability, Ch. Xanthopoulos-Palamas. The US Administration mistakenly found this reassuring. By September, when King Constantine visited Washington, he could obtain nothing from the Administration except promises of moral support. Opposition to the junta was limited to Congress and unofficial circles. The influential organization of Greek–Americans, AHEPA, gave no firm lead to public opinion.

In other western capitals there were protests from unofficial bodies but little action by governments. An exception was the Danish government, not least because both the Greek King and his young Queen were of Danish descent. In a note to all members of NATO on 5 May, the government expressed 'deep concern' over the abrogation of democracy and constitutional rights in Greece, and hoped that present conditions would be of short duration. The Greek Embassy in Copenhagen delivered a protest, which the Danish government rejected. Denmark also withdrew from the Salonika Trade Fair. Some support came from Norway, where a parliamentary debate showed strong feeling in favour of the expulsion of Greece from NATO.

Apart from the Scandinavians, the first protests were limited to groups and organizations which had no power to commit governments. A Greek–American committee, the 'Friends of Greece', published an open letter to the President on 9 May calling for action to overthrow the junta, especially as it had been set up with the help of American weapons.[12] At the Council of Europe the first of many attacks was made in the Parliamentary Assembly on 20 September, supported by the submission of a Scandinavian complaint to the European Commission of Human Rights. On 12 October came two further attacks: by the International Press Institute, denouncing censorship; and by the British Labour Party Conference, which voted for the expulsion of Greece from NATO. But in the latter case the majority was not large, and the Labour government ignored it.

Throughout the dictatorship, it was the various vehicles of public opinion rather than the executive authorities that sustained the resistance: the North Atlantic Parliamentary Assembly, not the NATO Council; the Parliamentary Assembly of the Council of Europe, not its constituent governments; the Parliaments and Assemblies of the European allies, not their Ministers; the US Senate and House of Representatives, not the Departments of State or the White House. Only in Scandinavia, with persistent determination, and in Italy, West Germany and the Netherlands on occasion, was the opposition in Greece supported by the state authorities.

Although two initial sanctions were imposed on the junta, both were half-hearted. First, in May 1967, the US Administration suspended the supply of heavy weapons to Greece, endorsing the prudent precedent set by Ambassador Talbot on 21 April. The suspended list comprised chiefly aircraft, tanks, armoured vehicles, artillery and minesweepers.[13] But the suspension was a two-edged weapon. Although tanks had helped the Colonels to power, most of the heavy weapons were needed for external defence rather than internal repression. In the interests of NATO, the suspension was first evaded and eventually cancelled.

In justice to the US Administration, it must be credited with being the only government which imposed a formal ban at all, at least initially. It was of course by far the largest supplier of weapons, but lesser suppliers among the allies had fewer scruples. The French government never interrupted supplies at all; the West Germans discontinued them only at the beginning of 1971; the British government negotiated the sale of three frigates to Greece in 1969, earning the qualified approval of a leader in *The Times*.[14] The argument in favour always rested on the needs of 'European defence'.

The second international sanction was the suspension of progress under the Treaty of Association between Greece and the European Economic Community. But there was no reversal of the terms already in operation. It was pointed out by Professor John Pesmazoglou, who had negotiated the treaty for Greece, that a number of loopholes were left unclosed. In this case no arguments from defence needs could be advanced; but equally, no pressure could be used by the Americans, the British or the Scandinavians, even had they wished to do so, because none of them was a member of the EEC.

The greatest stroke of luck for the junta was the outbreak, within two months of their coup, of the six-day war in the Middle East between Israel and Egypt. US facilities in Greece and Turkey then became essential for the defence of

Israel as well as for NATO. Without any formal announcement, the ban on heavy weapons was progressively lifted. A further consequence was that it became urgent to settle the problem of Cyprus. When the US Administration hinted that negotiations should be renewed between Greece and Turkey, the junta responded satisfactorily.

On 14 June, barely a week after the outbreak of the war between Israel and Egypt and just after the last shots were fired, a communiqué of the NATO Council recorded the agreement of Greece and Turkey to negotiate over Cyprus. But the Turks were not enthusiastic, and Makarios was unco-operative. The junta retorted sharply to Makarios' objections. On 1 July the censors gave the Athens press material criticizing 'persons holding the highest positions in the Cypriot state' who must be 'isolated and forced to give up their responsible offices on the eve of decisive developments'.[15] A milder tone was adopted by Papadopoulos when he visited Cyprus early in August. On his return he spoke of the aim of achieving *enosis* 'by peaceful methods . . . in co-operation with the Ethnarch [Makarios]'.[16] But it was increasingly taken for granted that Athens was the 'National Centre', whose policies the Cypriots must follow.

The next step was a conference between the Greek and Turkish governments, which met on 9 September at a frontier post on the River Evros. The Greek party included the Prime Minister (Kollias), his Deputy (Spandidakis), the Foreign Minister (Oikonomou-Gouras), as well as Papadopoulos and two other Colonels (Ladas and Mexis). The Turkish party included the Prime Minister (Demirel) and Foreign Minister (Çağlayangil) with a corresponding entourage. The results were disappointing, for the Turks had no idea what the Greeks intended to propose, and were unimpressed when they heard.

The Greek proposal was once more *enosis* with compensations for the Turks. It was based, with slight modifications, on a Greco-Turkish protocol which had been signed in Paris on 18 December 1966, immediately before the fall of the Stephanopoulos government.[17] The protocol had included an indirect reference to *enosis*, without commitment on the Turkish side, to be compensated by the cession of a Turkish base on Cyprus (perhaps the British base at Dekelia), the rest of the island being demilitarized. In addition, the Greeks now offered to cede a small area on the River Evros known as the 'Karagatch triangle'.

The Turkish delegation rejected the proposal. They insisted on either 'double *enosis*' (meaning partition of the island) or the maintenance of the 1959 settlement. Soon afterwards they were confirmed in their negative attitude by an assurance which Demirel obtained during a visit to Moscow, that the Soviet government remained opposed to the concession of *enosis* or any other change in the status of Cyprus. The junta had therefore suffered a serious rebuff. It was followed by the resignation of Oikonomou-Gouras as Foreign Minister a few weeks later, on grounds of health.

In Turkey anti-Greek propaganda was re-launched, starting with protests over the treatment of the Muslim minority in western Thrace. In Greece the clamour for *enosis* was also renewed. The King expressed his support for it on 25 September; so did Archbishop Ieronymos on the same day; so did Spandidakis on a visit to Cyprus in October. At the end of that month Raouf Denktash, the leader of the Turkish Cypriots, who had been forced to leave Cyprus in 1964, returned clandestinely to the island, but was arrested with two armed companions as they landed on the coast by night, and deported once more.

On 15 November there was an armed clash between Turkish Cypriots and Greek mainland forces under General Grivas. The next day the Grand National Assembly of Turkey met in secret session and resolved on war. The Colonels appeared to face the prospect with equanimity, no doubt relying on the Americans to rescue them. But strong warnings, from the King himself and the allied Ambassadors, persuaded them to see reason and submit. A wide-ranging reaction from the international community helped to camouflage their humiliation.

On 22 November President Johnson sent his Secretary of the Army, Cyrus Vance, to visit Athens, Ankara and Nicosia, with the Secretary-General of NATO and a representative of the Secretary-General of the United Nations to support him. Their object of averting war was achieved, but 'the basic problems of Cyprus remain unsolved', as the President said when congratulating Vance on his return.[18] War was averted only because the Colonels finally recognized that they faced inevitable defeat in Cyprus. Apart from the Turks' advantage in proximity to the island, the balance of forces on the land-frontier between Greece and Turkey was overwhelmingly in favour of the latter.

The junta capitulated on all points. They agreed to withdraw Grivas and his mainland troops from the island, leaving Makarios with only the Cypriot National Guard. The outcome was a new relation between Greece and Cyprus, but not a more propitious one. From this time forward, the Colonels were convinced that the problem of Cyprus could be solved only by eliminating Makarios, because the price of a settlement with the Turks would inevitably be beyond anything that Makarios could accept.

When Makarios attended a farewell parade of the Greek mainland force in Nicosia on 7 December, he was accompanied by his Minister of the Interior, Polykarpos Yiorkatzis, who was at that time Makarios' right-hand man. Yiorkatzis' subsequent role, for reasons which were presumably based on personal ambition, was perverse and fatal. He conspired for Makarios against the Colonels and then for the Colonels against Makarios. Since he came to a bloody end in 1970, when still only thirty-seven years of age, his motives are unlikely ever to be satisfactorily explained. Whatever they were, he contributed to the destruction of the Republic of Cyprus as well as himself.

In Athens too the fiasco over Cyprus had momentous consequences. Panayiotis Pipinelis, who had briefly succeeded Karamanlis as Prime Minister in 1963, undertook the post of Foreign Minister on 20 November, to apply his diplomatic experience to the task of retrieving the serious setback. He was thought at first to be an uncommitted professional, disapproving of the junta but willing to serve his country. Gradually, however, he became converted to the dictatorship, or at least to believe in its promises. The King, on the other hand, had no illusions. He was already involved in a scheme to overthrow the junta and restore constitutional government. He had little support to draw on, largely because of his indecisive reaction to the coup in the first place; but he made the most of such resources as he had.

The only potential allies with whom the King had close contact were senior officers, and few even of them. The head of his military household was Lieutenant-General K. Dovas, who was his chief adviser. Other serving officers on whom he could rely were Lieutenant-General C. Kollias (unrelated to the Prime Minister, though their names were identical), who commanded the First Army at Larisa; Lieutenant-General G. Peridis, commanding III Corps, whose HQ had moved from Salonika to Komotini in Thrace on account of the tension with Turkey; Brigadier O. Vidalis, who was still Chief of Staff at III Corps; and Brigadier A. Erselman, commanding 20 Armoured Divison, also at Komotini. There were others who had no troops under command: Lieutenant-General Manettas, who was still Inspector-General; Major-General Liarakos, in command of the War Academy at Salonika; and a number of staff officers. Finally, there were the Chiefs of Staff of the Navy and Air Force, Admiral Dedes and Air-Marshal Antonakos.

Indirect support could be expected from retired officers, though it was difficult for any of them to come into contact with the King. Colonel Opropoulos was active in recruiting his former colleagues, though he found some reluctant because of the enduring divisions between royalists and republicans. Among the retired Generals, a former Chief of the General Staff, Solon Ghikas, who was a close friend of Karamanlis, would certainly have given his support. So would the most senior of all, Th. Tsakalotos, though he expressed the pessimistic opinion that 'the King will never move', and that even if he did, the junta was too strong to be dislodged.[19]

Former politicians could also be contacted only indirectly. According to Andreas Papandreou (who was still in gaol), his father promised to support the King, but Andreas himself refused.[20] Kanellopoulos was not approached because he was too closely watched, but his support could be assumed; so could that of Averoff, now released from brief imprisonment in September. George Mavros, who was to succeed Papandreou as leader of the Centre Union (though the party was formally dissolved), was optimistic that the junta would collapse. The most important of the potential supporters was Karamanlis, with whom the King was in touch through intermediaries.

The King sent an ADC at the end of October to inform Karamanlis that he was preparing for a clash. Others were also approaching Karamanlis at this time. The Prime Minister, Kollias, wrote assuring him of his good intentions, and received a reply urging him to carry out his promise of restoring democracy. Makarezos sent an intermediary to seek his advice, but Karamanlis refused to meet him. On 9 November Karamanlis replied to the King expressing his despair of the junta. Later he was to say that he told the King 'seven times' not to launch his ill-fated coup.[21]

On 29 November, however, Karamanlis published an interview with *Le Monde* which was designed to give the King moral support.[22] He said that it was the duty of the Colonels to 'withdraw from power and put themselves at the disposal of the Palace'. The statement was well calculated to rally public opinion to the King, but unfortunately it also drew closer attention to him on the part of the junta. He found himself under even closer surveillance, but he had gone too far to draw back.

The junta was already well informed of the King's contacts. It was said that they expected him to launch his counter-attack on 28 October, the anniversary of Greece's defiance of Mussolini in 1940, but this was wishful thinking. When one of the senior Generals taxed him with the rumour, the King replied with dignity: 'The King does not conspire.'[23] Certainly no act by the King against an unconstitutional government could be called a conspiracy, but it was true that the King was planning a coup of his own.

On 28 October he was in Salonika with the Queen to celebrate the anniversary of the war. While there, he contrived to have a private meeting with General Peridis. During November all planning was suspended because of the threat of war with Turkey. On 6 December the King summoned Kollias (First Army Commander) and Peridis (III Corps Commander) for a meeting with General Dovas and himself. No doubt the meeting was observed.

The King explained his intentions to the Generals. He would announce the dismissal of the government and fly to northern Greece, accompanied by the Queen and Prime Minister. The Generals' task would be to rally the northern forces to his support and to control any dissident elements; but there must be no shooting. There were formidable difficulties. Not all the senior officers in the north would rally to the King. The rallying-point would have to be at Kavalla rather than Salonika, because the northern divisions were concentrated far to the east of the northern capital. A point which was overlooked was that there was no radio transmitter powerful enough to broadcast to the nation except in Athens and Salonika, so the junta would have control of the air.

General Kollias said that six or seven days' notice would be needed. The King could not risk a longer period for reasons of security. He decided to act on 13 December, because several indispensable officers were to be compulsorily retired soon after that date. On 12 December he summoned General Manettas and gave him a letter to be delivered to General Angelis at 11.00 on the following day.[24] The letter stated that the King had decided to take personal command of the armed forces, to dismiss Angelis as CGS and to appoint Manettas in his place. He explained to Manettas that by 11.00 on the 13th he himself would have left by air from Tatoi for the north. Manettas expressed his doubts: suppose anything delayed the King's take-off, would not the text of the letter endanger him by alerting Angelis? The King agreed to a modification: a telephone call would be made to Manettas as soon as the royal aircraft was airborne, so that the letter could safely be delivered.

On the same day, 12 December, the King informed the Prime Minister of his intention. Kollias agreed to go with him. At a party that evening the King met the American Ambassador, and asked him to call at Tatoi the next day at 09.00. About midnight certain key officers were informed that the King's coup was about to be launched. General Peridis informed General Liarakos, who was to take charge at Salonika until a sufficient force could be despatched there from further east. One of the King's ADCs arrived in Larisa to inform General Kollias, who was worried by the lack of earlier notice. His task was to cut telephone communication between Athens and the north at 11.00 on the 13th, and to secure the support of as many of his subordinate officers as possible. He still pressed for a postponement, but the King refused, using a coded phrase by telephone. Like most coded phrases, it was probably easy enough to interpret for anyone listening in.

Early next morning those who had been notified began to assemble at Tatoi. Two flights were to take off from the small aerodrome. In one aircraft, flying to Kavalla, the King was to be accompanied by the Prime Minister, Queen Frederika, Queen Anne-Marie and her gynaecologist (for she was again expecting a baby). In the other, Air-Marshal Antonakos was to fly to Larisa to join General Kollias, carrying a tape-recording of a proclamation by the King, which was to be broadcast by radio.[25] Although Antonakos had not been informed of his role until the last minute, he agreed at once. An attempt was made to locate Archbishop Ieronymos in the hope that he too would rally to the King. But he could not be found, or did not want to be.

At 09.00 Ambassador Talbot arrived at Tatoi. The King explained his intention, and asked for two gestures of support.[26] One was that the Voice of America should broadcast his proclamation, of which he gave Talbot a tape-recording. The other was that the 6th Fleet should make a show of force in Phaliron Bay. Neither of these requests was fulfilled. It is difficult in fact to see how either of them, particularly the latter, could have been fulfilled in time to influence the outcome. By 09.30 the Ambassador had left.

The flights from Tatoi were due to take off an hour later. During that hour, if not earlier, details of the King's plan became known to the junta. Between 09.30 and 11.00 the Deputy Minister of Defence, General Zoitakis, was closeted with Admiral Dedes, the Chief of the Naval Staff, in the latter's office. Their meeting was interrupted by an urgent telephone message summoning Zoitakis to the Pentagon. From there he telephoned Dedes to say that 'some irregularity' had occurred, so he had put the Army on a state of alert. Dedes, who knew nothing of the King's plans, assumed that he ought to issue a similar order to the Navy, which he did. It was not until midday that he learned the truth about the 'irregularity', but his action, taken without orders, fortuitously enabled the Navy to make a show of support for the King later in the day.

The King's party took off from Tatoi at 10.30, immediately followed by Antonakos. Ten minutes later Manettas received a telephone call in his office at the Pentagon confirming their departure. But at about the same time Angelis telephoned General Kollias at Larisa to tell him that the plot was discovered. Kollias nevertheless rejected Angelis' order to abandon the action. Shortly after 11.00 he cut off the telephone links between the Pentagon and northern Greece, in accordance with the King's instructions.

Meanwhile the die was cast almost simultaneously at 11.00 in a number of centres. Antonakos, in flight to Larisa, issued an instruction by wireless to all Air Force units, to prevent the Army from entering any aerodrome and to organize flights over Athens and other towns 'as a show of strength'.[27] Brigadier Erselman, at Komotini, told his officers in the Armoured Division of the King's action. General Manettas went to deliver the King's letter to Angelis.

Angelis received Manettas coolly, almost with contempt. Being forewarned, he was ready to disregard the King's orders; and he had communication by radio-telephone to replace the lines to the north which General Kollias had cut. He peremptorily told Manettas to go to his office, where he was kept under guard for the next twenty-four hours.

Outside Athens, however, things at first went better for the King. Antonakos joined General Kollias at Larisa, and gave him the tape of the King's proclamation, which was broadcast by the local transmitter at 11.30. The transmitter was not a powerful one, but the reactions of senior officers and public officials were said to be favourable at first. They may have been pleased by a phrase in the broadcast attacking 'the Communists who are working for the destruction of the nation', but by others it was regarded as an error of judgement.

At 12.00 Admiral Dedes, having learned the truth about the 'irregularity' in the Army, refused to take any more calls from the Pentagon and ordered the fleet to sea in support of the King. The main fleet sailed at 15.30 from Salamis, to be joined by squadrons from Crete and the Aegean. Admiral Rozakis, in command of the combined fleet, made for Salonika, which he assumed to be the King's destination. Later he received a radio message from Larisa redirecting him to Kavalla.

The King had already arrived at Kavalla, where he was met by a divisional commander who had been initiated into the plan only at the last minute by General Peridis from Komotini. Salonika was a much more difficult problem. Although there were comparatively few units there, they were mostly controlled by officers loyal to the junta. The exception was the War Academy under General Liarakos, which consisted of officers attending a course, without combat troops. As soon as Liarakos learned of the King's arrival at Kavalla, he sent individual officers whom he trusted with orders to take over the local units, and himself took possession of the building which had been III Corps HQ before it moved to Komotini. His intention was to hold on until he could be relieved by a force which was to be sent, according to the plan, from Komotini.

The King made a number of telephone calls soon after midday to the commanders of higher formations in the north. Their response was on the whole encouraging. At 14.00 he rang General Kollias at Larisa, and they assured each other that the plan was going well. But in fact it was not so. Support for the King was precarious, and would continue only so long as he seemed to have the upper hand.

Angelis had re-established communication from the Pentagon by radiotelephone. Many officers in the north were already wavering. Most units at Salonika refused to accept Liarakos' command. The force which should have rushed from Komotini to support him was delayed, perhaps by officers loyal to the junta. Brigadier Erselman was put under arrest by a unit of his own division, which then moved on III Corps HQ at Komotini. The King flew to Komotini by helicopter at 15.30 to see Peridis and Vidalis, but he was forced by bad weather to return before nightfall to Kavalla. One divisional commander whom he urged to move on Salonika was persuaded by a subordinate squadron-commander to order his unit against Kavalla instead. The King's own control centre was under threat.

By midnight it was plain that the chances of success had practically disappeared. About 01.30 on the 14th units loyal to the junta took over III Corps HQ at Komotini. At Kavalla, half an hour later, the King decided to leave Greece with his family and to take refuge in western Europe. They flew from

Kavalla without hindrance. Others, who did not know of the King's decision, held out for a time. Admiral Rozakis, in command of the fleet at sea, received a message from the Pentagon at 03.30 reporting the collapse of the King's coup, but he continued on his course until he learned from the radio news at 06.00 that the King had arrived in Rome. At 04.00 General Kollias restored the telephone link with Athens, and spoke defiantly to Angelis and Papadopoulos.[28] He refused to give up his command until 09.00. Some hours earlier, Liarakos had given up hope in Salonika and surrendered to the senior member of the junta in northern Greece.

The final seal was set on the misadventure when Archbishop Ieronymos administered the oath of office as Regent to General Zoitakis during the morning of the 14th. The King was deemed to have 'deserted his duties', but not to have abdicated or been deposed. Zoitakis' first act was to appoint Papadopoulos Prime Minister in place of Kollias, who was assumed to have resigned. Papadopoulos also took responsibility as Minister of Defence. Spandidakis was dropped and replaced as Deputy Prime Minister by Pattakos, who also retained the Ministry of the Interior. As a result of the fiasco, the junta was stronger than before.

Papadopoulos held a press conference on the same day.[29] He gave a brief account of what had happened in unimpassioned language. In answer to questions, he denied that he had any prior knowledge of the King's intention, and refused to speculate on the reasons for his 'incomprehensible action'. He confirmed that Pipinelis, the Foreign Minister, and Androutsopoulos, the Minister of Finance, would remain in office. The latter was insignificant, and became if possible more so when he was made Prime Minister in his turn six years later. But Pipinelis was an important recruit. This loyal servant of former monarchs now began loyally attacking Constantine.

The King's defeat made the prospect for Greece worse in many ways. Karamanlis, to whom the King telephoned from Rome, saw no point in meeting him. He expected Constantine to return to Athens under humiliating conditions. Pattakos said on 18 December that the King could return if he wished. Constantine himself said at a press conference in Rome on the 20th that he wanted to return, but only if the country were back on course to democracy.[30]

Despite visits to Rome by a number of intermediaries from Greece, no agreement was reached and the King did not return. Worst of all, the US Administration's attitude hardened in favour of the junta. A personal sorrow was also added to the historic tragedy of the monarchy: the Queen lost her unborn baby at the end of December. Papadopoulos sent his unwelcome condolences. He also assured those who were in doubt that he was, as ever, a devoted royalist.[31]

4 The monstrous regiment

1968

In its old sense, the word 'regiment' meant 'government'. That is how John Knox used it when he spoke of 'the monstrous regiment of women', referring to Mary, Queen of Scots. The Greek word *syntagma* means both 'regiment' and 'constitution'; and a *syntagmatarchis* is a Colonel. It is therefore peculiarly appropriate to speak of 'the monstrous regiment' of Colonels, who both demoralized the Army and made a shambles of the Constitution.

The Constitutional Commission, which the King had been forced to announce in May 1967, was already at work before his abortive coup. Only two days after his flight, the Commission held a public meeting which indicated that its work was near completion, and a week later its draft proposals were submitted to Papadopoulos. But until it was ratified – whatever ratification might mean – the status of the constitution and the head of state, with the King in exile and a General purporting to act for him, could only be regarded as fluid. This would have justified foreign states in refraining from recognizing the new government in Athens. For a time it seemed that they might do so, since on New Year's Day 1968 none of the allied Ambassadors attended the annual celebration in the Cathedral. But their circumspection proved short-lived.

When the Secretary of State, Dean Rusk, was asked on 16 December whether the US Administration would recognize the new Greek government, he replied: 'We'll wait and see.' But US recognition was granted little more than a month later, on 23 January. The Americans were not the first to do so, but the second, preceded surprisingly by the Turks, who had almost been at war with Greece a few weeks earlier. The British government followed the American example on 25 January. All the rest, including the Soviet bloc, soon did the same.

In a private note to Karamanlis from Washington the Greek Ambassador, Xanthopoulos-Palamas, reported that the US Administration was now more favourably inclined towards the Colonels. By mid-February the Americans were ready to give Papadopoulos a public accolade. He was entertained on an aircraft-carrier of the 6th Fleet anchored in Phaliron Bay. This must have pained the King, who had asked for exactly such support in vain during December. Rumours were already circulating that the supply of heavy arms would be resumed.

The junta celebrated its triumph by a characteristic combination of ruth-

49

lessness and reconciliation. On the one hand, the purges of senior officers and civil servants were intensified. Eighteen Generals and nine senior naval officers were dismissed for supporting the King; and Colonel Opropoulos was arrested and deported to a remote island, where he later suffered an almost fatal accident. On the other hand, an amnesty was granted to the ASPIDA group. Andreas Papandreou was released on Christmas Eve 1967, and given a passport early in the New Year.

Pattakos, who had twice visited Andreas in the Averoff prison, insisted on presenting the passport to him personally. These confrontations gave Pattakos the opportunity to question Andreas about his attitude towards the junta, which led to a series of almost comical exchanges about education, democracy, and the economy.[1] In characteristic form, Pattakos assured Andreas at their last meeting that 'elections will take place when you least expect them!' A few weeks later Theodorakis was also released, but his ordeal was not yet ended.

Andreas Papandreou received his passport on 15 January. When he and his wife presented themselves at Athens airport, however, their departure was delayed by an officious policeman who said that Andreas could not leave without a permit from Colonel Ladas, the Secretary-General of the Ministry of Public Order. After an angry argument and a telephone call to the Ministry, they were finally allowed to leave. This trivial episode was characteristic of government by junta. It showed, like many other examples, that Papadopoulos' right hand did not know what his left hand was doing; and that in a police state the correct action for a policeman was to be obstructive until ordered otherwise.

During the same period a number of other measures were brought forward to give the junta a more respectable appearance. On 26 December 1967 a decree was published demobilizing the triumvirate from the Army. Most of the other Colonels (except Ioannidis) were similarly demobilized in February 1968. While these steps theoretically civilianized the Council of Ministers, they also increased the ex-Colonels' authority, since in giving orders to the armed forces they were no longer addressing their superiors in rank.

The successful year was crowned by the publication on 28 December of Makarezos' five-year plan for 1968–72. But this was criticized from different directions by two of Greece's ablest economists. Professor John Pesmazoglou (who had resigned as Deputy Governor of the Bank of Greece in protest at the dictatorship) pointed out that the plan was simply an extension of the five-year plan already drafted for 1966–70.[2] It took no account in any case of the highly inflationary measures which the junta had already introduced. Andreas Papandreou, in his last interview with Pattakos, described the economic policy as 'deeply contradictory', because it tried 'to achieve rapid growth and deflation at the same time'.[3] The junta was in effect being carried on the crest of the wave of earlier development, and contributing nothing itself to the generation of long-term prosperity.

Although the regime seemed to be firmly consolidated at the beginning of 1968, there were serious troubles ahead. Andreas Papandreou, who arrived in Paris on 16 January, gave an interview to *Le Monde* on the 24th in which he made it clear that he would promote resistance to the junta in every possible way. He even declared – with the blithe confidence of one who had spent the years of the Second World War, the German occupation and the civil war in the safety of the United States – that guerrilla warfare would seem 'indispensable'.[4]

A month later he established the Panhellenic Liberation Movement (PAK) with its headquarters in Stockholm.[5] The Swedish government helped to finance it, which led to a severance of diplomatic relations by the junta. As a further reprisal, Archbishop Ieronymos announced that the Greek Church would not be represented at the forthcoming General Assembly of the World Council of Churches in Uppsala. But this decision was later reversed, in a manner characteristic of the junta; and even diplomatic relations were eventually restored between Greece and Sweden.

George Papandreou, still in Athens but no longer under house arrest, was more cautious than his son. He too made a public attack on the junta, using the first anniversary of the coup as his occasion, but he refrained from any call for revolutionary action, apart from a veiled appeal to the armed forces.[6] It appeared that he had begun to be embarrassed by Andreas' inflammatory language, which he said did not represent the policy of the Centre Union.

The Centre Union, technically dissolved, was also ceasing to be the party of either Papandreou, for the father was relinquishing the leadership to George Mavros and the son was dissociating himself from his former colleagues. From the middle of 1968, Andreas moved into closer relations with the Communists. On 4 August he and Brillakis, the leader of the KKE (Interior), announced an agreement between their respective organizations of resistance, PAK and PAM. There was already an agreement in effect between PAM and Democratic Defence (DA), the offspring of the Centre Union. On paper, therefore, it seemed that a united resistance was emerging, though its effectiveness in practice was doubtful.

International attacks on the junta were also resumed in 1968, but only by the lesser powers and by international bodies which did not necessarily represent governments. On 31 January the Parliamentary Assembly of the Council of Europe had before it two reports, one from Amnesty International and one from two of its own nominees, which both severely criticized the junta's disregard for human rights. The Assembly voted by sixty-six to one, with thirty abstentions, that if democracy were not restored by the spring of 1969, Greece should be expelled from membership.

Pattakos commented that the Council of Europe bothered Greece no more than 'a mosquito on the horns of an ox'. The junta was nevertheless taking steps, albeit clumsily, to improve its image abroad. On 1 January a contract was signed with a British firm of public relations consultants. Unfortunately for the junta, the firm's operations were so inept that by the summer its image was worse than before.[7]

Foreign criticism continued and increased. On 25 March the Scandinavians presented to the European Commission of Human Rights evidence of torture in Greek prisons. On 11 April a Foreign Office Minister confirmed in the House of Commons that there was 'strong *prima facie* evidence of people having been subjected to what one would regard as inhuman treatment under police interrogation'.[8] On 25 April the President of the Parliamentary Assembly of the Council of Europe, Sir Geoffrey de Freitas, repeated the warning of expulsion. On 8 May a Dutch member of the Parliamentary Assembly, Max Van der Stoel (later Foreign Minister of the Netherlands), presented a report containing even more damning evidence of torture.[9]

The major governments, however, were more tolerant towards the junta. All were conscious of the strategic importance of Greece, and many were more interested in trade and defence contracts than in human rights. Many attempts by the Danish and Norwegian governments to raise the Greek question in the ministerial committee of NATO were frustrated, chiefly by pressure from the United States with the help of successive Secretaries-General, Manlio Brosio and Dr Joseph Luns. Although glaring cases of maltreatment provoked occasional protests, the policy of the major western allies was 'business as usual'. Parliamentary missions from the House of Commons and the Bundestag appeared to notice nothing abnormal. France was the one country which sent a Minister from its Foreign Office on an official visit to Athens, but Ministers from other countries contrived to make visits under other pretexts.

The British Prime Minister, Harold Wilson, showed himself briefly an exception to the attitude of tolerance, when he spoke in the House of Commons on 25 June of 'the bestialities which have been perpetrated in Greece'.[10] But when the junta retaliated by breaking off negotiations for a contract to supply railway equipment, he authorized another Minister to withdraw the word 'bestialities' on his behalf, and to explain that he had meant only to repeat a phrase which he had used earlier about 'the barbarous methods in use in Greece today'.[11] Surprisingly, the amendment satisfied the junta, and negotiations were resumed.

In Moscow and Washington reactions were much the same. The Soviet government, which presumably saw nothing abnormal in the junta's treatment of its opponents, accepted a new Greek Ambassador in February 1968 and sent a new Ambassador to Athens in early June, after leaving the post vacant for several months. Trade relations were uninhibited. As usual, Moscow dissociated state policy from relations between Communist parties. In Washington also state policy took first place, but there was a dichotomy of a different kind. Andreas Papandreou, on a visit to the United States in March 1968, found the attitude of Administration officials discouraging, but members of Congress, together with journalists, intellectuals and students, more sympathetic. [12]

Clearly there was no serious threat to the junta overseas, either in the west or in the east. But an unsuspected threat from another quarter was already hanging over Papadopoulos. On 27 May 1967 a young reserve officer called Alexander Panagoulis had deserted from the Army. Nothing was heard of him for over a year. After hiding in Athens with friends in the Centre Union, he had obtained a false passport and travelled to Cyprus. What happened next was mysterious.

'Someone spoke about me to Makarios, to facilitate my departure,' he said afterwards. [13] Makarios saw him, and passed him to Yiorkatzis, his Minister of the Interior, with instructions that he should be helped. Yiorkatzis gave him a Cypriot passport, with which he travelled to the Lebanon and later to western Europe, returning to Athens on 15 May 1968. Panagoulis thus became an agent in the perennial feud between Nicosia and Athens. But his real purpose was more dramatic.

The affairs of Cyprus and Greece were more than ever intimately linked at this date. Makarios and Papadopoulos, while never quarrelling in public, were mortal enemies. Papadopoulos hoped to satisfy the US Administration's wish for a Cyprus settlement by achieving *enosis*, if necessary at the price of large concessions to Turkey. Makarios was relentlessly opposed to such a policy. On 12 January 1968 Makarios made a speech which hinted that *enosis* might no longer be obtainable. This annoyed not only Papadopoulos but also a number of Cypriot bishops. Anthimos of Kition warned Makarios that he ought to resign as President if he renounced *enosis*. Unrepentant, however, Makarios was re-elected President on 25 February.

He gave a further indication of his new attitude in the spring. He allowed Raouf Denktash, the acknowledged leader of the Turkish Cypriots, to return openly to Cyprus, and sanctioned inter-communal talks between Denktash and Glavkos Clerides, the President of the Assembly. The two men, who had both trained as lawyers in London, were personally friendly. Their talks continued for six years without achieving much, but at any rate inter-communal relations became no worse. Constitutional questions were, of course, excluded from their talks.

In this phase of the Cyprus problem the real antagonism was not so much between Greeks and Turks as between the Greeks of Nicosia and of Athens. This seems not to have been appreciated by the western allies. The Assistant Secretary for Near Eastern and South Asian Affairs in the US State Department, for example, delivered an address on 18 April which included seven paragraphs on the crisis in Cyprus without once mentioning the dictatorship in Athens.[14] But Makarios had no doubt where his real enemy was to be found.

There is no reason to suspect that he was aware of the use of Panagoulis as an instrument in his feud with Papadopoulos. The inspiration was probably that of Yiorkatzis alone. Makarios was naïve in his personal relations, and always disinclined to suspect the worst. He was genuinely shocked by the dramatic event of 13 August 1968.

In the early morning of that day Papadopoulos' car, travelling in an armed convoy along the coastal road from his residence at Lagonisi towards Athens, narrowly escaped the explosion of a powerful charge buried in a culvert. It was operated by remote control, and the perpetrator was caught on the spot. Unhurt, Papadopoulos went on at once to preside at the Council of Ministers. He added a new slogan to the philosophy of the junta: 'God was always a philhellene!'

On the same day a leaflet distributed in Paris claimed that the attack was the work of the Greek Resistance.[15] But the arrested man insisted that he had no accomplices. He was handed over to the Military Security Police (ESA), now commanded by Ioannidis. It was not long before all his accomplices were known. But although it was soon learned that his name was Panagoulis, he was at first mistaken for his brother George, who had also been posted as a deserter.

Once he was correctly identified, his Cypriot connections were quickly traced. The investigators' report, published on 20 October, implicated Yiorkatzis, who was alleged to have supplied Panagoulis with money and explosives through the diplomatic bag.[16] The junta demanded that Makarios dismiss Yiorkatzis, which he did after some resistance on 29 October. Three weeks later Alexander Panagoulis was convicted and sentenced to death. Fourteen others were tried with him, of whom four were acquitted and ten sentenced to terms of imprisonment.

The case of Panagoulis touched a nerve in the internal relations of the junta. There was already a marked division between hard-liners, such as Ladas, and pragmatists, such as Pattakos. They had disagreed about the treatment of the King and of Andreas Papandreou. Now they disagreed over the fate of Panagoulis. Ladas wanted the execution carried out, and it was so ordered by Papadopoulos. But during the night of 20–21 November a telephone message was received from Angelis and Pipinelis, who were in Brussels, reporting the catastrophic effect which it would have on the NATO alliance.[17] Papadopoulos cancelled the order, and Pattakos supported him.

But Pattakos was also in a troublesome mood. Only a week before the attempted assassination, he had sent a memorandum to Papadopoulos summarizing and partly endorsing the public criticisms which were being made of the junta (a term which he used himself). He spoke of illegal acts, of the 'asphyxiating centralization of power', of unemployment, and much else.[18] He also complained of the atmosphere of suspicion within the junta, directed especially against himself. In conclusion he demanded more responsible executive positions for Makarezos and himself.

There was pressure from other directions at the same time for the dormant Revolutionary Council to be convened.[19] Papadopoulos evaded the dilemma by temporizing and compromise. Although Panagoulis was not executed, he was not expressly reprieved. Ladas was moved to a new post as Secretary-General at the Ministry of the Interior, under Pattakos; but to make the change less noticeable, a general post of Secretaries-General was carried out. Pattakos' memorandum was forgotten in the drama of events which followed. Papadopoulos continued to alternate repression to please the hawks and concessions to please the doves. His principal ally in these manoeuvres was currently said to be Ioannidis, but theirs was at best a precarious alliance.[20]

Papadopoulos' policy of conciliation during 1968 was intended to pave the way for the new Constitution. More than 4,000 alleged Communists were released in the spring; six of the ten courts-martial were abolished in July, leaving only those in Athens, Salonika, Larisa and Tripoli; and most of the former politicians were released from house arrest. The draft of the new Constitution was published, after Papadopoulos had himself amended it, on 16 September.[21] The public was invited to comment on it. Averoff was the only politician who published express criticisms, but another bold critic was imprisoned for urging that it should be rejected.

A referendum was held on 29 September, which naturally approved the Constitution by a large majority. But it was noted abroad that more than twenty-two per cent of the electorate abstained, although voting was compulsory. Twelve articles, all concerned with human rights, were immediately suspended. They remained to be introduced later, by what were known as 'constructive decrees' (roughly equivalent to statutory instruments). The most striking innovation, which would remain even when the suspended articles were introduced, was the virtual autonomy conferred on the armed forces, which were exempted from political control and charged with defence of the state against internal as well as external enemies.

Prominent Greeks abroad were unanimous in condemning the constitution, mostly regarding it as unworthy of comment. The King prepared a draft statement on it, which Karamanlis advised him not to publish. Neither Karamanlis nor Andreas Papandreou made detailed comments on it at the time, but the latter published a severely critical analysis a year later.[22] The most elegant summary of the constitutional position was made by two French sociologists: '*La Grèce n'est, pour l'instant, qu'un royaume sans roi, un régime libéral sans libertés, un parlementarisme sans Parlement.*'[23]

Papadopoulos, however, had already promised, on 30 July, a return to parliamentary government. The date would depend only on Greece's response to his surgery. He renewed the promise at least once a year, but he did not survive to put it into effect. He also promised, on 10 August, that censorship would be ended, but he made it clear that other restrictions on the press would continue. On the day after the constitutional referendum, he announced that the 'revolution' was entering its second phase, and that the suspended articles would soon be introduced; but 'soon' turned out to be a long time.

Conciliatory promises were merely a counterpoint to real repression. Arbitrary arrest and administrative exile were regular practices. The case of Theodorakis was notable only because he was famous. On 21 August he and his family were exiled to a remote village in the Peloponnese. A year later, in October 1969, he was again imprisoned. At this date no charge was brought to court against him. Like hundreds of other cases, he was treated under martial law, which was based on an unconstitutional decree promulgated even before the military government was sworn into office.

The junta's disregard of constitutional procedure began to have consequences which went beyond personal hardship. Constitutionally, public servants had a right of appeal to the Council of State against dismissal. A decree of May 1967, which had no constitutional basis except in the initial decree setting up the dictatorship (and therefore none at all), deprived them of this right. Another decree of May 1968 empowered the government to dismiss judicial officials. The government then dismissed thirty judicial officials whose independence embarrassed them. All of those dismissed sought to appeal to the Council of State, which heard and granted their appeals during 1969, when the new constitution was in force. The junta nevertheless insisted, by virtue of the two earlier decrees, that they were in fact dismissed. A complex battle followed in the courts, which lasted until 1970 and culminated in a conflict of judgement between the Council of State and the Supreme Court (the Areopagus).[24] But for practical purposes, the junta had its own way.

If the courts were powerless to prevent such abuses of justice, they were still more powerless to prevent torture and even murder by the junta's agents. On 8 May 1968, the very day of Van der Stoel's first report to the Council of

Europe, a former Deputy of EDA, George Tsaroukhas, died in police custody, almost certainly from maltreatment. Panagoulis and others were certainly also tortured in prison.[25] The long arm of the junta reached even outside Greece. A former press attaché at the Greek Embassy in Denmark, George Mavroyenis, who had resigned and joined the resistance, was found dead in a wood near Copenhagen on 28 May. His death was described in the Greek press as suicide, but later investigation established that it was probably murder.[26]

It was difficult at the time, unfortunately, to produce convincing evidence against the junta. One attempt to do so, before the European Commission of Human Rights in November 1968, ended in a fiasco bordering on farce.[27] Three witnesses who had been imprisoned under the junta were brought to Strasbourg by government officials to testify that they had not been maltreated. But once they appeared before the Commission, they reversed their testimony. Two of them then sought asylum in Norway, where one of them reversed his testimony a second time, apparently under pressure from the Greek Embassy in Oslo. He subsequently returned to Greece, where he was greeted with great relief by his family, who had been threatened with reprisals if he failed to recant. The complexities of the story were such that the Commission could arrive at no conclusion. They could send representatives of their own to investigate conditions in Greece, but with little prospect of discovering the truth about what was happening in Greek prisons.

Those who spoke for the major allies did not much want to know the truth. The outlook for the junta became still more favourable when the Red Army and its allies invaded Czechoslovakia on 22 August 1968, to suppress what was known as 'the Prague spring'. Spiro Agnew, the Republican candidate for the Vice-presidency, who was himself partly of Greek descent, spoke favourably of the junta on 27 September. This was only a personal gesture, but a more substantial consequence was the restoration of US arms supply to Greece in October. The Administration told the Senate Foreign Relations Committee that the decision was due to 'recent events in Central and Eastern Europe', meaning not only the invasion of Czechoslovakia but also the concentration of Soviet ships in the Mediterranean.[28] It was limited, for that reason, to jet aircraft and minesweepers; but there was a general expectation that other armaments would eventually follow. For the rest of the year at least, the junta had little need to worry about allied criticism.

They had not much to worry about, either, on the domestic front, at least on the surface. The danger from Cyprus was neutralized by the dismissal of Yiorkatzis. The latent quarrel between Athens and Nicosia was kept under concealment on both sides. Early in September 1968 Makarios visited Athens, after calling on the King in Rome. He was anxious to promote a reconciliation with the King, whose exile caused him sincere distress; but nothing came of it. As he left Athens, the customary announcement was made of 'complete agreement' between the governments of Greece and Cyprus. Although certainly hypocritical, it at least indicated a state of truce.

In Greece the Resistance was still capable of occasional explosions, but for the most part it was confined to propaganda. Clandestine publications began to reappear. A student organization called Rhigas Pheraios, after an eighteenth-century revolutionary poet, succeeded in publishing an occasional newspaper, the *Thourios* ('battle-song'), which was the title of Rhigas' most famous poem. The Communists resumed publication of their newspaper *Rizospastis* in March 1968, but this too came out only occasionally. Towards the end of the year they refounded the Communist Youth of Greece (KNE). They were active also in other organizations, but their activities were restricted by the junta's efficient security services. Bombs were comparatively rare in 1968: an exceptional case in October was followed by some fifty arrests.

Shortly after disowning Andreas' enthusiasm for armed resistance, George Papandreou died on 1 November. His funeral, two days later, was the occasion of a massive demonstration against the junta. Kanellopoulos made a memorable speech in honour of his old colleague and opponent. Karamanlis sent a wreath, but noted regretfully that one of the former Deputies of the Centre Union took the opportunity to praise Papandreou's 'relentless struggle'. Later in November, Averoff made a statement offering the junta a 'bridge' back to legality, which again displeased Karamanlis.[29] Papadopoulos spurned the offer, but such signs of disarray in the opposition must have been gratifying to him.

On balance, the year 1968 was one of success for the junta. The momentum of the 'revolution' was not yet visibly waning. Domestic dissent and foreign disapproval were relatively muted. The economy was prosperous, and the 'deep contradictions' detected by Andreas Papandreou had not yet made themselves felt. A foreign economist remarked that it was impossible to tell from any of the normal indicators by themselves at what point any change of government had taken place since the end of the civil war in 1949. The general trend was one of steady improvement over twenty years, and the change in 1967 had proved no exception. By the end of 1969 Makarezos was able to make the bold announcement that a fifteen-year plan for industrial development was in preparation, though it was not completed until 1972.[30]

There were already abnormalities in the trend, however, which would have worried a more sophisticated economist than Makarezos. The junta had given a high priority to foreign investment in Greece, particularly from the United States. But the highest level of investment attracted from abroad, including the USA, had been reached in 1965, more than a year before the coup. The figures for investment both from the USA and from the rest of the world were lower in each of the first three years of the junta than in either of the two preceding years; and they did not begin to rise again until 1970. It was notorious that three of the four major contracts signed with foreign companies in the early days of the junta were later cancelled.[31] In addition, there was a heavy loss of capital funds from the EEC due to the suspension of progress under Greece's Treaty of Association.

Other weaknesses in the Greek economy became gradually apparent. The policy of encouraging consumption led to a higher rate of imports, not matched by exports. As the world moved into recession the rate of emigration (principally to West Germany, but also to the USA) declined, so reducing the flow of remittances and increasing unemployment. The rate of improvement in the remuneration of the unskilled relative to skilled workers deteriorated. Much publicity was given to the cancellation of agricultural debts, but this benefited the richer peasants, who could afford to incur debts, rather than the poorer ones, who had been obliged regularly to pay off old debts before they could obtain fresh credit. There was also a general decline in the rate of growth of agricultural income.

Public expenditure and taxation were both increased, but expenditure on education, health and social services declined relative to defence, sport and small local projects. Defence was naturally a high priority; sport was a kind of sedative against opposition; and small local projects were selected by officials loyal to the junta for their own benefit.[32] In general, the object of economic policy was to favour private capitalism, including foreign entrepreneurs, at the expense of Greek workers; and to give priority to measures of window-dressing and public relations.

At the popular level, a high priority was given to the promotion of tourism. This served the dual purpose of attracting foreign exchange and using the country's physical and cultural assets for favourable publicity. There was naturally a drop in the tourist influx immediately after the coup, but it was not long before numbers rose again, as it was seen that the country was safe for foreigners who were not too inquisitive. But the rapid expansion of tourism was not uncontroversial. A bishop denounced it as corrupting Greek morals and religion. The Federation of Industry published an article in its journal on 31 July 1972 criticizing the diversion of excessive resources to tourism, which was converting Greece into 'a nation of hotel managers'. This so enraged Makarezos that he published a reply at great length, justifying the government's policy and ending with a veiled threat against the editor of the journal.[33]

In all areas of economic policy, the effects took time to make themselves felt. At the turn of the year 1968–9 the benefits were more apparent than the disadvantages, except for the poorer peasants, who had no organization to speak for them, and the industrial workers, whose unions had been dissolved. For the military of all ranks, Greece had become a paradise. They enjoyed high pay, rapid promotion, improved living conditions, and at least the semblance of public respect. But where would it all lead?

The Colonels had no agreed long-term policy except to maintain themselves in power. They were responding to events and opportunities rather than creating the new social order which they professed to envisage. It was not surprising that even among themselves there was conflict about the nature of this new order, which never existed except in their dreams. As in all authoritarian regimes of the right, their ideology was an afterthought.

Because Papadopoulos had to contend with rival interpretations of the object of the 'revolution', his policy was to keep his colleagues regularly on the move in order to reduce their opportunities for forming an internal opposition against him. In June and November 1968, and again in January 1969, he partially reorganized his government. The purpose was steadily to consolidate his own power. To be sure of this, it was also necessary to be sure of the Army. There he reassured himself by appointing his old superior, and now faithful adherent, General Angelis, as Commander-in-Chief of all the armed forces on 13 December. This was a new post, hitherto held only by the Head of State, as distinct from the Chief of the Defence Staff, a post held by one of the Chiefs of Staff of the three services in rotation.

By another innovation in the New Year, Papadopoulos enhanced both his own status and his control of public funds. He assumed the presidency of the Royal National Foundation, which had been set up by Queen Frederika during the civil war. Two days later, in another fit of *folie de grandeur*, it was announced that the government intended to fulfil what was known as the 'Pledge of the Nation'. This pledge, which had originally been formulated no fewer than 140 years earlier at the Fourth National Assembly during the War of Independence, was to set up a huge church dedicated to Christ near the centre of Athens. It had never been executed, but never entirely forgotten. Papadopoulos evidently wanted not just earthly power but eternal fame.

In the end nothing came of the 'Pledge of the Nation'. Nor did anything come of most of his grandiose projects, such as the plan announced three years later to reconstruct the Colossus of Rhodes, which was to rise to a height of more than 300 feet. It seemed that the purpose of such plans was simply to be proclaimed, in order to deflect criticism elsewhere, to give an impression of constructive activity, and to conceal the actuality of stagnation. Papadopoulos would announce startling decisions – 'earthquakes', he sometimes called them – more or less at random, divorced from any coherent plan.

It would be a mistake to look for his theory of government either in his farrago of improvisations or in his speeches and writings. As a statement of policy, the publication which he, or his propagandists, called *Our Creed* (*To Pistevo mas*) does not bear comparison for coherence and logic even with Nasser's *A Philosophy of Revolution*, let alone Hitler's *Mein Kampf*. The Colonels had no conception of the future of Greece except as a parade-ground, which would be adjoined, of course, by a barracks, a guard-room and a military hospital. All that the officers in charge need do was to bark orders.

Papadopoulos himself thought most easily in slogans, of which his favourites were 'Greece of the Christian Greeks' and 'Greece is Risen' – a parody of the phrase 'Christ is Risen', which came to every Greek's lips at Easter. The function of his propagandists was to translate such slogans into a philosophy, which was to be the basis of 'Helleno-Christian civilization'. To study their feeble compilations is unrewarding. As was said of it when the junta's principal ideologist claimed that 'We are tomorrow', he might with more precision have claimed that 'We are yesterday'; for all that he had to offer was a rehash of the claims of Metaxas' dictatorship, the so-called Fourth of August.[34]

Pattakos and Ladas both fancied themselves as rivals to Papadopoulos in formulating ideology, but they incurred even greater ridicule.[35] Short of compiling an anthology of Pattakisms, his style of debate can best be illustrated by the single boast that the slogan which would for ever be associated with the 'revolution' would be 'Halt or I shoot!' Ladas was more intellectual. He claimed it as a universally recognized fact that 'civilization is an exclusively Greek creation'. Philosophy, he told an audience at the University of Ioannina, had been not merely invented but exhausted as a subject by the Greeks.

It followed logically enough that 'Helleno-Christian civilization' was an article for export to other countries. The campaign was launched in Italy, where the junta had close connections with the Neo-Fascist movement. K. Plevris, the leader of the 'Fourth of August Movement', which was founded to commemorate and revive the style of dictatorship imposed by Metaxas in the 1930s, became private secretary to Ladas in his capacity as Secretary-General of the Ministry of Public Order; and he was also intimate with Pino Rauti, a leading member of the Italian Social Movement (MSI), the reincarnation of the Fascist Party. Rauti often visited Athens, and Plevris visited him in Rome. Eventually the activities of the junta were to lead to diplomatic protests by the Italian government.[36]

It may be wondered why Greece's allies put up with this affront to the standards of western democracy for so long. Part of the answer is that they had no alternative once the Colonels were in power. Any hostile action would have been damaging to NATO, of which Greece was deemed an indispensable part. In the long run, however, tolerance of the dictatorship was even more damaging to NATO. This was less easily recognized. There were certainly some in the west – politicians, soldiers, officials, businessmen – who would have been horrified by military dictatorship at home but thought it quite acceptable elsewhere.

From an outsider's viewpoint, doing business or conducting negotiations with Greece became easier than before. One western Ambassador defended Papadopoulos with the argument that he was only doing for Greece what de Gaulle had done for France; and his was not a lone voice. There was also a more neutral view of the dictatorship, which held that the Greeks were an ungovernable people who had simply got what they deserved.

Foreign opinion was further confused by conflicts of evidence. Occasionally there seemed to be good reason for suspending judgement. The International Red Cross, for example, sent a team to investigate conditions of detention on Gioura early in 1968, and produced a surprisingly favourable report, in sharp contrast with a report by Amnesty International in the same period.[37] Towards the end of 1968 an OECD report gave a favourable view of the Greek economy which was equally gratifying to the junta and surprising to its critics.[38] Naturally the junta always referred to the more favourable verdict whenever less favourable verdicts were quoted against them. It was understandable that at the end of 1968 they seemed to have little cause for anxiety either at home or abroad. Papadopoulos could confidently announce on 7 December that 'no political developments' were to be expected, and no political parties were to be formed. The Christian soldiers were in absolute command.

5 Onward, Christian soldiers!

1969

The sense of security which the junta enjoyed at the turn of the year from 1968 to 1969 enabled Papadopoulos to override one or two setbacks without loss of confidence. On 28 January the Parliamentary Assembly of the Council of Europe, after studying Van der Stoel's report and hearing from him in person, virtually called for Greece's resignation. Papadopoulos retorted contemptuously on 1 February: 'Greece will not withdraw from the Council, in order not to put her great friends in an embarrassing position.'[1] He again reacted aggressively when the Italian Foreign Minister received Andreas Papandreou on 5 March. Pipinelis was compelled to make a formal protest; but a debate in the Italian Senate made it clear that the Minister's action had general support, so the matter was not pursued.

A more serious setback arose from the election of a new President of the United States, Richard Nixon, in November 1968. Although his Vice-president, Spiro Agnew, was well disposed towards the junta, when Nixon came into office in January he appeared at first more cautious. He allowed the partial resumption of arms supply by the previous administration to continue, and the first Starfighter aircraft were delivered to Piraeus on 18 February; but there was no general lifting of the ban, as had been expected. A more ominous development was the departure of Phillips Talbot, the US Ambassador, without replacement. It was normal for Ambassadors to resign on the election of a new President, but it was unusual for a post to be left vacant for over a year, as happened in this case.

The first opportunity to explore the significance of the change in Washington came in early April. Ex-president Eisenhower died on 28 March. Pattakos was sent to represent Greece at his funeral, which was also attended by Constantine, flying from Rome. The two men met at the Greek Embassy, where the King stayed, while Pattakos was put up at a hotel. Their meeting was unfriendly, and the King had the better of their tart exchanges. But Pattakos triumphed in the end, for he was received by President Nixon at the White House, and the King was not. Xanthopoulos-Palamas, the Ambassador, told Karamanlis privately that Nixon held Pattakos in high regard.[2] So the influence of Spiro Agnew, and perhaps also of Tom Pappas, was beginning to work.

The final lifting of the ban on heavy arms was now only a matter of time. The Secretary of State, William Rogers, told the Senate Foreign Relations

Committee on 14 July that the suspension of aid 'will not be removed unless they make some progress toward more parliamentary government'. Next day the Secretary of Defence, Melvin Laird, made a similar statement to the Committee about arms supply, but the Department explained that he was referring only to heavy arms.[3] On the other hand, a more revealing statement had been made earlier to the House Committee on Foreign Affairs by the Under-Secretary of State, Elliot Richardson, that over eighty per cent of military aid in 1970 would go to countries which provided important facilities, including the Republic of China (Taiwan), Korea, Greece and Turkey.[4] A later investigation by members of the Senate Committee's staff established that Greece probably received more military aid overall during the embargo than in the equivalent period before it was imposed.[5]

Although the Colonels were thus protected from serious sanctions by the requirements of the western alliance, they were astute enough to appreciate that an occasional gesture in the direction of liberalism would be helpful to their patrons in Washington and elsewhere. This would enable the allied governments to fend off criticism by affirming their belief that Greece was indeed on the way back to freedom and democracy. Experience soon showed that obeisance would suffice in the principal western capitals: the reality did not matter. So the junta obliged from time to time, in an idiosyncratic and unco-ordinated way.

For domestic purposes, it was made clear that change would not mean a return to democracy. Papadopoulos' warning in December 1968 that there were to be 'no political developments' was reinforced by Pattakos in the New Year. On 3 March, just over a year after he had told Andreas Papandreou that 'elections will take place when you least expect them', he announced that there was no question of early elections, because the Greeks were tired of them. A number of progressive schemes were canvassed, however, in order to generate a sense of movement at home and to attract favourable notice abroad, without necessarily leading to any changes of substance.

On 6 March, during a visit to the north-east, Papadopoulos announced that 'earthquakes' were about to take place. First, the administration was to be decentralized to the local authorities, leaving the central government with only 'staff functions' – a characteristically military phrase. Next, social insurance was to be totally reorganized and unified in a single system. These 'earthquakes' would provoke 'screams from the interests affected', he said: 'but don't listen to them!' In order not to alarm conservatives and businessmen too much, he went on to say that nothing would be done to prejudice the system of private enterprise. In the event there were no screams, because nothing was actually done.

A month later, on 10 April, Papadopoulos announced that several of the suspended articles of the constitution would soon be restored, and that a number of consultative bodies would be set up to prepare the way for the return of parliamentary government. This was the reverse of his announcement four months earlier. A month later again, on 10 May, he announced that civil servants who had been dismissed could be reinstated, and that the cases of those exiled or sentenced by court-martial would be reviewed.

In contrast with these encouraging statements, the month of May 1969 also recorded the highest number of trials and convictions for subversion in any month so far. The London *Times* reported on 24 May a total of eighty-four convictions in twelve days, including nine in Athens, twelve in Larisa and thirty-nine in Salonika. To crown the month's tally, ten royalist officers were sent into administrative exile at the end of May.

Warnings against over-optimism about the earlier signs of relaxation were hardly necessary, but they were delivered in June. On the 13th Papadopoulos told an audience of officials at the Foreign Office that 'we look to construct a state capable of confronting such necessities as will evolve up to the year 2000'. This cryptic phrase was calculated to discourage those who looked forward to the return of democracy, and they felt the force of it when a particular necessity evolved a week later. On 21 June the Council of State allowed the appeals of the thirty judicial officials who had been dismissed in May 1968, declaring that the decree of 1967 which purported to deprive them of their right of appeal was unconstitutional. In fury, Papadopoulos repudiated the judgement, and announced on the 27th that the resignation of the President of the Council of State had been accepted. In fact the President, Professor Stasinopoulos (later President of the Republic), had never resigned: he was under house arrest, with his telephone cut off. Seven other judges of the Council of State resigned in protest.

In this way the alternation of pretended reform and real repression continued through the summer of 1969. At the beginning of July the institution of Ombudsman came into operation, evidently with the idea that it would appeal to Scandinavian and British critics, who were familiar with it in their own countries. But their approval would have been chilled when it turned out that the first holder of the office was to be a retired Major-General who had formerly been head of the National Security Service (Asphaleia).

A more dramatic event made a deeper impression during the same month. Thirty-five members of Democratic Defence (DA) were arrested after an accidental explosion had seriously injured one of them, Professor D. Karayiorgas. It was true that he and his equally distinguished colleagues, including another professor and a retired General, ought not to have been involved in manufacturing bombs; and it was beyond doubt that most of them were guilty as charged. But the affair had a damaging effect on the junta's relations with the more sensitive of Greece's allies, especially when it became known that they were tortured in prison.

As opposition became increasingly vocal both at home and abroad, the junta found it necessary to maintain the flow of hints and promises of relaxation. The death of George Papandreou had acted as a catalyst in this respect. George Mavros, his eventual successor in the leadership of the Centre Union, was a less contentious figure and had no serious differences with Kanellopoulos. Nominally their parties had ceased to exist, but the junta had abandoned any attempt to prevent small numbers of them from meeting in private. The two leaders worked together in a team which was highly respected both in Greece and abroad.

Both had difficulties, however, with the more irreconcilable of their colleagues. The hard core of the Centre Union insisted on excluding the 'apostates', who had supported Stephanopoulos in 1965–6, from inter-party discussions of opposition to the junta. Andreas Papandreou's extreme views, as well as the echoes of his father's 'relentless struggle' against Karamanlis, were a further embarrassment. Karamanlis himself, writing from Paris, was not enthusiastic about inter-party co-operation.

Such difficulties hindered the efforts of Mavros and Kanellopoulos to form a united front over the following years. Kanellopoulos wrote to Karamanlis on 16 June about the talks which were in progress in Athens, explaining the difficulties. He said that it was impossible to co-operate with Andreas Papandreou so long as he continued abusing the Americans. He also reported the opinion expressed by Brigadier Vidalis, who had visited Washington since his compulsory retirement, that a merger of the parties under Karamanlis' leadership would favourably impress President Nixon. But neither Andreas nor Karamanlis was open to persuasion. Kanellopoulos sent an emissary to meet Andreas in England, where he was attending a conference of the Socialist International at Eastbourne during June, and found him intransigent against both the United States and the monarchy. Karamanlis strongly discouraged any notion that he might accept the leadership of a union of the old political parties.

George Papandreou had left what was called a 'political testament', the contents of which soon became known. In this document he had stressed the need for co-operation between Andreas and Karamanlis, not forgetting the King but excluding the Communists. Andreas was living in Canada when the document reached him. On 13 February 1969 he wrote to Karamanlis that he not only accepted but prayed for 'a Karamanlis solution'.[6] But Karamanlis was sceptical. He would not consider any future course until the junta was swept away. He too had received a copy of George Papandreou's 'political testament', but his comment on the idea of co-operation with Andreas was that 'one and one do not always make two: often they make zero'.[7]

So a possible partnership between Karamanlis and Andreas Papandreou never materialized. Karamanlis was contemplating a new initiative of his own, about which he forewarned his followers later in the year. Meanwhile Mavros and Kanellopoulos continued their hopeful talks, moving towards a united front of which they were the only significant members.

Another notable but non-political voice joined the opposition during March 1969. George Sepheris, the first Greek poet to win a Nobel prize, and formerly Ambassador in London, issued a carefully prepared statement of hostility to the junta, which was recorded and broadcast in Greek and English by the BBC. Emboldened by his support, a group of young writers published a collective protest against censorship a few weeks later. The colonels had a curious response already in preparation. On 13 April appeared the first instalment of a collection of short stories by left-wing writers, sanctioned by the censors. But publication was soon suspended when the writers proved insufficiently docile. It was not until more than a year later that independent writers dared to challenge the censorship again, with the publication in July 1970 of an anthology called *Eighteen Texts*.[8]

Opposition at home could be effectively silenced by the junta, but opposition abroad could not. It was gathering strength, thanks partly to the persistence of Andreas Papandreou and partly to the Council of Europe. Andreas travelled tirelessly across the Atlantic and between European capitals to stimulate opposition. He was more successful in Europe than in the United States. The interest of the US Congress in Greek affairs, however, was a new factor which perhaps owed something to Andreas' efforts, for his anti-Americanism was directed only against the Administration.

In the summer of 1969 the State Department received a letter critical of US policy, signed by fifty-one Congressmen. The reply, sent on 12 August, expounded the Administration's dilemma in terms which became increasingly familiar. It was faced with 'an autocratic government denying basic civil liberties' but also 'a NATO ally which has scrupulously fulfilled its treaty obligations'. Some of the Congressmen who signed the letter to the State Department had an opportunity later in the same month to confront Papadopoulos in Athens. When they taxed him with the accusations about torture, he replied that they were 'infuriatingly and basely false', and vowed that if a single such case could be proved, 'the only duty left to me as a man under solemn military oath is to commit suicide'.[9] This was another promise which was never carried out, although scores of such cases were abundantly proved at the torture trials in 1975.

In Europe, Scandinavian pressure against the junta in NATO gained some momentum, but the main forum of criticism was the Parliamentary Assembly of the Council of Europe. A distinction was explicitly drawn, by a

Foreign Office Minister in the House of Commons, between the Council of Europe as an appropriate body for such discussion and NATO as inappropriate because it was a 'defence alliance'.[10]

The prospect of Greece's expulsion from the Council of Europe could no longer be ignored in 1969. A motion to this effect was debated in the Parliamentary Assembly on 5 May, but it was agreed to postpone the final decision until the Council's meeting at ministerial level in December. Pipinelis at least was a sufficiently experienced diplomatist to take the threat seriously.

He had by this date committed himself wholeheartedly to the Colonels, but he did not share their reckless attitude towards foreign criticism. He was also a naturally cautious man. There was therefore probably no truth in the allegations which implicated him personally in a foolhardy plot to subvert the Italian government during 1969. The details were contained in what appeared to be a secret despatch from the Foreign Ministry to the Greek Ambassador in Rome, dated 15 May.[11] It was published in full only after the fall of the junta, but a summary of its contents was printed in the London *Observer* on 7 December 1969, together with a photograph of the seemingly authentic heading. Although the despatch was said to have been signed 'on the order of the Minister', it would have been grossly out of character for Pipinelis to have been associated with such irresponsible activities.

Somewhat less improbable was a story, published in the *Observer* on 23 November, that Pipinelis had presided on 26 August at a secret meeting in Switzerland of Ambassadors to western European capitals. There is no reason to doubt that the meeting occurred, but what happened at it is another question. Pipinelis was said to have told them that, no matter what might be said in public, there would be no restoration of democracy.[12] Even this story is hard to accept, because at the same date Pipinelis was strenuously trying to avert the expulsion of Greece from the Council of Europe by establishing a strict timetable for restoring constitutional government. To the end of his life, which was only eight months away, he appeared to believe sincerely in the validity of this programme.

He submitted his timetable to the Council of Europe on 25 August. It envisaged the restoration of freedom of the press by November 1969, the suspension of martial law throughout the country by September 1970, the progressive introduction of 'constructive decrees' based on the 1968 Constitution by the middle of December 1970, and the restoration of an elected Parliament by the middle of 1971.[13] Soon afterwards he wrote to Greece's permanent representative at the Council of Europe, K. Panayiotakos, instructing him to rebuff any hints from his foreign colleagues about elections, which were a matter purely for the Greek government to decide.[14]

Other indications suggest that Pipinelis genuinely believed, however mistakenly, that the timetable would be carried out. There was actually a beginning of progress in that direction, halting and deceptive as it turned out, during the next twelve months. When Pipinelis met King Constantine in Switzerland during October, he was said to have told him that 'with the timetable, the revolution is bound hand and foot, without possibility of escape'. He even added: 'I believe, Your Majesty, that in 1971 you will be back in Athens.'[15] Probably such really was his delusion.

He could claim that the first step actually was taken in October, when pre-censorship of the press was lifted. But what was given with one hand was immediately taken back by the other. A new draft Press Law was published in November. This formulated much the same restrictions as the censors had imposed, but with the proviso that newspapers were to censor themselves, under the threat of severe penalties, including imprisonment. Among the offences specified were 'provoking dissident activities', 'inflaming political passions', 'identifying agents of the secret services', and even, with an ironic gesture to the past, 'insulting the royal family'. The government could also control the press by limiting supplies of newsprint and holding up distribution.

While the Council of Europe was considering its response to Pipinelis' efforts, the North Atlantic Assembly added its modest weight to the campaign against the junta. In October 1969 it passed a motion urging the other fourteen governments in NATO 'to utilize all appropriate means to bring about, promptly, a return by Greece to free elections, parliamentary democracy and the rule of law, and to concert their actions in this respect'. The force of the motion was increased by the participation of elected representatives from the United States and Canada, which had, by definition, no standing in the Council of Europe. But although Scandinavian representatives at subsequent meetings of the Ministerial Council of NATO repeatedly pressed for action on the basis of the North Atlantic Assembly's resolution, their efforts were persistently blocked by the major allies and the Secretary-General.

The junta showed a surprising air of confidence as the day of decision in the Council of Europe approached. But its confidence was soon to be undermined. A secret report by the Commission of Human Rights was leaked to the press at the end of November, which virtually ensured a vote of expulsion from the Council, with its account of the junta's disregard for the rule of law and its practice of torture and imprisonment without trial. On 9 December the British Prime Minister, Harold Wilson, announced that his government would vote for expulsion. This decision was likely to be influential, since the British government had hitherto taken an ambiguous attitude towards the junta.

Influential Greeks abroad added their voices to the general condemnation. Constantine explicitly supported expulsion – of the junta, that is to say, rather than of the Greeks whom it did not represent. Karamanlis published on 1 October the statement of which he had forewarned his colleagues in Athens.[16] Without specifically supporting expulsion from the Council of Europe, he denounced the junta as a 'tyrannical and illegitimate institution', whose political ideas were 'medieval and theocratic'. He was sure, he said, that the Colonels never intended to restore democracy, but their eventual downfall was inevitable. Either they must resign or be overthrown.

In a simultaneous letter to his friend Solon Ghikas, the retired CGS, he made it clear that he expected the senior Generals to take some initiative against their former subordinates. But although the party leaders in Athens publicly endorsed his statement, Ghikas had to report with regret ten days later that the Colonels were obdurate, and there was no reaction among the military hierarchy to Karamanlis' appeal. The junta publicly repudiated it on 23 October, and accused Karamanlis of responsibility for 'terroristic activity' in Greece. The King was also attacked in the press at this time, for complicity in a royalist conspiracy which the junta claimed to have uncovered.

Opposition to the junta within Greece was faring equally badly. The talks between Kanellopoulos, Mavros and their colleagues about a united front of the major parties were making little progress. Plots against the junta were regularly uncovered by its efficient security services before they could reach fruition. There was a mood approaching despair as it was realized that even if the Council of Europe finally decided to expel Greece, it would make little difference so long as the US Administration was prepared to tolerate the junta.

The immediate reason for the United States' tolerance was simple. On 1 September 1969 the Libyan monarchy was overthrown by the revolution of Colonel Gaddafi. One of his first targets was the US Air Force base at Wheelus Field. Two days after Gaddafi came to power, the Americans were required to cease all flights and to prepare to evacuate the base as soon as possible. Shortly afterwards the British naval station at Tobruk was similarly required to close.

American activity in the Mediterranean had already begun to expand under President Nixon, in reaction to the emergence of a Soviet fleet and the development of a close relationship between the Soviet Union and Egypt under President Nasser. It was to be expected that the US Administration would seek compensating facilities elsewhere. Greece under the junta provided the likeliest opportunity.

Consequently a noticeable change began to take place in relations between Washington and Athens. Earlier in 1969 the US Administration had spoken severely of the junta, and had been in no hurry to replace its Ambassador. On 27 March the Secretary of State, William Rogers, had told the Senate Foreign

Relations Committee that he shared the concern it expressed about torture in Greece and the infringement of civil liberties. After September the tone of official comments was different. The State Department gave no support to Karamanlis' denunciation of the junta on 1 October. In European capitals, US Embassies were reported to be urging restraint on the proposal to expel Greece from the Council of Europe. Later it became known that the National Security Council had decided during September to end the embargo on heavy weapons, though officially the decision only came into effect a year later.[17]

It was also decided to send a new Ambassador to Greece for the first time since the departure of Phillips Talbot at the beginning of the year. President Nixon nominated Henry Tasca for the post. He was a career diplomat, like his predecessor, and no difficulties were to be expected. The Senate Foreign Relations Committee began its hearings on the appointment on 4 November. Although several Senators spoke critically of the situation in Greece, others were more tolerant.

The Committee recommended approval of Tasca's appointment on 8 December, without pressing him personally to answer embarrassing questions about US policy. Immediately afterwards, however, the Committee inserted a clause in the Foreign Assistance Authorization Bill, initiated by Senator Claiborne Pell, banning aid to Greece.[18] But the full Senate, on 12 December, deleted the amendment and substituted an anodyne resolution urging that 'the United States Government exert all possible effort to influence a speedy return to a constitutional government in Greece'.[19] The Senate in its totality thus proved more amenable to pressure from the Administration than its specialist committee.

The substituted resolution was carried in place of the Pell Amendment by forty-five votes to thirty-eight. This was the first time that opposition to the junta was measured by a formal vote in the US Congress. It was a conspicuously small majority, which suggested that the White House and the State Department would not always prevail.

Both in the Senate and in the House of Representatives there was a number of liberals, including some of Greek descent, who had made their opposition to the junta clear from the first, but without making much impression on the Administration. Almost all of them were Democrats; but there was also a number of active supporters of the junta in Congress, and these too were mostly Democrats.[20] This division within the Democratic Party made it easier for the Administration to carry its policy into effect.

Across the Atlantic, in the House of Commons the situation was different. Practically no members of the Labour or Liberal Parties supported the junta, and very few Conservatives actively opposed it. But the Labour Party was in office, and its Ministers exercised an embarrassed tolerance of the junta for reasons of expediency. The difference in attitudes between Washington and London was a natural reflection of the difference between parliamentary government as practised in Britain and the separation of powers established under the US constitution.[21]

But the results in the two cases were much the same. Whichever administrations were in office in London and Washington, the sanctions against the junta amounted to little more than words, and only words were needed in response to neutralize them. The Colonels were ready with an abundance of words, some of them contradictory, some irrelevant, and almost all hypocritical. During the months before the decisive meeting of the Council of Europe, indications about the junta's intentions were particularly hard to interpret. Pipinelis was still talking as if the country was on its way back to democracy, but the junta was assuming that it had many years of office ahead. On 6 September, at the opening of the Salonika Trade Fair, Papadopoulos declared that 'leaps forward are not achieved with a parliament.'[22] He might have offered as an example of a leap forward not to be so achieved the fifteen-year development plan, which was announced by Makarezos on 21 November.

A few last-minute efforts were made to placate the junta's critics at the Council of Europe, but they did not carry conviction. On 3 November Pattakos held a press conference to explain away the newly proposed restrictions on the press, but he ended by abusing the journalists present instead.[23] On 4 December the Minister of Justice announced that eleven out of the eighteen 'constructive decrees' required to bring into operation the suspended clauses of the 1968 Constitution were ready in draft.[24] On 11 December Pattakos announced that 'elections are being methodically prepared, and will be conducted by the majority system'.[25] Opponents were unlikely to forget that one year earlier he had declared that the Greeks were tired of elections, and two years earlier that elections would take place when they were least expected. They could hardly be less expected than at the end of 1969.

None of this impressed the junta's critics at the Council of Europe, which was virtually certain to suspend Greece from its membership. Pipinelis therefore forestalled the vote by announcing Greece's 'permanent withdrawal' on 12 December. The ministerial committee of the Council would not be deterred, however, from passing a resolution that Greece was in breach of the Charter. It added an expression of hope that conditions would soon be established in Greece which would justify her return to membership.

When Pipinelis returned to Athens from Strasbourg on 19 December, he was greeted at the airport by the entire government, as if he had achieved a diplomatic triumph. Although he made a short speech full of admiration for Papadopoulos, he cannot have been under any delusion about the outcome. On the following day he told a press conference that his timetable of reforms would none the less be carried through.[26] It would be published, he said, within three or four days. Three or four days turned into four months: the timetable was published on 17 April 1970. But at least it was published, which argues in favour of Pipinelis' sincerity. He did not live to see his hopes belied by experience.

6 A new era

1970

The US Air Force began to evacuate its base in Libya on 8 January 1970. Two days later Henry Tasca took up his post as Ambassador in Athens. That second week of the New Year marked the opening of a new era in the junta's relations with the United States. The improvement was timely, for a current of anti-American feeling was making itself felt in Turkey. A few weeks earlier, on 19 December, sailors of the 6th Fleet had been attacked by a mob of students and others at Smyrna (Izmir), which had forced the US ships to withdraw from the harbour. It needed no emphasis that such an episode would be unthinkable in any Greek port so long as the junta remained in power.

There was an evident connection from the first between Tasca's appointment and the American need for secure facilities in the eastern Mediterranean, for the 6th Fleet in particular. But it took three years for negotiations to reach an acceptable conclusion, because bargaining on defence was one part of foreign policy in which the Colonels were competent and sure of their own strength. Karamanlis, who was equally aware of their bargaining power and fearful of the purposes to which they might put it, took the opportunity early in 1970 to offer his personal advice to President Nixon for the first time. He chose as his intermediary Archbishop Iakovos, the head of the Orthodox Church in America, who passed through Paris on his way from Athens to Washington in February.

On 20 February the Archbishop delivered to the President a long memorandum which Karamanlis had given him.[1] It started with an outline of the crisis in Greek affairs, and went on to list three possible courses: first, a forcible overthrow of the junta; secondly, its voluntary surrender of power; thirdly, elections to be held under its continuing control. Since force ought to be avoided at all costs, and elections under the junta could not possibly be satisfactory, there remained only the second course. The junta was bound to resist making a voluntary surrender, so it must be put under pressure. Such pressure, by implication, could come only from the US Administration. There is no evidence of the President's reply, but the advice clearly ran counter to his current policy. It was not until a year later that the Administration began to become impatient with the junta. As usual, however, members of Congress were less tolerant.

One of the problems in which the Administration hoped that the junta

74

could play a useful role was that of Cyprus. But even the President might have been shocked by the methods used by the Colonels in trying to liquidate the problem, and Makarios with it. Early in January 1970 Makarios visited Athens, where he appeared to be warmly received. A communiqué on his visit contained the usual announcement of 'complete agreement' on matters of common interest. On 8 January Papadopoulos explicitly repudiated rumours that his government was supporting a so-called 'National Front' in Cyprus, hostile to Makarios.

Makarios had little confidence in this assurance, for the existence of the National Front had been common knowledge for the best part of a year. It consisted mainly of ex-members of EOKA who were now enrolled in the police; and it was supported by Makarios' old rival, Bishop Anthimos of Kition. Before long it was to become better known as EOKA-B. Soon after his return from Athens, Makarios introduced a Preventive Detention Bill to restrain it.

He also had an even more dangerous antagonist: Polykarpos Yiorkatzis, his former Minister of the Interior, whose idle hands were itching for mischief since his enforced resignation in the aftermath of Panagoulis' attempt to kill Papadopoulos. Enigmatic though Yiorkatzis' motives always were, it seems probable that towards the end of 1969 he had allowed himself to be recruited by the junta as an agent against Makarios. Papadopoulos' motives are not in doubt. He needed to eliminate Makarios as a step towards the final settlement of the Cyprus problem, which was to be his contribution towards the pacification of the eastern Mediterranean in the interests of the United States.

On 8 March an unsuccessful attempt was made to assassinate Makarios in Nicosia, as his helicopter was taking off from the grounds of the presidential palace. A number of the participants were arrested on the spot. It was at once suspected that Yiorkatzis was involved in the plot. On 12 March, before sufficient evidence could be established to bring him to trial, Yiorkatzis was prosecuted for a separate offence of possessing two revolvers without a licence. He pleaded guilty. The next day he tried surreptitiously, but undisguised and carrying his own passport, to leave Cyprus by air. On Makarios' orders he was prevented from embarking, but not placed under arrest. Two days later, on 15 March, he was found murdered in an isolated spot.

The complexities of the bloody affair were past unravelling. But there was one seemingly concrete piece of evidence. A document came into Makarios' hands containing a plan, under the code-name 'Hermes', for the Cypriot National Guard (whose high-level officers were mainland Greeks) to seize power in the island.[2] Makarios pronounced it a forgery, however, and declared his disbelief in any suspicion of a plot against him mounted in Athens. Few Greeks shared his credulity, which may have been assumed.

The common suspicion was that the Hermes Plan really existed; that

Yiorkatzis was behind it; that the junta was behind Yiorkatzis; and that when the plot failed, officers from the Greek mainland murdered Yiorkatzis in order to silence him. The Cypriots arrested for the attempt on Makarios told different stories at different stages of their interrogation, but the court which tried them in September 1970 was in no doubt of the complicity of Yiorkatzis nor of the genuineness of the Hermes Plan. The accused men were convicted and sentenced to long terms of imprisonment. After a short time, however, Makarios pardoned and released them, with a truly Christian clemency. It was rumoured that when they went to thank him, one of them told him that they were really guilty, and that the plot had indeed been concerted between Yiorkatzis and a group of Greek officers from the mainland.[3]

On the assumption that the complicity of the junta was a fact, the purpose of the plot could hardly be in doubt. It was to enforce some form of *enosis*, with compensation to the Turks – a policy to which Makarios was the chief obstacle. Nobody could afford to say this openly in Athens, but one newspaper, *Ethnos*, published an interview with a leading member of the Centre Union, I. Zigdis, who hinted at it in veiled language. The offending issue was confiscated and a prosecution was launched against Zigdis, together with the proprietor of *Ethnos* and four members of the editorial staff. Many of the former politicians, including George Rallis and Kanellopoulos, came to give evidence for the defence. But on 1 April the defendants were all convicted and sentenced to terms of imprisonment, ranging from thirteen months to five years, together with heavy fines. Three days later *Ethnos* was obliged by financial difficulties to cease publication.[4] It was thus shown that censorship of the press was no longer necessary.

Another spectacular trial was in progress at the same time. The thirty-four arrested members of Democratic Defence (DA), including General Iordanidis (who had served as Greece's senior representative at NATO headquarters) and Professors Karayiorgas and George A. Mangakis, were on trial for conspiracy and possession of explosives. Many of them, giving evidence in court, revoked the testimony they had given under interrogation, on the ground that they had been tortured. Although they were men of high character, they were no doubt guilty as charged, but it was really the junta that was seen to be on trial. Very heavy sentences were imposed on them: a life sentence for Karayiorgas, eighteen years for Mangakis. Iordanidis, an elderly and sick man, was imprisoned in harsh conditions on Corfu, in a gaol which had been condemned years before.

Their treatment led to a further protest from the Scandinavians at the Council of Europe. The Council also received a new report on 15 April from the Commission of Human Rights, as a result of which Greece was declared to be in breach of ten articles of the international Convention. These further condemnations of the junta evidently convinced Papadopoulos that some pretence of reform must again be presented to the world, especially since the US Senate was about to begin another round of hearings on military aid.

The junta's reactions were often predictable in the sense that they were regularly contradictory. One step forwards or to the right was followed quasi-automatically by one backwards or to the left. This was not merely a matter of caprice. The likeliest explanation is that the junta was far from united: supporters of different lines of policy outweighed each other in turn, while Papadopoulos tried to maintain a balance between them. A hint of this explanation became public in May 1970 from an unexpected but well-informed source. Colonel D. Stamatelopoulos, an original member of the 'revolutionary group', had lost faith in the junta, particularly Papadopoulos. But he suffered no penalty for his defection. Although he criticized his fellow officers in the press, he remained nominally a member of the Revolutionary Council, which itself had no more than a nominal existence.

On 11 May Stamatelopoulos published an article in *Vradyni*, the most outspoken of the surviving newspapers, in which he openly criticized Papadopoulos for acting irresponsibly. The occasion was one of the Prime Minister's perverse decisions, taken a month earlier, to release the musician Theodorakis and allow him to leave the country.[5] Theodorakis arrived in Paris in the private aircraft of Jean Servan-Schreiber, the flamboyant Secretary-General of the French Radical Party, who claimed the credit for his release. He also claimed to have been supported in his efforts to free Theodorakis by several prominent Greeks, including Aristotle Onassis and Tom Pappas; but they denied his story.

Even more unexpectedly, Theodorakis' wife and children were able to escape clandestinely from Greece a few weeks later, obviously with official connivance. In his article in *Vradyni*, Stamatelopoulos sharply criticized Servan-Schreiber for exploiting the affair, but he also implied that the Prime Minister had no right to take such arbitrary decisions. Papadopoulos, he argued, was not an autocrat but only first among equals. The leadership was supposedly collective, but clearly it had not acted collectively in this case.

Papadopoulos continued to take his own initiatives, however, in pursuing a conciliatory line towards the junta's foreign critics. In March 1970 he released a further fifty-five alleged Communists from detention, and in April over 300 other detainees. On 10 April he announced that the articles on human rights in the 1968 Constitution would come into immediate effect. At the same time he forecast the establishment of a Consultative Committee, which would be partly elected and would serve as a 'mini-parliament'. He allowed several other opponents of the junta to leave Greece during the summer, including Amalia (Lady) Fleming, the Greek widow of the discoverer of penicillin, as well as a number of politicians. How far his colleagues supported these decisions is not known, but before long the internal dissensions of the junta, though not publicized, were to become acute.

It was undeniable that Papadopoulos' experiments in relaxation brought him some rewards. Most of those whom he allowed to leave Greece did little to stimulate opposition abroad. Some, like George Sepheris, were not temperamentally inclined to do so. Lady Fleming did not give any immediate sign of commitment to active resistance. Theodorakis made a statement to the French press on 29 April calling for the formation of a government in exile, but nothing came of it. The only man outside Greece who could have formed such a government with any hope of recognition was Karamanlis, and he had no intention of doing so. Apart from his natural disinclination, he could see from his long residence in France that opinion abroad, particularly in France, was by no means wholeheartedly opposed to the dictatorship.

At the meeting of Ministers of the Council of Europe on 15 April, the French Foreign Minister abstained from the vote condemning Greece for breaches of the Convention of Human Rights. It was speculated that the price of his abstention had been a secret agreement by Papadopoulos to release Theodorakis; and that Servan-Schreiber, having learned of this agreement, had contrived to exploit it for his own interests. On 30 April, the day after Theodorakis' statement in Paris, the Greek government published its own account of the discussions which Papadopoulos and Servan-Schreiber had held in Athens about Theodorakis and other detainees. By this account, Servan-Schreiber had said that he himself approved of much that Papadopoulos was doing, that he opposed any suggestion of cutting off Greece from the body of Europe, and that he would speak to this effect in the Parliamentary Assembly of the Council of Europe. He was also said to have given an assurance that Theodorakis would not involve himself in politics. If this was true, the undertaking was not respected.

Evidently Servan-Schreiber was swimming with the tide of French political opinion rather than influencing it; but the direction of the tide was unmistakable. Nor was it confined to France. It was noticeable also in NATO, where the French were absentees. At the ministerial meeting of the NATO Council in Rome during the last week of May 1970, Danish and Norwegian attempts to persuade the allies to put pressure on Greece, even to the point of suspension from NATO, were frustrated. The argument against such a policy was that it would weaken NATO.

This argument had been presented in its most sophisticated form by a Foreign Office Minister in the House of Commons in December 1969:

> Actions against Greece in NATO would not necessarily help the Greek people, but would undermine the security of the south-east flank of NATO, thus putting at risk democratic ideals and parliamentary institutions on a scale far wider than Greece.[6]

If a Labour Minister could so argue, the Greeks had no hope of relief from a Conservative government, which was elected in June 1970.

Papadopoulos could therefore claim to have neutralized opposition abroad. But at home reactions were less satisfactory for him. Stamatelopoulos' article in *Vradyni* on 11 May appeared to reflect a division within the junta. It led to a brief controversy in the press, of a kind that would have seemed impossible a year earlier. An editorial on 17 May in *Acropolis*, a right-wing but not pro-junta newspaper, called for explanations of Stamatelopoulos' article. Stamatelopoulos replied in cryptic terms in *Vradyni* on 23 May. *Acropolis* commented on the 27th that Papadopoulos' status appeared to be confused and uncertain. In particular, it was unclear whether the Revolutionary Council still existed or not. The points raised by *Acropolis* were never clarified, but the impression of internal conflict was corroborated by a number of incidents during the summer.

Early in June the former President of Parliament, D. Papaspyrou (a member of ERE), was prosecuted for failing to vote in the plebiscite of 1968, when voting was compulsory. Although he admitted the offence, he was acquitted by the court. The prosecution would hardly have taken place without the approval of the junta, yet no outburst of wrath followed. There was an equally surprising silence when a group of young writers published their *Eighteen Texts* in July. Although the political content of their essays, and its hostility to the junta, were unmistakable, no sanctions were taken against them.

Papadopoulos had other business to distract him at the time. At the end of June he was engaged in a reconstruction of his government, with the introduction of twelve new names to the Council of Ministers. One of the newcomers was G. Yiorgalas, the ex-Communist who was engaged in writing *The Ideology of the Revolution*. Yiorgalas described the reconstruction as 'an opening to the new generation'.[7] It was true that the comparative youth of the new Ministers was a feature of the changes. But this was not the case with Yiorgalas himself, who had many years of political agitation behind him.

It is likely that the US Embassy played a part in encouraging the attempt to create an improved image of the junta. Ambassador Tasca had become an important figure in the calculations of the Colonels, so much so that Pattakos took a personal interest in his welfare. On 26 July Pattakos sent a note to Papadopoulos reporting a fear expressed by 'American sources' that Tasca might be kidnapped, and urging that precautions should be taken.[8] The fear may have been real, for all Europe was troubled at the time by terrorism, kidnapping and hijacks. Athens was not exempt: only a few days before Pattakos' warning a group of Arab hijackers in Athens, who had been held in prison for over a year, had been released under threat of an aircraft and its passengers being blown up at Athens airport. Precautions were duly taken to protect Tasca, who was not molested during his tenure of the US Embassy.

Good relations with the United States were essential in 1970 because otherwise the US Congress was unlikely to confirm any agreement on 'homeporting' for the 6th Fleet in Greece, which was the chief object of Tasca's mission. In the early months of 1970 scepticism in Congress and pressure from the Administration were evenly balanced. The House Foreign Affairs Committee heard a senior General on the importance of military sales abroad, to Greece among other countries, on 17 February;[9] and its Subcommittee on Foreign Assistance heard the Secretary for Defence (Melvin Laird) with two more Generals on 10–11 March, and the Deputy Assistant Secretary of State responsible for the area (Rodger Davies) on 10 April.[10] Such hearings were to be annual events, and to become increasingly critical.

The most serious confrontation during 1970 was between the Subcommittee of the Senate Foreign Relations Committee on Security Agreements and Commitments Abroad, and the two key officials of the State Department and the Department of Defence, Rodger Davies and Robert Pranger, which took place on 9–11 June.[11] This was the occasion on which Senator Fulbright bluntly accused the Administration, though not the two officials personally, of deceiving Congress about its relations with the junta. He referred to the surreptitious breach of the embargo on heavy weapons, and went on:

> Your actions are so sympathetic to the Greek Colonels that it lends very little credence to your declaration that you are opposed to them, because you have done everything really that they needed to do to keep them in power and to give the impression that we approve of them. The pressure was very great, to be sure to send a sympathetic Ambassador there, and you did send a sympathetic Ambassador there...[12]

He might have added, but perhaps he did not know, that the Administration had exercised strong pressure only a few weeks earlier to neutralize an attack on the junta by the Scandinavians at the meeting of the NATO Council in Rome.

Although the two officials were obliged to make a somewhat evasive defence of the junta, the Subcommittee was less hesitant in its conclusions. It adopted an amendment to the Military Sales Act for 1971, in the name of Senator Vance Hartke, to ban the supply of any 'defence article or defence service' to Greece, subject to exceptions for expenditure already obligated; but it allowed the President a right of waiver on grounds of overriding national interest. The full Senate, however, under strong pressure from the Administration, overruled the Hartke Amendment on 29 June. Again the majority of fifty to forty-two was significantly narrow.[13]

In the eyes of Congress the junta's progress towards respectability suffered a further setback a few weeks later, when Pipinelis died on 19 July. He believed to the last that his timetable of reforms would be carried out, but this seemed unlikely when Papadopoulos took over the Ministry of Foreign Affairs in his place. The succession caused some consternation. Apart from international opinion, which regarded Papadopoulos as a poor exchange for Pipinelis, the internal relations of the junta were also upset. Papadopoulos' accumulation of offices as Prime Minister, Minister of Defence and Foreign Minister aggravated the jealousy of some of his colleagues. His pre-eminence was emphasized by the appointment of three junior Ministers in the Prime Minister's office, which was more than any previous Prime Minister had needed.

The rivalry which had been latent at the time of Stamatelopoulos' article in May came to a head in August. Pattakos, who remained at heart loyal to Papadopoulos, later described a crucial meeting of the junta on 27 August.[14] The storm burst over matters of only indirect relevance. One was the marriage which Papadopoulos had recently contracted with a second wife, after divorcing his first. Some held it to be irregular, and therefore unacceptable in the chief Minister of the 'Greece of the Christian Greeks'. Another item was the enforced retirement, on Papadopoulos' orders, of an officer believed to have been involved in the recent attempt to kill Makarios. But the real issue was the concentration of power in Papadopoulos' hands.

After listening to several hours of criticism, Papadopoulos delivered a furious retort, accusing his colleagues of working against him and undermining his policies. He then left the room, saying: 'I cannot continue shouldering the burdens I have undertaken.' But he had not lost his head: he shrewdly gave his colleagues two months to clarify their disagreements, after which he would decide whether or not to resign. Much less than two months was required.

As he implied, the criticisms directed at him were largely contradictory. By some he was accused of aiming to end the dictatorship, by others of trying to maintain it indefinitely; by some of failing to carry out reforms, by others of undermining the social system; by some of being too soft towards Makarios, by others of promoting violence in Cyprus. But all blamed him for the stagnation and inertia into which the junta had sunk. In this at least they were right. His efforts to create a semblance of momentum had failed, but his tactic of threatening resignation was another effort of the same kind. It could only succeed if he were judged irreplaceable.

For some days the outcome was in doubt. On 28 August Pattakos called on Papadopoulos to calm him down, and to find out the exact nature of his grievances against his colleagues. Papadopoulos promised to put them on paper. What exactly he wrote to Pattakos is not known, but some indications of it can be found in a letter of reply from Pattakos, dated 8 September.[15] Two things are made clear by Pattakos' letter: that Papadopoulos' complaints were chiefly directed at Ladas, who was now Secretary-General of the Ministry of the Interior under Pattakos; and that Pattakos himself was desperately anxious to persuade Papadopoulos not to resign.

He need not have worried, for by the date of his letter the crisis was already to all intents and purposes over. Papadopoulos had repeated his threat of resignation over the telephone on 2 September to Rouphogalis, the Director of KYP, saying that he would announce it at the Council of Ministers on the 7th. Rouphogalis had told Angelis, the Commander-in-Chief, who seemed unmoved. But Rouphogalis also told Pattakos, who tried to telephone to Papadopoulos himself. Having failed to reach him, Pattakos set about drafting a desperate plan to reform the whole system of government.[16] The most significant feature of his draft plan was a provision for the recruitment into a re-established Revolutionary Council of the leaders or representatives of the old political parties, excluding only the extreme left. The plan was never submitted to Papadopoulos, however, for he changed his mind and reached a compromise with his rivals before the need for it had come to a head. Temporarily, the crisis was resolved and Papadopoulos remained in office.

It seemed that Papadopoulos enjoyed crises, and caused this one as a diversion. He was conscious of the dilemma of the junta: whether to move forward to liberalization or backward to repression. To stand still, as they had been doing for so long, was to stagnate without achieving anything. Papadopoulos and Pattakos were, on balance, in favour of moving forward, though uncertain of their direction. A majority of their colleagues, led by Ladas, believed that only a hard line could keep them permanently in power. Papadopoulos' personal problem was to satisfy international opinion, particularly in the United States, without losing control of his colleagues. Allied officials were fairly easily satisfied, but his colleagues were not. Their case against him was that he was taking too much into his own hands. His defence was that it appeared to work, and anyway it was only cosmetic.

In the late summer of 1970 Papadopoulos raised hopes abroad by his conduct and public statements, which led to corresponding concessions. In August, during his own personal crisis, it was announced that some 500 more detainees were to be released. In September he repeated the promise of a Consultative Committee, though he qualified it later in the month by repudiating any notion of a return to democracy. Early in October Pattakos gave an interview to the German periodical *Der Spiegel* in which he said categorically: 'Elections will take place.' But Yiorgalas, speaking with the authority of a Minister in the Prime Minister's office, half-withdrew the promise with a cryptic phrase: 'Elections are not a theme of the present moment but of the immediate future.'[17] It was to appear later that all of them were more or less telling the truth as they understood it.

Papadopoulos was also working to improve his relations with Makarios, at least on the surface. In a letter to the Archbishop in mid-June, he wrote that he was disgusted with the rumours of hostility between them. They met again in September, shortly after Makarios had once more visited the King in Rome. There was discussion of the possibility of the King's return, which Makarios strongly favoured, but as usual nothing came of it. The purpose of such occasions on Papadopoulos' part was to create an illusion of reasonableness and expectations of progress, which would never be fulfilled.

The allies hopefully put the most favourable interpretation on Papadopoulos' words and gestures, and responded accordingly. In September 1970 the British Minister of Defence, Lord Carrington, visited Greece. It was said that he was on holiday, but it cannot have been unforeseen that, rightly or wrongly, a more far-reaching interpretation would be put on his visit. No one in Athens believed the statement that he had not met any member of the junta, nor that his sudden departure was due to illness, even if both were true. The tactlessness of the visit was offset a day after the Minister's departure by the news that a Greek Air Force pilot had defected to the Soviet Union with his aircraft (which was returned). Fortuitously, the propaganda value of the Minister's visit was diminished by this distraction.

A much more important advantage accrued to the junta ten days later. On 22 September it was announced in Washington that it had been decided to 'resume normal military shipments to Greece'.[18] The decision had in fact been taken in principle a year earlier, though this was denied by the Secretary of State, William Rogers, at a news conference on 13 May.[19] Even a year later, on 3 August 1971, Ambassador Tasca evaded answering questions from the House Foreign Affairs Committee about the date of the decision.[20] The Administration was excessively sensitive on this topic, knowing that it was certain to attract Congressional criticism.

The announcement in September 1970 was so phrased as to imply that there had been no change of policy since May 1967. In effect, the partial relaxation of the embargo on heavy weapons since October 1968 was ignored. Strategic reasons alone were now invoked: the cohesion of NATO, together with Greece's contribution to the security of the west, the importance of which had been 'sharply underlined in recent months by events in the eastern Mediterranean'.[21]

So far as the internal affairs of Greece were concerned, it was only possible for the State Department to find cosmetic excuses. Although it admitted that the United States 'had hoped for a more rapid return to representative government', nevertheless 'the trend toward a constitutional order is established'. Major sections of the 1968 Constitution had been implemented; there had been a 'partial restoration of civil rights'; and the Greek government had stated its intention 'to establish parliamentary democracy'. Like the rest of NATO, the United States continued to expect 'steady progress toward restoring the country to political government'.

In return for these speculative advances, Greece was to receive a substantial share (with Taiwan and Turkey) of an extra 100 million dollars which President Nixon proposed to Congress on 18 November in his supplemental Military Aid programme.[22] More important than the scale of aid in financial terms were the categories of armaments to be licensed. It was unofficially forecast that they would include jet aircraft, tanks and other armoured vehicles, artillery, mortars and helicopters. The supposition was that such items were more appropriate to external defence than to internal repression, but recollection of the way the junta came to power made this seem naïve.

The changed atmosphere between the US Administration and the junta was soon made even clearer. Early in October the Secretary for Defence, Melvin Laird, made an official visit to Athens. It was not an unqualified success as propaganda, for on 3 October a bomb exploded near Papadopoulos' office in the old Parliament building while he was in conference with his visitor. But at least he was able to represent to his colleagues that his policy was bearing fruit in real terms. Many other prominent Americans were to be welcomed to Athens during the following months. Even in Congress there were faint signs of increasing tolerance: for example, in November the Senate Armed Services Committee recommended an extension of the loan of a submarine to Greece, though not without individual expressions of dissent.[23]

It need not be supposed that the US Administration was deceived by Papadopoulos' gestures, although its Embassy tried hard to present them in a favourable light. Strategic necessity rather than delusion determined the shift of policy in Washington. There was serious trouble again in the eastern Mediterranean in September 1970, when the expulsion of the Palestinian Commandos from Jordan into Syria caused a threat of war, which the US 6th Fleet intervened to forestall. The death of President Nasser at the end of September increased the atmosphere of uncertainty and tension in the area, especially as his successor, Anwar Sadat, appeared at first to be inclining even further than Nasser towards an alliance with the Soviet Union. Since Turkey was in a state of political chaos, and Libya was under the erratic control of Colonel Gaddafi, Greece under the junta could be regarded as practically the only remaining bastion of stability, apart from Israel.

Meanwhile the junta had passed through the crisis which split it at the end of August. Pattakos continued his role of conciliator. Although the memoran-

Armoured vehicles outside
Parliament, 21 April
1967   Topham

King Constantine poses
with Cabinet Ministers of
the National Government:
From left to right, first row:
Colonel George
Papadopoulos, Premier
Constantinos Kollias, King
Constantine, General
Grigorio Spatidakis
Second row:
Lieutenant-General George
Zoitakis (on right of King),
Brigadier-General Stylianos
Pattakos (on left of King),
26 April 1967   Associated Press

Above: Three leaders of the Greek Revolutionary Junta receive the Grand Cross of the Orthodox Crusaders of Saint Sepulchre of Jerusalem: Papadopoulos (left), Pattakos (centre), Makarezos (right), 5 July 1968   Topham

Left: Rome: King Constantine and Queen Anne-Marie fly into exile, 14 December 1967   Topham

Opposite: Archbishop Makarios, President of the Republic of Cyprus, and General Grivas   Topham

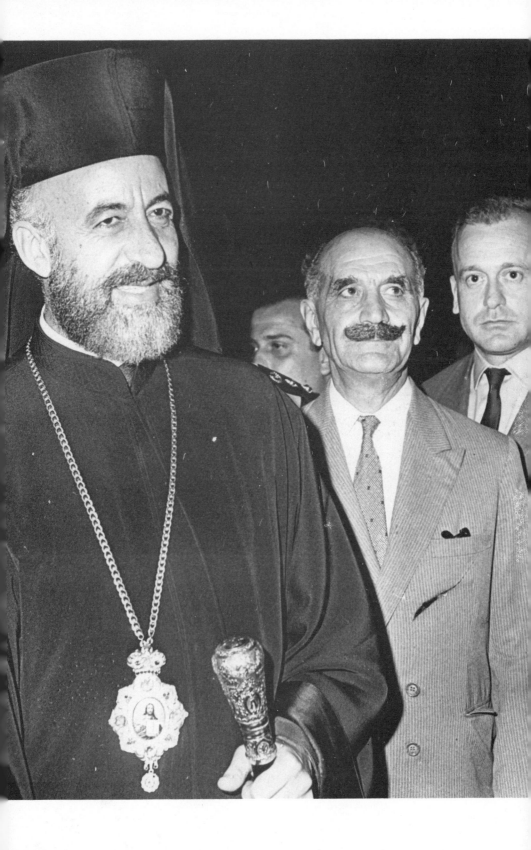

Right: Papadopoulos and colleagues dancing at a popular festival

Below: G. Papadopoulos and General Angelis inspecting a guard of honour at the Memorial to the Unknown Soldier

Opposite above: The tank at the gates of the Polytechnic, 17 November 1973

By kind permission of the Greek Ministry of Press and Information

Opposite below: The palace of Archbishop Makarios after the attempt to murder him, 15 July 1974

By kind permission of the Greek Ministry of Press and Information

Below right: Mrs Helen Vlachos, a newspaper proprietor and prominent antagonist of the dictatorship

Below left: Andreas Papandreou and Lady (Amalia) Fleming, leading figures in the opposition to the dictatorship

The three leaders of the former Greek dictatorship listen
to the death sentence passed on them in the Athens
court: 23 August 1975. Left to right: Papadopoulos,
Makarezos, Pattakos   Associated Press

Opposite above: Constantine Karamanlis returning to
Greece to restore democratic government, 24 July 1974

Opposite below: Turkish troops near Kyrenia, Cyprus,
23 July 1974   Popperfoto

The author and Panayiotis Kanellopoulos at a meeting
in Athens, 15 April 1981

dum which he had drafted on 2 September, proposing an entirely new system of government, was never submitted to his colleagues, some of its ideas were to be brought to their notice in another way. On 26 September Colonel Stamatelopoulos again published an article in *Vradyni*, which was probably inspired by Pattakos. In it he hinted at the possibility of the King's return to Greece, perhaps as early as New Year's Day. Although he did not say so in the article, it would clearly have been impossible for the King to return unless at least some reforms on the lines of Pattakos' suppressed memorandum were carried out. Stamatelopoulos argued that the aims of the dictatorship had virtually been achieved, so that the time was approaching for the 'closure of the parenthesis'. He suggested that an electoral law might be published not later than 31 December.

Once again these hints could expect a welcome in western capitals, especially as they seemed to be officially inspired. But there were warning voices against too favourable a reception, and these were not without justification. On 30 October a group of twenty-four Greek journalists delivered an open letter to President Nixon at the US Embassy in London, protesting at the decision to resume the supply of heavy weapons.[24] On 11 November they received a reply from the Deputy Assistant Secretary of State responsible for Near Eastern and South Asian Affairs, Rodger Davies, indicating that the Administration's view of developments in Greece was more optimistic than their own.[25] Among other indications, he must have had in mind the Consultative Committee or 'mini-parliament', which was about to be brought into being. But the unacknowledged reason for his defensive reply was that Greece was indispensable to US strategy.

Elections to the Consultative Committee were due to take place on 29 November. As the title implied, the Committee was to have no executive or legislative functions. Its conception failed entirely to satisfy the demand for parliamentary government. Curiously, it was almost the only measure introduced by the junta which could literally be described as 'fascist' – a term loosely but wrongly applied to most of the junta's actions – because its basis of representation was to be corporative.

The Consultative Committee was to comprise fifty-six members – forty-six elected plus ten nominated by the Prime Minister. Some of the elected members would be chosen by academic and professional organizations, others by localities. The electors were to be the presidents and functionaries *ex officio* of bodies representing lawyers, doctors, chemists and merchants, together with workers' clubs, agricultural co-operatives and boards of trade. These electoral bodies would choose ninety-two candidates between them, from whom the President would choose the final forty-six. He would then add his own ten nominees. Thus every single member of the 'mini-parliament' would be approved by Papadopoulos personally. The whole

85

exercise was presented with much solemnity, and with a precise timetable; and the timetable at least was strictly executed.

Elections for the Consultative Committee duly took place on 29 November. Papadopoulos hinted that if it behaved itself, it might even provide a training-ground for a real Parliament later on. On 31 December he named the first fifty-six members. But he had already announced on 20 December that 'as regards the constitutional state order, there will be no change in the coming year'.[26] Naturally public opinion did not take the innovation seriously.

The limited scope of the junta's concessions to liberalization was illustrated by the publication on New Year's Day 1971 of fifteen out of the eighteen 'constructive decrees' which were required to bring the 1968 Constitution into full operation.[27] Five of the fifteen were no sooner published than suspended. Among those suspended were three on which civil liberties and the prospect of democracy depended: one on martial law, which was to continue in force; one on political parties, which were to remain dissolved; and one establishing the post of Parliamentary Commissioner to license political parties, which was unnecessary because political parties were not to be formed. In this way Papadopoulos sought to please Greece's allies by a display of progress, and his colleagues by making sure that it was only a display.

7 The American commitment

1971

Kanellopoulos published a message on New Year's Day 1971, which made a deep impression, as his words always did.[1] His language was everything that the Colonels' language was not: lucid, logical, precise and persuasive. He pointed out that the junta advanced two principal arguments against the right of the Greek people to political freedom. One was the Communist danger; the other was the lack of political maturity. As the last constitutional Prime Minister of Greece, he could assert that the so-called Communist danger was non-existent. As for the lack of political maturity, this was merely an insult. But even if it were true, how could it happen that those currently governing Greece were alone in possessing the requisite maturity? The armed forces were as Greek as any other Greeks, 'a part of the Greek people, flesh of its flesh'. But it was simply not true that the armed forces were governing Greece. Greece was governed by 'a tiny group of men', who were creating a dangerous gulf between the armed forces and the people.

Almost simultaneously, the US State Department took the opportunity of the New Year to make a statement defining its policy towards Greece. Under the heading 'Greece: US Policy', it pointed out that when the Colonels seized power, the US government had to choose between three courses: first, to support the military dictatorship; secondly, to sever relations with it; thirdly, to maintain relations with it while encouraging it to return to constitutional government. The US Administration also had to bear in mind the importance of Greece as a member of NATO and an ally in the Mediterranean, especially in view of the growing activity of the Soviet fleet in that area. Therefore the third course was chosen, and this was still US policy. The Administration continued to make its position clear to the Greek leadership, and believed that this policy had contributed decisively to certain changes in the direction of reform.

Many Congressmen considered this statement unduly complacent. As a result of representations by Senator Fulbright in correspondence with the State Department, it was substantially revised later in the year to give its criticisms a sharper edge.[2] But at best there was no doubt that Kanellopoulos was closer to the mark than the State Department. Both saw that the signs of movement were very slight, but the State Department was mistaken in trying to interpret them as moves in the right direction.

Not everyone in Washington, however, was allowed to be taken in. Two staff members of the Senate Foreign Relations Committee, Richard Moose and James Lowenstein, visited Greece early in 1971 and formed the opinion that the US Embassy as well as the Administration was taking too optimistic a view of the junta.[3] They reported that among the Greek opposition there was a feeling that the United States had betrayed its true friends. That feeling undoubtedly existed, partly because Embassy officials thought it unwise to have direct contacts with the opposition.

The two investigators also noted that the confinement of official contacts to a limited circle around the junta had led members of the Embassy staff to adopt the language of the junta itself: for instance, they referred to it, almost unconsciously, as the 'revolution', a term which in Greek usage begged the very question of its legitimacy. Apart from their initial scepticism, the two had opportunities to observe for themselves what was happening. A number of trials were in progress during their visit, including one of seventy defendants charged with subversion. Other contemporary episodes no doubt came to their ears: a villager sent to prison for playing a record of Theodorakis; a man convicted simply of 'insulting authority'; a number of magistrates held in solitary confinement, whose offence was to have condemned the accused in the Lambrakis case seven years earlier.

The Senate Foreign Relations Committee was favourably impressed by its investigators' report, which provided it with further justification for criticism of the Administration's attitude towards the junta. But that attitude did not change, even if some pressure was exercised on the junta behind the scenes. Outwardly, the habitual ambiguity remained. The Assistant Secretary for Near Eastern and South Asian Affairs, Joseph J. Sisco, drew attention to the dilemma once more in a television interview on 14 February.[4] 'Candidly,' he said, 'we have been disappointed in the fact that there hasn't been more progress toward the establishment of parliamentary government.' But he added that Greece was a loyal NATO ally, so there was no alternative but to pursue 'a two-pronged policy' – support for Greece in the context of defence and hope for more progress in internal liberalization. To the Senators, however, it appeared that the two prongs were not equally sharp.

The same point was made against the Secretary of State, William Rogers, by an interviewer on 9 March. When Rogers claimed to be disappointed that 'they haven't moved toward representative government more quickly', the interviewer interjected: 'There's a question as to how clear we've made that.' Rogers retorted sharply: 'We've made it crystal clear.'[5] In a paradoxical way, he could draw some comfort from the fact that at the end of March a spokesman for the junta criticized the United States for interfering in Greek domestic affairs. At least this underlined the dilemma.

But at the top level the Administration was less sensitive to the dilemma than its officials were obliged to be. Only a few weeks after the State

Department was embarrassed by these exchanges, President Nixon gave the junta a very different signal. On 22 April his Secretary for Commerce, Maurice Stans, arrived in Athens in the course of a tour of six nations. At a lunch in his honour given the next day by the Greek–American Chamber of Commerce, with Tom Pappas in the chair, he praised both the economic and the political stability of Greece. He emphasized the 'sense of security' which the United States felt in Greece. In an *extempore* comment afterwards, he spoke of an 'economic miracle'. Since he also carried a letter to Papadopoulos from the President, which expressed his best wishes 'for the continued welfare and prosperity of the people of Greece', it was clear that Stans spoke with the full authority of the US Administration.[6]

Stans' glowing testimonial to the junta naturally received ample publicity in the Athens press, which also published Nixon's letter. Even in the United States it rated front-page treatment in the *New York Times* on 24 April, under the headline: 'Stans in Athens, Hails the Regime'. Senator Hubert Humphrey called Stans' remarks 'careless and callous'; and his was not a lone voice. It was plain that the split was widening between the US Congress and Administration. But in the minds of the Colonels there was no doubt that the latter would prevail.

The report of Moose and Lowenstein to the Senate Foreign Relations Committee was particularly timely because it came immediately after the inauguration of the Consultative Committee or 'mini-parliament', on which both the junta and its overseas supporters relied for the rehabilitation of the dictatorship. Much publicity was given to the inaugural meeting of the 'mini-parliament' on 21 January, which was attended by Papadopoulos himself. But it was a dispiriting occasion, made remarkable only by Papadopoulos' bizarre speech. He particularly puzzled his audience with a statement which, literally translated, appeared to say: 'There are two presuppositions for the movement of the Revolution towards completion of the constitutional order: the achievement of objective aims and the danger of the imposition of a *kathestos*.'[7] Leaving aside the confused vocabulary, what exactly was the danger he implied?

The word *kathestos* means 'that which has been set up'; in other words, an established state of affairs or *status quo*. It was the word currently used for the dictatorship itself. But clearly Papadopoulos could not be warning his audience against the imposition of what he had himself imposed. Almost as if puzzled himself by what he was saying, he went on to restate his point, using the word *kathestos* twice more, in each case to mean something undesirable. He said that if it proved impossible to avoid 'conditions of a *kathestos*', he would act 'regardless of consequences'. He went on: 'I will interchange all the highest public servants, whether recalled or in service, by others at regular intervals, in order to confront the tendency towards the creation of a *kathes-tos.*' So far as any sense can be made of these remarks, Papadopoulos appeared to be worried lest the administration should stagnate under the control of a bureaucracy unresponsive to the stimulus of military leadership. But it is impossible to be sure.

There was indeed stagnation, but it was the stagnation of the junta itself. Perhaps he was inviting the Consultative Committee to help him in the task of stimulating a fresh initiative. For he went on to speak of the need for 'criticism in good faith', emphasizing that it must not raise the question whether it was right or wrong for the 'Revolution' to remain in power, 'because that last is a matter for others – it is a matter for those who applied the fuse to the dynamite for the explosion aimed at the rebirth of the state on the night of 21 April'.[8] So there was no question of an end to the role of the Army, but there was a role for constructive criticism.

It was not easy for the Consultative Committee to judge how far this directive entitled them to go. They were soon to learn from experience. Their first substantive debate took place on 12 February, on three draft items of legislation. One of the items, 'on meeting defence needs in time of peace', could be considered of some importance. But there was to be no amendment nor even criticism of these drafts, which were simply discussed with no discernible purpose. This initial experiment seemed to satisfy the junta, for the official attendance at the debates was gradually upgraded. At first the appropriate civil servants attended, later the responsible Ministers, and then occasionally Pattakos himself.

But as the 'mini-parliament' gained in confidence, it began to go too far. On 1 April it actually dared to vote against a measure on taxation, which provoked a protest from Androutsopoulos, the Minister of Finance. Four weeks later, on 29 April, it voted against another measure involving finance, and did so in the presence of Pattakos and other Ministers. Although these negative votes had no effect in reality, the government agreed in the second instance to reconsider the draft legislation. But in the end, of course, it was the Council of Ministers and not the Consultative Committee which always prevailed.

A new development had now to be taken into account. Almost simultaneously with the inauguration of the Consultative Committee, a National Resistance Council was formed outside Greece. This was the nearest approach that the opposition ever achieved to the establishment of an alternative government abroad. Four organizations took part: the Free Greeks (largely an organization of officers), the Defenders of Freedom on the right, Democratic Defence (DA) in the centre, and PAM on the left. But Papandreou's organization, PAK, would not join because the Council's programme did not provide for a plebiscite on the monarchy. In the event the National Resistance Council made little headway, and gained little international recognition.

Papadopoulos perhaps succeeded in neutralizing its influence by his policy of limited liberalization. In March 1971 he made soundings among the former politicians in the hope of enlisting their support. One of those whom he approached was Averoff, who wrote to Karamanlis on 21 April that he was treating the approach with extreme caution and would take no steps without consulting him. To improve the atmosphere for these soundings, Papadopoulos released more than 250 exiled politicians in April, the majority of whom were allegedly Communists. In June even Manoli Glezos, a Communist who had been more than once condemned to death (though not under the junta), was allowed to return home. At the end of August Papadopoulos announced his intention to abolish the system of 'certificates of social conscience', which had been introduced a generation earlier by Metaxas in order to deny to Communists and their families any access to higher education or the professions.

He seemed also to be growing more tolerant of Communism abroad as well as at home. This policy could have had a dual purpose: to assert a degree of independence of the United States, and also to neutralize the left-wing opposition. From the autumn of 1970 he supported the Soviet proposal for a European security conference.[9] In 1971 he established diplomatic relations with Albania for the first time since the war, and invited the Foreign Ministers of Bulgaria and Rumania to Athens. In later years he went still further, recognizing the People's Republic of China in 1972 and the German Democratic Republic in 1973.

To stress that he was not a satellite of the USA, Papadopoulos also sought better relations with western Europe, but with little success. The only significant European visitor to Greece during 1971 was the Spanish Foreign Minister in August. This relative failure was noticeable, because the junta was in the habit of posting up news-sheets on the walls of the main towns illustrating its successes. The eminent visitors shown in the photographs were mostly from black Africa, the Middle East or eastern Europe, but seldom (apart from the United States) from the west.

In western Europe, on the contrary, a new form of opposition emerged through the formation of the European–Atlantic Action Committee on Greece (EAACG), which was inaugurated at a press conference in London on 1 June. Its chairman was Sir Hugh Greene, formerly Director-General of the BBC, who was attacked in virulent terms by the junta's newspapers. Although the Committee was a private organization, it included many influential names among the western allies, chiefly European but also American and Canadian.

At the official level, the western allies remained divided. Two days after the Action Committee's first press conference, the Greek government was again under attack from the Norwegian and Danish Foreign Ministers at the NATO Council in Lisbon. Xanthopoulos-Palamas, the former Ambassador in Washington who had now become Deputy Foreign Minister, made a vigorous reply, challenging their criteria of democracy. It was received in silence, but not supported by the other Foreign Ministers. Six months later much the same happened again when the NATO Council met in Brussels. Although in the meantime yet another hostile resolution had been passed by the North Atlantic Assembly of parliamentarians, meeting in Ottawa, the Ministers and officials of the allied powers preferred to bury the subject in embarrassed silence.

The US Administration did not waver in its policy towards Greece during 1971, but it found increasing difficulty in carrying Congress with it. A new Chairman of the House Foreign Affairs Committee, Benjamin Rosenthal, set a tone of vigorous criticism. The annual round of hearings on overseas aid by the Committee and its subcommittees began in March and continued through the summer. It compelled the attendance of the Secretary for Defence, Melvin Laird, on 24 March; the Supreme Allied Commander in Europe, General Goodpaster, on 2 June; and numerous other senior officers and officials.[10] On 12 July the Subcommittee on Europe heard, as usual, a defence of the Administration from Rodger Davies.[11]

He began by redefining the problem created by the coup in 1967. The problem was: 'how to support our mutual interest in free-world security in the Eastern Mediterranean while encouraging a return to representative government which we believe is requisite for Greece's longer term stability and progress'. He described the suspension of 'certain deliveries of heavy equipment in our military assistance program' (which was a tacit admission that not all types even of heavy weapons had been banned). But he added that 'we felt that our influence in Greece could be used in the most constructive way if we maintained our working relationship with the regime'. This was done 'through continuous quiet exchanges'. The Greek government had always said that authoritarian rule would be temporary, and proof that they were sincere was to be found in the new constitution, in the release of political prisoners, in the relaxation of censorship, and in the curtailment of martial law.

Meanwhile, he said, the arms embargo was weakening NATO, and also failing to influence the Greek government in the desired direction. Even opposition leaders such as Averoff had advised the United States 'to keep the security aspects of our relationship with Greece separate from the political'. The majority of NATO allies agreed that the embargo should not continue indefinitely. The Administration had therefore decided to 'resume normal military shipments', but to emphasize that 'our assistance does not imply our support for or endorsement of the form of government now existing in Greece'. It was believed that the resumption of supplies would enhance the ability of the Administration to influence the outlook of the Greek government.

Lest this should seem too complacent a view, he went on to express disappointment in Papadopoulos' statement in December that no further steps would be taken towards elections in 1971. But he insisted that 'the situation has been by no means stagnant'. He cited progress in the restoration of civil rights, the creation of the 'mini-parliament', and Papadopoulos' discussions with former politicians. The US Administration was not satisfied with this progress, and was urging further curtailment of martial law and further releases of political prisoners. But US influence could be used constructively only if it was used with restraint. That was why 'we have carefully avoided any direct interference in the domestic politics of Greece'.

A final sentence summarized the whole argument and set the key-note for all future statements:

Our basic policy toward Greece has been to protect our important security interests there and in the broader area of the Eastern Mediterranean and Near East while preserving a working relationship with the regime through which we can exert our influence to encourage a return to representative government.

He spoke similarly to a Senate Subcommittee two days later.[12]

These statements were undeniably ambiguous, since US policy was undeniably ambivalent, but that is not to say that Davies was being untruthful. He was closely questioned by the House Subcommittee, which gave, on the other hand, a much more sympathetic hearing to witnesses hostile to the junta. Among the latter were Sir Hugh Greene, chairman of the European–Atlantic Action Committee on Greece, and John Brademas, the first American-born Greek ever elected to Congress, both of whom were heard on 14 July; Mrs Helen Vlachos on 9 September; and Andreas Papandreou's American-born wife Margaret on 14 September. The powerful attacks of these witnesses were supported by a joint statement from Kanellopoulos, Mavros, Zigdis and Papaspyrou submitted on 10 July. The defence of the junta was supported only in evasive terms by Ambassador Tasca on 3 August.

In the upshot the Subcommittee recognized that Davies was an honest witness, but there nevertheless appeared to be another policy behind and above that which had been disclosed. This suspected but undeclared policy was generally associated with the influence of people and agencies over whom the State Department had no control. Prominent among them, it was thought, were Vice-President Agnew, Tom Pappas, the CIA and the Chiefs of Staff.

The hearings ended on 15 September. As a result of the Subcommittee's adverse report, the Bill to update the Foreign Assistance Act of 1961 had an unusually difficult passage through Congress. The House adopted an amendment in the name of Representative Wayne Hays to ban aid to Greece unless the President certified in writing that there were 'overriding require-ments of the national security of the United States'.[13] The Hays Amendment was passed without a division, whereas the Bill itself was approved only by 200 votes to 192. The Senate Foreign Relations Committee, which had also heard hostile evidence from representatives of private organizations on 14 June,[14] supported the Hays Amendment. But the full Senate unexpectedly voted to reject the Bill outright by forty-one votes to twenty-seven, through a coalition of conservative Senators opposed to foreign aid in principle and liberal Senators opposed to the subsidy of dictatorial regimes.[15]

Since the matter clearly could not be left at that, a compromise Bill with a lower total of expenditure was introduced in November. There continued to be serious debate on the principles of foreign aid, but the Senate finally approved the revised Bill, with the Hays Amendment intact, on 18 December. It was also passed by the House, and became law on 7 February 1972. But on 17 February President Nixon signed the waiver required by the Hays Amendment.[16] So the hopes of the Greek opposition were dashed once more.

Despite the Administration's victory over Congress in the matter of aid to Greece, the uneasiness in Greek–American relations showed itself in a number of other ways during the summer and autumn of 1971. In July the visit of an American Admiral to Greece was cancelled, and in August the Greek government postponed work on a rest centre in Crete for the 6th Fleet. On 13 August Papadopoulos remarked to an American journalist that it seemed to be the Americans rather than the Russians who were pushing Greece towards a neutralist policy.[17]

A more serious conflict occurred early in October. Tasca had held private meetings with Karamanlis in Paris and with Constantine in Rome. He had already had contacts with Kanellopoulos, Mavros and other politicians. The junta, or at least Papadopoulos, would probably not have objected if these meetings had remained secret. But when they became known, the junta published a severe rebuke. The State Department, however, firmly defended the Ambassador.

The damage was repaired later in October, when Vice-President Agnew arrived in Athens on an official visit. He was returning from Iran, where he had attended the lavish celebrations at Persepolis of the supposed twenty-fifth centenary of the imperial dynasty, at which Constantine was also present. Agnew's arrival, on 16 October, was welcome to the junta because of his Greek ancestry as well as his political eminence. But it was publicly regretted in a statement on the 15th, signed by 183 former Deputies, including Kanellopoulos and Mavros.

The visit was also marked by a series of minor explosions near the airport, organized by a retired officer of the Air Force, Tasso Minis, who was a highly decorated hero of the wartime Resistance and the civil war. He was caught with two accomplices and severely tortured before being sentenced to a long term of imprisonment and held for 111 days in solitary confinement.[18] A striking indication of the character of the opposition to the junta was the fact that Minis' accomplices were a paediatrician and an architect by profession. It was particularly exasperating to the junta that Minis was the son of a distinguished General, for they expected the officer corps to be solidly on their side.

Hostility to the junta was in fact becoming markedly stronger in the officer corps, but open expression of it was necessarily confined to retired officers. On the basis of figures compiled between April 1967 and April 1972, it appears that a total of 3,047 army officers were removed from active service over five years. The figure represents an annual rate of retirement between two and three times as high as the rate during the preceding five years. The result, in the words of Brigadier Vidalis, was that the Army had been transformed 'from a national institution, serving all the people, into a political instrument, serving the dictatorship in enslaving the people by force'.[19] In the Navy, which suffered less severely from purges, plotting against the junta was almost continuous, though without culmination between December 1967 and the summer of 1973.

In other sectors of Greek society, after a period of relative quiescence, the Resistance became active again in 1971. On 5 June one of Panagoulis' accomplices escaped from prison on Aigina, with the help of members of the prison staff. By coincidence, on the same day Pattakos had a narrow escape from death when his aircraft caught fire on landing in north-west Greece and was completely destroyed. Almost certainly the cause was sabotage, though in no way connected with the simultaneous escape of Panagoulis' accomplice.

A startling event some months later, however, certainly was connected with that escape. On 1 September an attempt was made to free Panagoulis himself from a military prison, but it went badly wrong. The attempt involved Lady Fleming, who was caught waiting with a car outside the prison. She was convicted of complicity and sentenced to sixteen months in prison on 27 September; but on 21 October she was released on grounds of health. On 14 November she was forcibly deported to London, which was possible because she had dual nationality by marriage, and her Greek passport was declared invalid. This sensational incident made the Resistance international news on a major scale.

The junta could count another success against the Resistance at the same time. On 18 October two leading Communists, D. Partsalidis and Ch. Drakopoulos, who had returned clandestinely to Greece, were arrested in Athens. Partsalidis was a veteran of the wartime Resistance; Drakopoulos was Secretary-General of the KKE (Interior). Their arrest was evidence that the junta's security services were even more skilful than the KKE's secret organization. Little more was to be heard of the Communists until the last days of the dictatorship. In the meantime Partsalidis and Drakopoulos, after being held in prison for over a year, were both sentenced to long terms of imprisonment, along with fifteen other Communists.

Papadopoulos' tactics during 1971 displayed the same dualism as before: releasing some opponents while arresting others; closing some prison-camps while expanding others; easing legislative controls on trade unions while crushing dissident organizations; depriving some opponents of their Greek nationality while encouraging others to return from abroad; holding talks with former politicians while keeping most of them under surveillance. The politicians who agreed to meet Papadopoulos were not of the front rank, but they professed themselves optimistic about the outcome. The leaders of ERE and the Centre Union were more sceptical. The one practical outcome was to create confusion about Papadopoulos' intentions; and that was probably one of his intentions.

Despite his occasional gestures of independence in 1971, Papadopoulos' primary concern continued to be his relationship with the United States. The visit of Spiro Agnew in October was in effect the first step in the negotiation of homeport facilities for the 6th Fleet, which had been formally requested by the US Navy Department on 21 September. The Administration's anxiety to improve its defence facilities in Greece had become more urgent since a general election in Malta on 14 June was won by the Labour Party under Dom Mintoff, who made no secret of his intention to deprive NATO ships of the use of the Grand Harbour of Valletta. For the same reason, it also became urgent to solve the problem of Cyprus, which continued to weaken the southern flank of NATO.

There were both encouraging and discouraging developments over Cyprus in 1971. On 13 March the senior Turkish Generals seized power in Ankara, where military rule was usually, unlike Athens, welcomed as an interruption of civilian misrule. But the prospect of negotiations proceeding amicably between two military governments was soon frustrated by the opposition of Makarios. In early June he visited Moscow, and found that he could rely on Soviet support against any attempt to impose a settlement on his Republic. Soon afterwards he secretly ordered a consignment of arms from Czechoslovakia. It began to look to the Americans as if Cyprus was slipping into the Soviet orbit.

There were rumours during the summer of 1971 that the Greek and Turkish military governments might try, with American encouragement, to impose their own solution on the island. On 12 July the German magazine *Der Spiegel* published the text of a letter from Papadopoulos to Makarios, dated 18 June. The letter denied the existence of any plan to impose a settlement, but suggested that Makarios should appoint a Turkish Cypriot Minister in his government to look after the problems of local self-government. It was also hinted that if Makarios were uncooperative, 'the Greek government will find itself faced with the harsh necessity of taking the measures which the national and well-considered interests of Cypriot Hellenism require, however painful they might be'.[20]

The authenticity of the letter was neither denied nor admitted at the time, though it was confirmed years later, after the fall of the junta. The same was true of Makarios' reply, dated 24 June, of which extracts were also published in *Der Spiegel* on 6 September.[21] Makarios rejected the proposal for a Turkish Minister, and also the threat at the end of Papadopoulos' letter; but he asserted that he had never believed there was a plot against his independence. This correspondence certainly reflected accurately the tension between Makarios and the junta at that date.

An explanation of their tart exchanges emerged early in 1972 from a statement by Spyros Kyprianou, who was Makarios' Foreign Minister and later his successor as President of the Republic. Kyprianou claimed to have evidence that Papadopoulos' Deputy Foreign Minister, Xanthopoulos-Palamas, had been holding secret talks in Lisbon and Paris with the Turkish Foreign Minister, about the possibility of imposing a jointly agreed settlement on Cyprus, based on partition. Whatever the truth of this claim, it is certain that Palamas reinforced Papadopoulos' letter of 18 June with a diplomatic note to Makarios on 20 July, which again contained almost undisguised threats.[22]

The note pointed out that although Cyprus was independent, Athens was the 'National Centre'. In a matter affecting national interests, the Cypriots must follow the policy laid down in Athens. To this Makarios replied uncompromisingly on 4 August.[23] He insisted that: 'Greece should not contribute to the creation of the illusion in Turkey that it would ever be possible for Athens to be a party to imposing a solution to the Cyprus question which is unacceptable to Cypriot Hellenism.' He went on to conclude: 'In what concerns its national interest Cypriot Hellenism must have the last word. If there is disagreement between Athens and Nicosia, each must bear responsibility for its own actions.'

This tension between Athens and Nicosia was further aggravated at the end of August, when it became known that General Grivas had disappeared from his home in Athens. It was naturally, and rightly, assumed that he had gone back to Cyprus with the connivance of Papadopoulos. The junta was undergoing one of its perennial crises during that summer. It is a reasonable conjecture that the crisis was at least partly connected with the tense relationship between the Greek and Cypriot governments, and with Papadopoulos' personal handling of it.

The main source of evidence on the crisis, as on most of the internal affairs of the junta, is Pattakos.[24] It appears that the ringleaders of the internal opposition on this occasion were the two hard-line ex-Colonels, Ladas and Aslanidis. They had in mind the replacement of Papadopoulos by a new head of government, perhaps Makarezos, or perhaps even Karamanlis if he could be persuaded to return, but in any case still under the guidance of the Army. It was ludicrous to suppose that Karamanlis would have agreed, but the junta was fertile in ludicrous ideas.

Ioannidis was privy to the plot. He was already in a powerful position, being not only the head of the ESA but also of the branch of GHQ which controlled officers' postings. He undertook on behalf of the conspirators to take soundings among the officer corps on their feelings about Papadopoulos. When the crucial meeting of the junta took place, at which Papadopoulos found himself faced with a demand for resignation, to the general astonishment Ioannidis brought the argument to an abrupt end by declaring himself on Papadopoulos' side because that was the general wish of the Army.

The result was that Papadopoulos was again in a position to assert his personal ascendancy. He did so in two drastic steps. On 24 August all the Secretaries-General of the fifteen Ministries were asked to resign, including seven ex-Colonels who had been members of the original revolutionary group. Six of the seven were then appointed regional Under-Secretaries in the provinces, thus simultaneously depriving them of a base in Athens and also creating the appearance of carrying out Papadopoulos' earlier promise to devolve government from the centre to the provinces.

Two days later the Council of Ministers itself was reconstructed. The number of Ministers was reduced to thirteen, including two Deputy Prime Ministers without portfolio (Pattakos and Makarezos). This step simultaneously enhanced the prestige of Papadopoulos' two colleagues in the triumvirate, and reduced their power. Papadopoulos, who retained the Ministries of Defence and Foreign Affairs, was now without serious rivals. The one possible exception was Ioannidis, whom he regarded as entirely loyal.

There was another remarkable measure which Papadopoulos took as a mark of his growing self-confidence. He had foreshadowed it in his speech at the opening of the Trade Fair in Salonika at the end of August. Now he announced on 6 October that the 'certificates of social conscience', introduced by Metaxas in 1938, were abolished except in the armed forces and security services.[25] Thus after thirty-three years the imposition of one dictator was lifted by another. Papadopoulos could argue that his decision showed the strength of the junta: the only guarantee which it needed was absolute control of the Army and the Police. But to his critics within the junta it seemed like a symptom of weakening resolve, as did any relaxation of their dictatorial power.

8 Towards a home port
1971–72

Negotiations on the provision of a 'home port' for the 6th Fleet in Greek waters began in the autumn of 1971, and lasted nearly fifteen months. The proposal was important for Papadopoulos, if only because it was also important for the United States. Greece under the junta would become more than ever a vital component in the alliance if she provided docks and other facilities for the American Navy, and above all temporary homes for thousands of American sailors. It was therefore essential that the junta should present the right image throughout the negotiating period. Greece must appear to be a secure and disciplined country, but also one in which human rights and civilized standards were maintained. The familiar problem of balancing liberalization to placate external criticism against repression of the opposition to placate the hard-liners was intensified.

The solution was also familiar. Every step in one direction was compensated by another in the opposite direction. After the 'certificates of social conscience' were abolished, a series of exercises in thought-control followed. In October 1971 the code of ethics came into force for the press. In November several journalists were gaoled on charges of propaganda against the regime. The young writers who had published *Eighteen Texts* in 1970 produced two more volumes (*New Texts* and *New Texts II*) in 1971.[1] The junta fulminated against them, but refrained from prosecution.

On balance, November 1971 was a bad month for freedom of expression. A poet was jailed for publishing insults to the Army; suspended sentences were passed on the writers of anti-regime slogans; and on 25 November the Directorate of National Security published a new list of banned books and periodicals. Among the names on the list were Chekhov, Brecht, Marcuse, Gorky, Troyat, Deutscher, Peter Brook (for a work on the theatre) and Lampedusa (for *The Leopard*).[2] It was also the month in which Lady Fleming was deported, but in which, on the other hand, a judge imprisoned for his role in the Lambrakis case was released.

These were all overt manifestations of the junta's policy. There were also more perplexing incidents over which the junta wished to draw a veil of secrecy. The attempt to release Panagoulis had clearly involved many accomplices, some of them based in Italy; and even if the plot had been frustrated, the last had not been heard of it. An even more mysterious episode was the murder in October 1971 of an English girl, Ann Chapman, who was on holiday in Greece but had apparently become involved in seeking intelligence on the junta. A man was convicted of her murder, and he lost an appeal twelve years later, but there was a widespread suspicion that the crime had really been committed by the security services.

Of all the semi-clandestine activities of the junta during 1971, the most immediately serious was the departure of Grivas for Cyprus. He disappeared from his home in Athens on 28 August, the day on which Papadopoulos was speaking in Salonika at the opening of the Trade Fair. It was no chance coincidence. Although Grivas later denied it, his clandestine journey must have been facilitated by the junta, with the object of making trouble for Makarios. Presumably this was Papadopoulos' concession to his hard-line colleagues for the measures of liberalization which he was initiating at the same time. If it resulted in the elimination of Makarios, it would also be a way of settling the Cyprus problem for the benefit of the Americans, though it could not be acknowledged as such.

Within a week of Grivas' disappearance, Makarios came to Athens on 3 September. He knew, but concealed his knowledge, that Grivas was back in Cyprus. His comments to the Athens press were characteristically cool and sardonic: 'No one, I think, ought to be happy about the disappearance of the General.' He did not exclude the possibility that Grivas was in Cyprus, but added that 'our principal interest is that he should not vanish'. It almost appeared as if he were concerned about the General's safety.

Grivas' new mission was in fact to form the force which became known as EOKA-B, based on the existing organization known as the National Front. In response Makarios also formed a new force, the Tactical Reserve Police, usually known as the Reserve Corps for short. There followed a covert and bitter struggle between the two irreconcilable rivals. On 26 September Makarios said in a press interview that he would never accept a Greco-Turkish settlement reached without regard to the Cypriot people. Grivas would no doubt have said the same. Yet he allowed himself to be used as an instrument of the junta for the destruction of Makarios, presumably believing that he would be able to manipulate the consequent crisis in such a way as to achieve *enosis* without undue concessions to the Turks.

On 29 October Makarios openly accused Grivas of leading the way towards civil war in Cyprus. The tension between the two men simmered menacingly through the winter until it reached the point of explosion early in 1972. On 21 January a Danish ship arrived on the north coast of the island, carrying a cargo of weapons from Czechoslovakia which Makarios had ordered after his visit to Moscow in the previous June. The weapons were unloaded in an unfrequented bay. They were intended not for the official National Guard, in which Makarios had little confidence because it was under the command of officers from the Greek mainland, but for his newly formed Reserve Corps.

Grivas learned of the arrival of the arms, and sent a unit of EOKA-B to seize them. But his men were beaten off by the Reserve Corps, who carried off the arms. Once their delivery became known in Athens, the junta demanded that they should be handed over to the National Guard. Makarios denied that any such arms had arrived. On 9 February a meeting was held at the Regent's residence in Athens, attended by Zoitakis, Papadopoulos, Pattakos, Makarezos, Angelis and senior officers from Cyprus. It was decided to demand that Makarios should surrender the arms instead to the United Nations force in Cyprus (UNFICYP); and also that he should dismiss his Foreign Minister, Kyprianou, who had accused the junta of plotting with the Turkish government against the independence of Cyprus.

A diplomatic note to this effect was sent to Nicosia on 11 February, carried by K. Panayiotakos, who had been Ambassador to Cyprus since leaving the Council of Europe, and was now a junior Minister in the Foreign Office.[3] The note was also published in Athens, contrary to normal custom. Makarios rejected it, in a statement issued on the 15th,[4] though some months later he made the single concession of accepting Kyprianou's resignation. Panayiotakos announced in response that the Greek government would not intervene further, but added that 'for the future Greece will, however, exercise her rights under the treaties if the national interest requires it'.[5]

As a Minister, albeit a junior one, Panayiotakos was speaking on behalf of the government, but he was also expressing his personal antagonism towards Makarios. Some years later, after the fall of the junta, a document attributed to him was published, purporting to record a conversation between him and the Turkish Ambassador in Athens during February 1972.[6] Panayiotakos was represented as describing the Greek government's hostility towards Makarios and its determination to remove him from the political scene. He also appeared to be soliciting Turkish help in the plot against Makarios. When the document was discussed in Parliament on 13 June 1975, reasonable doubt was cast on its authenticity by Bitsios, who was then Foreign Minister. Panayiotakos denounced it as a fabrication, and a judicial enquiry reached the conclusion that this was probably the case.[7] But the document corresponded closely in many respects to the actual course of Greek policy in subsequent years.

In any case, the repercussions of the crisis did indeed seriously threaten Makarios' position. On 2 March 1972 the three senior Metropolitans in Cyprus, led as usual by Anthimos of Kition, called on Makarios to resign from the Presidency, on the ground that to combine it with the Archbishopric was contrary to canon law. Grivas supported them; so did Archbishop Ieronymos at first, hinting in a letter to Makarios that he might become

Patriarch of Constantinople if he gave up his secular power.[8] But within a few days Ieronymos withdrew his advice. The reason for his reversal, which was mysterious at the time, became known years later: it was due to strong pressure on the junta from the United States, Britain and particularly the Soviet Union, which attached great importance to Makarios' survival in office.[9]

He was therefore able to reject the demand for his resignation once more. He went even further, inviting Grivas to a secret meeting at which he persuaded his rival to relax the pressure on him. No doubt he argued that it was unpatriotic to pursue a policy which weakened the unity of the Greek Cypriots for the benefit of the junta, the Turks and the Americans. For the moment, then, the crisis passed.

In Athens, however, the crisis left renewed doubts in the minds of Papadopoulos' critics among the Colonels. On this occasion the Regent, Zoitakis, was on the side of his critics, for a number of reasons. He considered the policy of undermining Makarios highly dangerous, since the chief beneficiaries would be the Turks. He disapproved of the policy of making approaches to the former politicians, which might portend a return to parliamentary democracy. He had disagreed with Papadopoulos over the abolition of 'certificates of social conscience'. On the last point, as on others, he had adopted the practice of delaying his signature on legislative decrees, much to Papadopoulos' annoyance.

Zoitakis now reached the same conclusion as Ladas and other hard-liners, that Papadopoulos must go. But it was not easy to remove him. The most active of the critics had themselves been removed from Athens in the last reshuffle of the government. Besides, Zoitakis himself had annoyed other senior Ministers by his practice of delaying legislation. Pattakos and Makarezos in particular were becoming impatient with Zoitakis' tactics. Papadopoulos thus still had the support of his oldest allies, who were both Deputy Prime Ministers. Thanks to them, he was able to turn the tables on Zoitakis.

On 21 March 1972 a startling announcement was made: Zoitakis had been removed from the Regency and replaced by Papadopoulos himself. The decision had been taken that morning, at a meeting of the Council of Ministers, with Pattakos in the chair in the absence of Papadopoulos. It was said to have been a unanimous decision. Next day Papadopoulos wrote a warm letter of thanks to Pattakos for the way he had acted. The contents of his letter can be inferred from Pattakos' reply, which was enthusiastic to the point of ecstasy.

Papadopoulos' letter was delivered to Pattakos by hand of Ioannidis, whose support for the decision can therefore be assumed; though perhaps he hesitated, for the letter only reached Pattakos two days after it was written. Pattakos replied on the 24th that he had received it 'just this moment', and went on:[10]

> To tell you I was moved would be too little. So I say: 'Indeed yes, with tears in my eyes'. I know your humanity, your affection (even if you sometimes conceal it), but above all I know your goodness, which perhaps, for the exercise of power, goes too far to a dangerous degree.

After further professions of admiration and love, he concluded:

> May God protect you and enlighten you, speaking always what is good in your heart for the benefit of our country and its people to the end of your life, whose duration I pray may be very long.

Clearly, despite all his tribulations, Papadopoulos was still capable of commanding an unquestioning and almost religious loyalty, even from a hard-bitten soldier who had been his senior in rank.

He was now approaching the apogee of his revolutionary career. He retained all the offices which he already held, as well as the Regency: Prime Minister, Minister of Defence, Foreign Minister. Only the formal abolition of the monarchy was needed to make his power absolute. But the internal crisis of the junta was still not over.

There were valid grounds for the hard-liners' distrust of Papadopoulos. His capricious policies of relaxing repression and hinting at constitutional reforms, without consulting his colleagues, were exasperating to them. In one of the most remarkable examples, he failed even to inform Pattakos. On 15 April Professor George A. Mangakis, who had been sentenced to eighteen years' imprisonment two years earlier as a member of Democratic Defence (DA), was released by a court order for eight months on grounds of health. As soon as he was released, he was driven with his wife to the US Air Force sector of Athens airport, where a German military aircraft was waiting to fly them to West Germany.

It seems hardly possible that his escape could have taken place without official connivance, though Xanthopoulos-Palamas, the Deputy Foreign Minister, seems to have believed it,[11] and Pattakos angrily denied any knowledge of the plan of escape. On 22 April the government demanded the recall of the German Ambassador. He left at once, but the German Foreign Office denied any impropriety. The Greek Foreign Office supported Pattakos in denying collusion with the Germans in what it called the 'kidnapping' of Mangakis. Nevertheless it seems probable that Papadopoulos contrived the whole operation. As he was Minister both of Foreign Affairs and of Defence, it could hardly have taken place without his connivance.

His arbitrary policy was presumably designed to impress European and American opinion. To underline its effect, an announcement was made by the Greek Embassy in Washington at the end of 1971 presenting statistics which showed a substantial reduction in the number of convictions by court-martial: only eight in 1971, compared with 837 in 1967. The favourable signs encouraged a group of retired senior officers to issue an appeal a few weeks later for a general amnesty. But Papadopoulos ignored it, while continuing to release those whose names would make an impression abroad.

The policy was capricious as well as arbitrary. Glezos, Theodorakis, Lady Fleming, Professor Mangakis had been released; but fresh arrests and deportations took place at the same time. On 20 March, fifteen members of PAK (the resistance group of socialists, formed by Andreas Papandreou) were put on trial by court-martial. On 10 May, seven members of two legal organizations, the Society for the Study of Greek Problems and the Greco-European Movement of Youth, were sent into administrative exile. These organizations had been formed by Professor Pesmazoglou, formerly Deputy Governor of the National Bank and Professor of Economics at Athens University, and Virginia Tsouderos, the daughter of a war-time Prime Minister. When they protested, Pesmazoglou was also exiled to northern Greece, and Mrs Tsouderos was arrested and held without charge.

The US Administration had to consider with some embarrassment how to react to the perversities of Papadopoulos' policy. It could hardly be pretended that Greece was moving towards constitutional government in the way that official spokesmen regularly urged. On the other hand, the need for homeport facilities was imperative. Conflict between the Administration and the more liberal members of Congress was therefore inevitable during 1972.

The House of Representatives was particularly resentful of the President's cavalier action in overriding the embargo on arms supply which had been embodied in the Hays Amendment. Early in 1972 the House Armed Services Committee sent a special Subcommittee on NATO Commitments to conduct hearings in a number of European capitals, including Athens. They were not favourably impressed by Ambassador Tasca's evidence, which they heard on 12 January.

Tasca claimed that 'there is just no place like Greece to offer the facilities that we have got with the back-up of the government you have got here'.[12] He admitted that there were certain weaknesses in the armed forces, most of which were due to budgetary limitations. He said that the training and maintenance systems were excellent, and 'they have an outstanding mobilization system and experienced officer corps'. Much of this was to be proved wishful thinking in the event. But what was more immediately serious was his admission that he had no idea when Papadopoulos would carry out his promise to restore democracy.

The House Foreign Affairs Committee was examining the outlook in Greece even more sceptically at the same time. On 7 March a joint meeting of its Subcommittees on Europe and on the Near East began hearing evidence on the proposal for the homeporting of the 6th Fleet in Greece.[13] Among those who gave evidence against the proposal were George Rallis and D. Papaspyrou on 8 March and Brigadier Vidalis on 13 April. Naturally their chief concern was that the establishment of homeporting would greatly strengthen the junta and increase the United States' commitment to supporting it. But they were also conscious of the prospect of growing antagonism between the Greek people and their American allies, which would result from the creation of a large resident colony of Americans in the Greek ports.

The weightiest testimony, however, came from Admiral Elmo R. Zumwalt, the Chief of Naval Operations, who was supported by the familiar figure of Rodger Davies from the State Department. The Admiral limited himself to logistic arguments. He explained that, after examining fifteen ports in the Mediterranean, it had been concluded that 'the port of Athens' (which meant principally the Bay of Elevsis) was the most suitable. Davies added the political arguments in favour of the plan.[14] It would help to promote stability in the area of the eastern Mediterranean, and even to facilitate a peaceful settlement of the Arab–Israeli dispute. With deliberate under-emphasis, he added that the proposal was 'an administrative measure to ameliorate the human problem' for naval personnel, several thousands of miles from home, and that it involved no 'major new facilities'. As for its potential effect on the aim of promoting a return to democracy, he made no optimistic claims. 'Our mutual security relationship with Greece,' he said, 'has not implied in the past and does not now imply our support for any particular government in Greece.'

The same message, in effect, was conveyed by the Assistant Secretary of State for Near Eastern and South Asian Affairs, Joseph Sisco, to the Senate Foreign Relations Committee on 9 March and to the House Foreign Affairs Committee on the 20th.[15] Less explicitly, but even more effectively, the message was twice underlined at the highest level of the Administration during July. On 4 July the Secretary of State, William Rogers, visited Athens. The fact that it was Independence Day enabled him and Papadopoulos to veil their real thoughts with amicable platitudes, which included such words as 'liberty' and 'democracy' without any detectable trace of irony. Then, even more significantly, President Nixon told a press conference on 27 July: 'Without aid to Greece and aid to Turkey, you have no viable policy to save Israel.' Again without a trace of irony, he was invoking Jewish support for a dictatorship which was perhaps the most anti-Israeli government outside the Arab world and the Soviet bloc.

Despite these strong indications of the Administration's wishes, there was still disapproval in Congress. At the end of July the House Foreign Affairs Committee failed only by a narrow margin to adopt amendments restricting aid to Greece in the Foreign Assistance Act for 1973.[16] This was only the preliminary to a much more hostile gesture against the junta by the Committee later in the year, when the issue of homeporting was at stake.

The scale of opposition to the junta in Congress should not be exaggerated, however. It was led by a few determined individuals, but it did not amount to a running battle between the legislature and the executive. As often as not, it consisted merely of personal statements. In May 1972, for example, Donald Fraser read into the record of the House of Representatives a criticism of the junta's economic policy by Professor Pesmazoglou, which had been one of the contributory causes leading to his arrest and exile.[17] On 28 October Senator McGovern issued a statement to the effect that 'while the Greek dictatorship has the support of the Nixon Administration, the resistance of the Greek people to that dictatorship has the support of the American people'. But McGovern was the Democratic presidential candidate seeking votes, and 28 October was the anniversary of Greece's entry into the Second World War.

Occasionally Congressional supporters of the Greek opposition could mobilize their colleagues into confrontation with the junta by an indirect route. In December 1972 the House Subcommittee on Foreign Operations began an examination of the arrears in payment of Greece's public debt – a perennial complaint by western creditors against Greek governments, not confined to the junta.[18] By then, however, Nixon had been re-elected, and Papadopoulos' future looked secure, debts or no debts.

There still remained the danger that untoward incidents would mar the good impression which Papadopoulos had made on the US Administration. Student unrest, for example, was beginning to make itself felt during 1972. This was indeed a world-wide phenomenon, which had its roots in the west, and especially in American universities. In most of the democratic countries, the state authorities had learned to deal with it firmly. But it was a relatively new phenomenon in Greece, and it had several distinctive features. Its aim was to recover legal and democratic rights which had been destroyed by a dictatorship, not to promote a revolution against authority as such. Unlike the student unrest in western Europe and America, it was sometimes supported by the university authorities themselves.

The opportunity for a trial of strength was provided by one of the early actions of the junta itself. In 1968 the Colonels had appointed unelected committees to represent the interests of the students, with a tenure of three years. By the end of 1971 their term of office had expired, but they had not been replaced. The students demanded the right to elect their own committees, and took their case to the courts. The courts upheld their application, but the junta still ignored it. When the students held demonstrations in protest during May 1972, more than forty of them were arrested, and six Cypriots among them were deported.

These events were pregnant with consequences, but not for more than a year. They would not have disturbed Nixon or Agnew, and they no doubt passed unnoticed by the American negotiators occupied in discussing the proposal for homeporting. But there were other events at the time which even busy negotiators should not have overlooked. A new wave of bombing incidents occurred in 1972, and on 3 August a guerrilla-style attack was made on the US Embassy. Although it was repulsed without difficulty, it was a bad omen for the future of Greek–American relations.

On the day after the attack on the Embassy, however, President Nixon addressed a message to the Senate which virtually committed the United States to the proposed agreement on homeporting, although it also had an unforeseen consequence. He repeated his statement that the support of Greece and Turkey was indispensable for the protection of Israel. This argument had been implicit in the requirement for improved facilities in the eastern Mediterranean from the first. But the Greek government felt obliged to qualify Nixon's statement, in view of Greece's close relations with the Arab states.

Greece had never given *de jure* recognition to the state of Israel, partly out of sympathy with the Arabs and partly because of the importance of oil supplies from the Middle East. It was also unwelcome to the Greeks to be associated with the Turks in Nixon's statement. The Deputy Foreign Minister, Xanthopoulos-Palamas, who knew from his previous experience as Ambassador in Washington how sensitive the matter was, explained publicly that there was no question of Greece taking part in operations against Arab states. A White House spokesman replied that the President's words had been misinterpreted, but he did not offer a corrected interpretation.[19]

From his dealings with the United States as Foreign Minister, Papadopoulos had begun to understand more than his colleagues of the complexities of diplomacy. He was also learning the value of extending his diplomatic contacts with other countries, and amending his conduct accordingly. For most of the last four years Greece had been a defiant pariah. The junta had tried to make up for its isolation from the west by offering its good will to any country that would accept it. But there were not many. The news-sheets posted up on the walls of provincial towns sometimes showed the Prime Minister shaking hands with unrecognizable Africans and Arabs, but seldom with anyone else except Americans.

In 1972, however, there were signs of improvement. The French Under-Secretary for Foreign Affairs visited Athens in January; so did Lord Carrington, for the second time, in September. The release of Professor Mangakis, who was highly regarded in West Germany, was an attempt, which misfired, to bring about a similar improvement there too. In June diplomatic relations were restored even with Sweden.

It was impossible, however, to liquidate entirely the legacy of international mistrust. With Italy mutual hostility was undiminished. During August 1972 the junta accused the Italian Socialists of helping political detainees to escape from Greece, and the Italians accused the junta of complicity in the explosion of a bomb at a bank in Milan. Parliamentarians of other European countries regularly attacked the junta, but with little effect on their governments. Such was the annual experience of the North Atlantic Assembly in passing hostile resolutions, which were ignored by the NATO Council of Ministers.

Papadopoulos' critics in the junta could understand the need for some degree of conciliation towards Greece's allies, but they were shocked by another of his diplomatic innovations – an 'earthquake', he might have called it. He had already extended his friendship towards the Soviet bloc. Now, in June 1972, he took the surprising step of recognizing the People's Republic of China. He could claim some countenance from President Nixon, who had himself visited Peking in January (though not yet granted *de jure* recognition). But the hard-liners in the junta disapproved both Papadopoulos' decision and the autocratic way it was taken without consulting them.

They were beginning to suspect that he was ideologically unsound. Neither at home nor abroad could much difference be seen, in their eyes, between his long-term aims and those of any bourgeois government in the past. Abroad, the policy appeared to be one of loyalty to the western alliance coupled with normalized relations with the Communist states. At home the policy was to move towards a more conventional style of government, perhaps leading even to a presidential democracy. It was as if Papadopoulos had become tired of dictatorship.

On 18 December 1971 Papadopoulos had made a speech in which he hinted that the role of the Consultative Committee might be enlarged. He had qualified the forecast by adding that there was no prospect of an old-style Parliament. Later in the same month it was announced that martial law was to be suspended everywhere except in the main urban areas of Athens, Piraeus and Salonika. In Papadopoulos' eyes, these moves were evidence of the security of the regime, but to his critical colleagues they were departures from military orthodoxy.

The Consultative Committee had been re-elected on 12 December 1971, and met again four weeks later. Promises were given that any legislation of which it disapproved would be withdrawn, and that it would have the right to criticize the government. But when the Committee ventured to exercise this supposed right at its sitting on 8 March, a furious row broke out with Pattakos.[20] In a debate on an item of labour legislation, the President of the Committee complained that a specific court decision had not been carried out by the Minister concerned, 'contrary to the principles of sound administration'. This rather pompous rebuke infuriated Pattakos, who ordered him to sit down and declared, no less pompously, that 'no one is permitted to criticize the state, which is protected by the Revolution'. After this revealing definition of the junta's political theory, an angry dialogue followed between Pattakos and the senior officers of the Committee.

Naturally, in the end the will of the government prevailed. But it seemed that nobody, not even Ministers nor the junta itself, had a clear idea how far licence was permissible. The same uncertainty recurred in the autumn of 1972, when *Vradyni*, on 11 September, sharply criticized Papadopoulos' speech at the opening of the Salonika Trade Fair. Pattakos sent a memorandum to Papadopoulos demanding that the newspaper should be prosecuted, and even that the Press Law should be amended to introduce harsher penalties.[21] But nothing was done, so the limits of the permissible were slightly expanded. They could equally well be contracted again if the junta so decided. What was legal and what was illegal were determined simply by the Colonels' whims.

But they no longer all had the same whims; nor did their whims have equal weight. In phraseology which had been introduced during the journalistic argument between Stamatelopoulos and the *Acropolis* in 1970, Papadopoulos was far advanced on the way from being *primus inter pares* to becoming *primus solus*.[22] At the same time resentment of his primacy was growing stronger within the junta. Internal criticism was reinforced as the political opposition to the dictatorship became bolder towards the end of 1972, taking both active and passive forms. During September bombs began to explode again in Athens. A new organization called the '20th October Movement' appeared to be responsible; but it was short-lived, for four of its members were quickly arrested, court-martialled and sentenced early in October.

In the same month a number of former members of ERE and the Centre Union issued a manifesto of common purpose, but their initiative was not approved by their party leaders. Such symptoms of dissidence were perhaps unimportant to the junta, whose control of the country seemed unbreakable. But more serious in the long run, though seemingly less significant at the time, was a new spirit of rebellion in the universities and polytechnics. Students were again demanding the right to elect their own committees. The junta's commissioners, however, were still in control.

None of the minute advances and retreats on the domestic front during

1972 had any impact on the negotiations with the US Administration. As early as January the Greek government agreed in principle to grant homeport facilities to the 6th Fleet. It gave permission for a destroyer squadron to anchor in Phaliron Bay before any formal agreement had been concluded. All that remained was to settle such details as the legal status of US naval personnel in Greece. The decisions were taken exclusively by the military leadership: Xanthopoulos-Palamas was simply informed of what had been decided by a telephone call from the Commander-in-Chief.[23] When Nixon was re-elected in November 1972, the formal agreement could be taken for granted.

President Nixon was now in a strong position to override the residual obstacles. One was the attitude of the Soviet government, which naturally saw the homeporting agreement as directed against itself. On 28 December, as the day of signature approached, the Soviet Ambassador in Athens stated that 'there are difficulties in Greco-Soviet relations'. In the same month Radio Moscow, which had hitherto been neutral towards the junta, began to attack it. These reactions were foreseeable, and had to be accepted.

A more serious obstacle was to be encountered in the US Congress. On the last day of 1972 the joint Subcommittees on Europe and the Near East of the House Foreign Affairs Committee had their last word on the subject of homeporting.[24] Although they had been assured since January, by Admiral Zumwalt and other spokesmen of the Administration, that the agreement was essential to US defence policy, they concluded nevertheless that 'the decision ... is a serious mistake'. Out of twenty-five members of the two subcommittees, only seven expressed dissent or reservations. The recommendations of the majority were that relations with the junta should be restricted to the minimum, that a search should be made for an alternative 'homeporting' site, and that Congress should become more involved with the State Department in formulating such decisions.

None of these recommendations was likely to be taken seriously in the White House. Not only was Nixon about to be inaugurated into a second term with a greatly increased majority: in addition, he had the support of his Chief of Naval Operations, who confirmed that there was no possibility of finding an alternative location; and of his Assistant for National Security Affairs, Dr Henry Kissinger, the former professor of history at Harvard, whose style in foreign policy was based on that of his nineteenth-century hero, Count Metternich. Papadopoulos was entitled to assume that his future was guaranteed.

9 Turn of the tide
January–November 1973

President Nixon did not carry the Congressional elections with him in his overwhelming victory: the Democrats retained control of both the House and the Senate. He had also laid up trouble for himself by the folly of what became known as the Watergate scandal. But these hazards lay in the future. At the turn of the year 1972–3 Nixon's prospect, and therefore that of Papadopoulos, seemed bright.

Despite the reservations of Congress, the agreement on homeporting was signed on 8 January, with a duration of five years in the first instance. The group of harbours adjacent to Athens could now be described as 'the American Navy's largest home port in Europe'.[1] The Greek government celebrated the occasion by voluntarily renouncing the supply of free military aid from the United States. An offer of fifteen million dollars for 1973 was declined. Papadopoulos made it known that in future Greece would pay cash for US weapons. The proud implication was that Greece was more indispensable to the USA than the USA to Greece. It might be called the junta's 'finest hour'.

But despite its brilliant opening, the year 1973 brought Papadopoulos' nemesis. In the first instance, it brought to a head the schism within the junta. The hard-liners remained convinced that the only purpose of staying in power was to stay in power. Papadopoulos, almost alone, had to some degree matured in the exercise of responsibility. He recognized that the purpose of a revolution must be to produce something new. He could only vaguely imagine what it was to be, but he was confident that he alone among his colleagues would eventually succeed in identifying it and bringing it to fruition. Whether he really contemplated ever renouncing power of his own volition can never be known; but in fact his days were numbered through circumstances beyond his control.

He failed to recognize which of the potential threats to his position in 1973 were real and which were not. An easily recognizable group of opponents were the naval officers, who had never accepted the defeat of the King's coup in 1967. Their hostility was perhaps aggravated by the overwhelming presence of the US Navy since the homeporting agreement. Less easy to identify were the dissident officers of the Army, who now comprised not only the surviving loyalists to the old regime but also the hard-liners loyal to the original junta. The latter could become dangerous if they formed an alliance with Ioannidis and the ESA, as eventually they did.

A third source of danger, which Papadopoulos never took sufficiently seriously, was the body of students in higher education. Their grievances were at first concentrated on purely internal matters, such as the right to elect their own representative committees and to discuss the content of their educational curriculum. But they could present a more serious threat if they had the support of a disciplined organization of the working classes, drawn from the same age-groups as themselves. Papadopoulos flattered himself, however, that he had put the workers' organizations out of action for good.

The organizations expressly formed for purposes of resistance presented relatively little threat to the junta in 1973, because they had few secrets from the secret police. The junta was not to be overthrown by leaflets or even bombs. The better-known organizations survived by inactivity; lesser-known ones emerged and vanished at short intervals. One of them, the Greek Anti-dictatorship Youth (EAN) caused a bomb explosion in April, which killed an Arab visitor. But within a few weeks its leading members were arrested. One of those who was compromised as a result, with disastrous consequences for the conspirators in the Navy, was Major Moustaklis, commander of the military garrison on Syros. Although Papadopoulos was thus justified in having confidence in his security services, it led him to overlook less obvious sources of danger.

The greatest danger to his personal position lay within the junta. He was plagued by uncertainty about his future direction. Was the military dictatorship to become permanent, or was it to guide Greece back to constitutional government? Was the Consultative Committee to evolve into a Parliament or was it to remain a mere debating society? Was the façade of the monarchy to be preserved, or was Greece to become a presidential republic? Papadopoulos had no ready answer to these questions. He was soldiering on from day to day, like a disciplined subordinate awaiting directions from above; but there was nothing above to direct him, except his own capricious imagination, for he would not accept subordination to the Revolutionary Council, nor even its right to be convened. His colleagues demanded certainty, but he was conscious only of perplexity.

One uncertainty was still Greece's relationship with the western allies, other than the Americans. The British presented a problem typical of many others. After the Labour government was succeeded in June 1970 by the Conservatives, the junta expected to find itself on firmer ground. But Edward Heath proved just as unpredictable a Prime Minister as Harold Wilson. Ministers were sent to Athens in pursuit of trade, and awkward questions were parried in the House of Commons. So far, so good. But there were also hints of disapproval directed at the junta. Early in January 1973, during a celebration of Britain's accession to the European Communities, in the presence of the

Queen and the Prime Minister, Laurence Olivier was allowed to read out a moving passage from Professor Mangakis' account of his experiences in the Averoff prison. Naturally, the Greek Ambassador in London made a protest, but the damage was done.

Soon afterwards, however, came a compensating gesture of reassurance. In April 1973 Britain's most senior Admiral, Sir Peter Hill-Norton, made a highly publicized visit to Athens. He went ostensibly not in his capacity as Britain's Chief of the Defence Staff, but rather as Chairman of the Military Committee of the NATO Council. For the Greeks, and especially for the junta's propagandists, this was a distinction without a difference. The effect was to give the junta a certificate of approval from both NATO and Britain. While he was in Athens, he spoke with admiration of Greece's armed forces, as he could hardly avoid doing. No doubt he had in mind primarily the Greek Navy, where his judgement was valid; but it was doubtful whether he was even aware of the demoralized state of the Army.

A few weeks later came a gesture which was harder to interpret with any confidence. In early May the British government invited members of the 'mini-parliament' on a visit to London. The invitation presented Papadopoulos with a dilemma. Was it another certificate of respectability? As such, it was welcome. But was there not a danger that the mini-parliamentarians might be corrupted by exposure to British democracy, and get ideas above their station? Fortunately for both sides, the course of events soon rendered the invitation abortive.

Besides the western alliance, the people's democracies also troubled Papadopoulos with uncertainties. He gave particular attention to them in 1973, but the results were not always satisfactory. In March the first Ambassador from Communist China arrived in Athens, and a week later Makarezos began an official visit to Peking. In May the Bulgarian Foreign Minister visited Athens, and diplomatic relations were established with the German Democratic Republic. But with Greece's chief Communist neighbour, Yugoslavia, relations deteriorated, as they had done with the USSR. Propaganda agencies in each country persistently attacked the other. Papadopoulos had not the skill which Karamanlis later exercised in managing Greece's relations with all the mutually antagonistic people's democracies at the same time. His clumsy efforts only convinced his colleagues that they ought never to have been undertaken.

Cyprus was another perennial source of perplexity. Makarios was still vigorously resisting attempts to depose him as Archbishop, and preparing for re-election as President. Grivas and the National Front (now better known as EOKA-B) had launched a new campaign of violence against his supporters. On 8 February 1973 Makarios was nevertheless returned unopposed to the Presidency. A month later the dissident bishops declared him deposed from the Archbishopric, but he refused to receive the notice of deposition. Although Papadopoulos longed to see the last of Makarios, he felt it impossible to take sides with the Archbishop's enemies so soon after he had been shown to have wide public support. It was left to the Deputy Foreign Minister to issue a statement on 17 March repudiating the purported deposition of the Archbishop, on the ground that it had not been recognized by the Orthodox hierarchy in general, which included Archbishop Ieronymos of Athens. But the statement added an expression of 'anxiety about the consequences'.[2]

The anxiety was justified. A virtual state of civil war prevailed in Cyprus between Makarios, supported by his Reserve Corps, and Grivas' EOKA-B. In April the bishops repeated their claim that Makarios was deposed. A few days later Makarios issued a public challenge to Grivas to come out of hiding and explain his intentions. There was no response. The deadlock was one from which only the Turks could benefit. Papadopoulos had to consider afresh how to rid himself of the turbulent priest, who was upsetting all his plans for the pacification of Cyprus in the interests of his American patrons.

Even more troublesome than these uncertainties in the outside world was the unanswered question at home: what was to be the constitutional future of Greece? Papadopoulos' chief allies, Pattakos and Makarezos, both recommended that the fate of the monarchy should be decided by a new plebiscite. Makarezos made the suggestion indirectly through a new political journal, *New Directions* (*Neai Katevthynseis*), which was published for the first time on 17 January. Its first leading article attacked the King personally (which was still technically a criminal offence), and proposed that a plebiscite should be held on his future.[3] As the editor of *New Directions* was a former Minister of the junta and a relative of Makarezos, it was assumed that the article had the latter's authority.

It was followed by a private memorandum from Pattakos to Papadopoulos on 2 February, which contained a detailed plan for a plebiscite based on three choices: first, a constitutional monarchy with Constantine as King; secondly, the same without Constantine, which would mean a continuation of the Regency; thirdly, a republic under the presidency of Papadopoulos.[4] Pattakos even drafted a proclamation for Papadopoulos to issue, setting out a programme and timetable for the introduction of a new constitution.[5]

Nothing came of these ideas immediately, but Papadopoulos kept them in mind for future use. Meanwhile he took a new step in April which might be seen as a move in the direction of democracy. He formed a political organization called the National Cultural Movement (EPOK). The two middle letters of the acronym stood for *politistikon*, which means 'cultural' or 'civilizing', being derived from the same root as 'politics', the occupation of the citizen or civilized man. Papadopoulos, or his propagandists, no doubt intended the subtle ambiguity. Two days later he announced that others would be free to form similar organizations. The inaugural meeting of EPOK took place on 15 April, in the presence of members of the government. No one could be sure how great a degree of licence was to be permitted to other such organizations. But before anyone dared put the matter to the test, dramatic events occurred which shifted the dictatorship on to yet another new course.

On 23 April a long statement by Karamanlis was published in *Vradyni*, and also in one newspaper in Salonika.[6] Both issues were seized, and the publishers were prosecuted. The statement was couched in familiar terms, denouncing the junta for creating 'a psychological gulf between the armed forces and the people, with incalculable damage to the nation', and calling for 'the restoration of democratic normality'. The greatest offence lay in one key sentence: 'Let the government recall the King, who is the symbol of legality, and surrender its position to a strong, experienced government.' The junta, which was already aware of a revived conspiracy among naval officers, chose to believe that Karamanlis' statement was designed to provide 'political cover' for their movement.

In fact there had been few periods since 1967 when naval officers were not considering in one way or another how to remove the junta from power. The ringleader, Commander N. Pappas, had begun cautiously sounding fellow officers as early as September 1968. During the following months a plan was formed to kidnap Papadopoulos when he was expected on shipboard during naval exercises in August 1969, but it was abandoned as impracticable. Another plan was formed in 1970 with the support of Garouphalias, the former Minister of Defence and a close friend of the royal family, to seize Crete as a base of operations. Crete was suitable because it had an important naval station in Souda Bay, and a vigorous population with a strongly liberal tradition. But the plan became known to Papadopoulos, who installed army units loyal to the junta in the island. So this scheme also lapsed, as did a number of others.

But Commander Pappas and his colleagues were persistent. In 1973 they thought they had a feasible plan, which included trustworthy officers of the Army as well as the Navy. The occasion for their operation was to be a NATO exercise, in which naturally many ships would be at sea without attracting suspicion from the security services. Thus the naval officers were to act in the shadow of the western alliance, as the army officers had done six years earlier.

Their plan was first to seize the island of Syros, a naval station which had only a small military garrison. The commander of the garrison was Major Moustaklis, who was a party to the conspiracy; but unfortunately, unknown to the conspirators, his involvement in the resistance was already known to the junta. Once control of Syros was gained, the plan was that naval units from the island should sail in two directions, to blockade Piraeus and Salonika. A summons would be broadcast calling on the junta to resign. If necessary, the ships off Piraeus would cut the routes into Athens by gunfire until the junta surrendered. The operation was to start at 02.00 on 23 May.

On this occasion the naval Commanders had recruited officers at the highest level, including two retired Admirals, Konophaos and Rozakis, who had supported the King in December 1967. But they also insisted on 'political cover'. Their first approach was made to Averoff by Commander Papadongonas, who had planned the details of the operation. Averoff did not think that his backing would suffice to guarantee public support, and he was also doubtful about the security of the planning. But he undertook to approach Karamanlis in Paris. When Averoff and Karamanlis met (after the publication of Karamanlis' statement in April), the latter was even more doubtful whether the plan was feasible. But he undertook to make a statement approving the action if it took place successfully.[7] There was clear evidence in early May, however, that the plan was already compromised. Karamanlis' response was therefore at best neutral, as Averoff emphasized in relaying it to Papadongonas.

By 21 May the prospect of success was virtually extinguished. Major Moustaklis, among others, was arrested and brutally tortured.[8] That night, Commander Pappas received a telephone call from the Navy GHQ which warned him that the plot was betrayed. He decided nevertheless not to surrender, and put to sea on the 22nd in his destroyer, the *Velos* (*Dart*), as if to take part in the naval exercise. His was the only ship which escaped the clutches of Papadopoulos' security services.

On 24 May the junta announced that a naval conspiracy, which it called 'a piece of comic opera', had been frustrated and the ringleaders arrested.[9] As soon as Pappas heard the announcement by radio, he made for Italy in his destroyer, with the agreement of his crew. On arrival at Fiumicino, he was granted political asylum, together with those of his crew who wished to defect with him. The rest returned to Greece with their ship. Their brief adventure was over, but the consequences of the conspiracy were still to come.

The first consequence was to convince Papadopoulos that his colleagues were right in recommending the abolition of the monarchy. Although the King had not supported the conspiracy, his restoration would presumably have followed if it had succeeded; for even Karamanlis, who was no devotee of the royal family, had urged only a month earlier that sovereignty should be restored to the King. It was therefore announced on 1 June that the Council of Ministers had decided to establish a 'presidential parliamentary republic'.[10] (By a convenient ambiguity, the Greek *dimokratia* means both 'democracy' and 'republic'.) There would be a plebiscite on a new constitution within two months, and a general election before the end of 1974. On 4 June the first decree was promulgated in the name of the 'President of the Republic'. On the 15th the presidential powers were defined by a further decree. The effect was to give Papadopoulos' allies abroad the impression that he was at last moving towards democracy; but his colleagues at home were still more uneasy.

The failure of the naval plot also seemed to Papadopoulos to give him the opportunity of eliminating Karamanlis as a potential threat. The connection between Averoff and the conspirators was no secret. Averoff was arrested on 3 July. Under interrogation, he admitted his conversation with Karamanlis in Paris, but insisted that Karamanlis' words had been neutral, not an endorsement of the plot. Nevertheless a court order was issued on 21 July for Karamanlis' interrogation, though naturally it could not be enforced since he had no intention of returning from abroad.

By chance a curious story, which was partly true, came to the assistance of the junta in its campaign against the King and Karamanlis. The story was that on 9 July the Commander of another Greek destroyer, on a visit to the French port of St Raphaël, was approached by Commander Pappas and a civilian with a proposal that they should sail together to Fiumicino, where they would take on board the King and Karamanlis to return to Greece. Such an encounter had in fact taken place, as was confirmed by the civilian named in the story, who was a member of the Venizelos family; but neither the King nor Karamanlis knew anything about it. This did not prevent Papadopoulos from exploiting the story to discredit them.

Among the allied governments, the abolition of the monarchy was received with muted acquiescence. But there were significant exceptions. At the meeting of the NATO Council in Copenhagen on 14 June Van der Stoel, who was attending for the first time as Dutch Foreign Minister, made a veiled attack on the junta by means of a statement emphasizing the ideological and political foundations of the alliance and 'the basic requirements of individual liberty and political democracy'. It could not be contested, least of all in the Danish capital. Even Dr Luns, the Secretary-General, admitted that Greece's military capacity was impaired. But US protection again ensured that there was no formal censure or positive action against Greece.

The US Congress was less easily satisfied. On 5 June eighty-one Congressmen signed a letter to President Nixon calling for 'a serious review of our policy regarding Greece'.[11] On 25 June the Senate adopted by forty-six votes to forty-one an amendment in the name of Senator Claiborne Pell to the Foreign Assistance Act, which would authorize military aid to Greece 'only when that government fulfils its obligations under the North Atlantic Treaty'.[12] That phrase included, by definition, the political principles of

NATO. The Senate's attitude was supported in July by the House Foreign Affairs Committee, when its Subcommittee on Europe held hearings on the implementation of homeporting. Despite strong arguments from Admiral Zumwalt and Rodger Davies, the Chairman of the Subcommittee, Benjamin Rosenthal, wrote a preface to its report severely criticizing the policy.[13]

The prospect of giving practical effect to these criticisms depended on the passage through Congress of the Pell Amendment. Its progress was delayed by a disagreement between the House and the Senate on other aspects of the Foreign Assistance Act. This disagreement was not resolved until after dramatic events in Athens during November had set Greece once more on a new course. It was partly due to those events that the Pell Amendment, though modified, was not lost. But there was little doubt that President Nixon would in any case have used his executive privilege to override the embargo, just as he had done with the Hays Amendment in 1972.

The plebiscite on Papadopoulos' new constitution was held on 29 July. The question was presented in such a way that to vote Yes was not merely to accept a republic but also to approve Papadopoulos as the first President. From London the King issued two statements, on 9 June and 24 July, denouncing the whole proceeding, and promising that after the removal of the junta the future constitution would be submitted to a genuine plebiscite. From Paris Karamanlis issued a supporting statement on 19 June, and another scathing attack on the junta on 16 July.

In Athens Kanellopoulos organized a group of former colleagues and opponents, including Mavros, Rallis and Zigdis, to campaign for a negative vote. Andreas Papandreou advised his supporters to return blank ballot-papers. But Spyro Markezinis, the former leader of the small Progressive Party, announced that he would vote Yes, with reservations. There was naturally no way of expressing reservations in the ballot, so his decision was taken as a decisive move in the direction of the junta.

As was to be expected, Papadopoulos' Republic won a substantial majority, though the figures were not to be taken seriously apart from the abstentions, which reached a significant total of twenty-five per cent. Papadopoulos immediately reconstructed his government once more on 30 July. The reconstruction was remarkable in two respects: it brought into office for the first time two former Deputies of the defunct Parliament; and it brought back to office two hard-liners of the junta, Ladas and Aslanidis, who were generally regarded as antagonists of Papadopoulos.

The new government was therefore a kind of coalition. Its composition drew attention again to the declared intention of the Constitution, to establish a 'presidential parliamentary republic' (or democracy). This marked a startling innovation, which people began to suppose might actually be intended.

Certainly Markezinis was convinced. The intention was indeed real, at least in Papadopoulos' mind, but it was to be a democracy still under military control.

Along with Papadopoulos as President, General Angelis was to be Vice-President. He was replaced as Commander-in-Chief of the armed forces by another General, D. Zagorianakos. In other words, the precedent followed in the days when there was only a Chief of the Defence Staff – of rotating the appointment between the three services – was no longer to be followed. The Army was the only service which Papadopoulos could trust. If evidence were needed, it was clear in July, when he attended a naval review under extraordinarily strict security precautions; and in the same month a number of Air Force officers were arrested on charges of conspiracy.

In other respects Papadopoulos appeared to be making real concessions; and thanks to these, foreign reaction to the constitutional upheaval was surprisingly favourable. Nowhere was any question raised of recognition *de jure* of the new Republic. The US Administration seemed to be positively enthusiastic. After a cautious but not hostile comment on the impending changes by the Deputy Secretary of State, Kenneth Rush, on 14 June, a much warmer welcome was given to Papadopoulos as President by the Secretary of State himself, William Rogers, on 20 August, the day after his inauguration.[14] Rogers' statement was made at a press conference, which covered other areas of foreign affairs. Questions followed, but none of them touched on Greek affairs. It was as if even the journalists shared the Secretary of State's confidence in Papadopoulos' intentions.

On the surface, this was understandable. His statement had confirmed that 'parliamentary democracy' was to be restored, martial law ended, and courts-martial abolished throughout the country.[15] There was also to be an amnesty for all crimes committed since 21 April 1967. These provisions were enacted by decrees published on 20 August.[16] In addition, a separate proclamation extended the amnesty to Panagoulis by name.[17] Averoff and the naval conspirators were released under the amnesty, but the latter were not restored to their careers. Although no one had expected such far-reaching concessions, the reaction of informed opinion in Athens, to Papadopoulos' disappointment, was unfavourable.

Several concurrent symptoms suggested that the new measures were only a smoke-screen. Since the amnesty covered only crimes 'within Greece's jurisdiction', it excluded Karamanlis, whose alleged crime was committed abroad. Thus the leading Greek politician could not return, even if he wanted to. Another unfavourable sign was the establishment at last of the Constitutional Court, whose function was to monitor political parties when they were allowed to re-emerge. To the politicians this seemed merely an insulting restriction on democracy.

In one curious manoeuvre, Papadopoulos appeared to be trying simultaneously to satisfy both his hard-line colleagues in the junta and the demands of liberal opinion at home and abroad. Some twenty members of the opposition who had been living abroad for several years were declared to have been tried *in absentia* by a secret court-martial on 22 June. They included Andreas Papandreou, Mrs Vlachos, Costa Mitsotakis, Brigadier Vidalis and other well-known personalities. After the amnesty, it was announced that they had all been acquitted, although none of them knew that they had been tried.[18] Mrs Vlachos commented that it sounded like a cross between Kafka and *Alice in Wonderland*. But those who had been deprived of Greek nationality, such as Melina Mercouri and Lady Fleming, were not allowed to recover it nor to return to Greece, as Lady Fleming found when she flew hopefully into Athens on 29 August, and was at once flown out again.

Markezinis alone might perhaps have felt justified in voting Yes in the plebiscite, given that he had at least expressed reservations. Between July and September Papadopoulos began negotiations with him on the possibility of forming a quasi-political government.[19] Markezinis made efforts to consult some of the former politicians before accepting, but most of them, including Karamanlis, refused all contact. The only success he could claim, after several rebuffs, was with Kanellopoulos, who reluctantly received him on 17 October, after Markezinis had accepted office. By agreement, Kanellopoulos then issued a statement confirming that his opposition to Markezinis' decision was unchanged. Markezinis, who was easily pleased, took it as a success that at least Kanellopoulos' hostile statement was published in the press.[20]

The announcement of Markezinis' appointment as Prime Minister had been made on 1 October, and his government was sworn in a week later. His first statement of policy promised that 'impeccable elections' would be held shortly. This was almost the only area of policy over which he had any prospect of exercising control, for Papadopoulos was to retain exclusive responsibility as President for defence, foreign affairs and public order. The Ministers in those three departments were to be appointed by the President, not the Prime Minister. Papadopoulos also intended to preside at the Council of Ministers, and in his absence Angelis would do so. These arrangements did nothing to satisfy the demand for democracy in Greece, but they had a surprisingly favourable reception abroad.

Papadopoulos had not only failed to go far enough for Greek democrats, however; he had also gone too far for his critics in the junta and the Army. He no longer had the support even of his closest colleagues. Makarezos and Aslanidis had resigned in the last days of September when they saw which road Papadopoulos was taking. Pattakos and the rest were simply relieved of their posts a few days later to make way for Markezinis' government.

Pattakos in particular was a disappointed man. In July Papadopoulos had offered him a meaningless role as 'assistant or pilot' to the prospective government, which he refused. The offer prompted him to compose yet another of his memoranda on the future course of the 'revolution',[21] little knowing that he was simply to be dropped.

Other senior officers, not necessarily members of the original junta, were asking themselves what had been the point of the 'revolution' if this was to be its outcome. Their discontent led them to look to Ioannidis, the only member of the revolutionary group who was still on active service, as head of the ESA. Those who were in a position to know said later that the plot in the Army to overthrow Papadopoulos began to take shape in September, even before Markezinis had accepted his derisory office.

Markezinis admitted in retrospect that he hardly even knew the two men appointed by Papadopoulos as Ministers of Defence (N. Ephesios) and Public Order (P. Therapos). He did succeed, however, in securing the appointment of his own nominee, Xanthopoulos-Palamas, as Minister of Foreign Affairs. This posed no difficulty, since Palamas had already served Papadopoulos as Ambassador in Washington and as Deputy Foreign Minister. Markezinis was thus able to claim at least a minimal influence over foreign policy.

His major ambition in foreign policy was to restore the Treaty of Association with the EEC to full operation, but that would become possible only after the conduct of 'impeccable elections'. The first and only opportunity he had to play an international role came with a visit by Makarios to Athens on 6 November. Markezinis welcomed him, and they had a long private talk, at which none of the military leaders was present. Markezinis professed himself optimistic, and thought that the Archbishop left the meeting satisfied.[22] But the fact was that relations between Makarios and his enemies had already reached a point of crisis which made disaster almost inevitable.

The crisis over Makarios' dual role as Archbishop and President had finally come to a head in July 1973. A Holy Synod met in Nicosia under the presidency of the Patriarch of Alexandria to examine the vexed question of his purported deposition. On 14 July the Holy Synod supported Makarios, and deprived the dissident bishops of their sees. This did not settle the quarrel, but merely transferred it to the field of guerrilla warfare. On 27 July men of Grivas' EOKA-B kidnapped one of Makarios' Ministers. They sent Makarios a letter on 1 August setting out conditions for his release, one of which was a new election to the Presidency. Makarios could not use his official force, the National Guard, against them because its officers were mostly drawn from the Greek mainland and sympathized with Grivas. His one recourse was to his unofficial Reserve Corps.

On 8 August men of the Reserve Corps retaliated by capturing the deputy commander of EOKA-B. They also seized documents containing evidence of a plot against Makarios, in which mainland officers were clearly implicated. Makarios demanded the removal of the Commander of the National Guard by the government in Athens. The demand was met, and a new officer, also a mainland Greek but less suspect in Makarios' eyes, was appointed on 13 August.

A fortnight later, after an appeal by Papadopoulos on 25 August for an end to terrorism on both sides, Grivas released the kidnapped Minister.[23] He still did not renounce his feud with Makarios: on 6 September he published a long letter in *Acropolis*, giving his own version of the events of 1964–7 and accusing Makarios of having abandoned the cause of *enosis*.[24] But by this time Grivas was convinced that he himself, and not Makarios, was the target of Papadopoulos' enmity. From his secret hiding-place he sent an insulting message on 27 August in reply to Papadopoulos' appeal for peace.[25]

Soon afterwards he went further. On 22 September, in a secret interview with *Vima*, Grivas accused Papadopoulos of sending Greek officers to Cyprus to murder him. Papadopoulos denied the charge on the 26th; Grivas repeated it on the 28th; but nothing more was heard of it.[26] No doubt Papadopoulos would have been glad to be rid of both Grivas and Makarios. On 7 October an attempt was made to murder Makarios by means of mines laid on a road over which his car regularly passed, but the attempt failed. It was impossible at the time to identify the source of the violence which was tearing Cyprus apart, but suspicion naturally fell on Papadopoulos and Ioannidis as well as Grivas.

A still more serious crisis erupted simultaneously in the eastern Mediterranean. On 7 October, the same day as the latest attempt on Makarios' life, the Yom Kippur war broke out between Egypt and Israel. This time the Egyptians took the initiative, and almost achieved an astonishing victory. The US Administration, as always, gave strong support to Israel, but the Greek government, in conformity with the national policy of friendship for the Arabs, declared itself neutral in the conflict. An announcement to this effect was made by the new Foreign Minister, Xanthopoulos-Palamas, on 13 October. He stated that 'Greek sea and air space is not being used for any activity whatever related to the state of war in the Middle East'.[27] A similar statement had been made by the Turkish government on 10 October, which Kissinger thought had prompted the Greek statement.[28]

At one moment, when the Israelis were gaining the upper hand, President Nixon feared a Soviet intervention and declared a world-wide nuclear alert by US forces. This was an alarming prospect for the Greeks, since the US 6th Fleet, which now had the use of port facilities close to Athens, was known to carry nuclear weapons. Fortunately the fighting between Egypt and Israel was brought to a halt almost immediately afterwards, on 23 October. The nuclear threat subsided, but the dilemma of Greek policy remained.

It was later suspected by many Greeks that the US Administration was disappointed by Greece's neutrality, and decided accordingly to abandon support for Papadopoulos and Markezinis. An American diplomat visiting Greece soon afterwards was heard to say as much at a reception in his honour.[29] Markezinis, who shared the suspicion, attributed it to his refusal to agree to a request for an extension of US military facilities, including the use of Elevsis airport.[30] But the suspicion was not confirmed by American statements in the aftermath.

The most significant statement on behalf of the US Administration was made four months later, at a joint session of the Subcommittees on Europe and the Near East of the House Foreign Affairs Committee, on 19 February 1974. Evidence was being taken from two officials of the State Department, Arthur Hartman and Rodger Davies.[31] The evidence was on balance favourable to the Greek government, and partially contradicted Palamas' statement on 13 October. Since Papadopoulos and Markezinis had in the meantime fallen from office, there was no current need for such support of them from Washington. The officials' evidence was therefore probably correct.

Hartman confirmed that Greece had declared its neutrality in the Yom Kippur war, as had Spain and Turkey. But Davies pointed out that this was due to historic, geographical and commercial links with the Arab states rather than hostility towards Israel. Greece recognized Israel, maintained diplomatic relations, and supported all the United Nations resolutions bearing on the Arab–Israeli conflict. It would have been more accurate if he had pointed out that Greek recognition of Israel was only *de facto*, and that diplomatic relations were not established at the level of Embassies. But the crux of the matter came in the following statement.

The Greek government, Davies said, had offered to provide observers or military units for a UN force in the area, if required. More important, Greece had co-operated in allowing the United States to use 'communications facilities' in Greece, and also the airports at Athens and Souda Bay in Crete. No restrictions had been placed on the movements or the resupply of the 6th Fleet. All this amounted, according to Davies' statement, to a constructive role within the framework of a policy of neutrality. It could be inferred that the Administration had no reason at the time to be displeased with Papadopoulos or Markezinis.

Such was the state of affairs in the eastern Mediterranean when Markezinis and Makarios met in Athens on 6 November. Markezinis' memoirs show that their exchanges followed a familiar pattern: complaints from Makarios about the Turkish Cypriots, Grivas and the dissident bishops; attempts by Markezinis to urge reconciliation.[32] The absence of the military leaders from the meeting was thought to be a good sign. Markezinis said later that if his government had survived, he was sure that the catastrophe of July 1974 could have been avoided in Cyprus.[33] In reality his government was already doomed, and so was Papadopoulos' presidency, but for reasons unconnected with foreign policy.

Although foreign opinion might approve Papadopoulos' initiative in appointing a quasi-political government, he had practically no friends left at home. Few of the former politicians had even an expression of tolerance to utter for Markezinis' decision to accept office. The few exceptions were somewhat surprising: Averoff and Stephanopoulos on the right, Mitsotakis in the centre, Brillakis and Iliou on the left; but Kanellopoulos, Mavros, Papandreou and the official KKE were unanimously critical. On the other side, Ioannidis and the group of officers who supported his hard line were already plotting another coup. The prospect of 'impeccable elections' was a mirage.

There was also another force opposed to Papadopoulos which he did not take sufficiently seriously. This was the resentment among students in higher education, all over Greece but especially in Athens, of six years of humiliating oppression. The sequence of events made it appear at first sight that it was the students' revolt which precipitated the downfall of Papadopoulos, but this was not in fact the case: it was a mere coincidence in time. The students certainly struck a memorable blow in November 1973 against the whole principle of the military dictatorship. But unfortunately the fall of Papadopoulos only brought to power a tyranny which was, if possible, even more odious. For this the students could not be held to blame.

10 The students' revolt

November 1973

Student resistance to the junta was spontaneous and improvised. This was so from the first day, when the students of Ioannina University demonstrated on 21 April 1967. Their organization was like all student organizations in the democratic world: amateur, enthusiastic, spasmodic and often reckless. They were greatly excited by the dramatic eruption of May 1968 in Paris, but they were facing a far more ruthless enemy than the French students. The excitement soon subsided. Even the group called Rhigas Pheraios, which was the most durable and best organized, was only intermittently effective.

The strict discipline and conspiratorial secrecy required for a clandestine movement were in any case alien to students. They did not know how to use the weapons of their enemies. They were also, by definition, a short-term and shifting group in the population. All they wanted at first, in the words of their own touching slogan, was 'Bread – Education – Freedom'. Papadopoulos, at his trial in 1975, claimed to have given them all three;[1] and he was obtuse enough to believe it.

At first the junta had indeed made a show of benevolence towards the student population. University textbooks were to be made available free of charge; numbers in higher education were increased; so was expenditure on education, though not as a proportion of total public expenditure. But everything was to be centrally regulated: the syllabus, appointments, methods of teaching, and even the language of instruction, which was to be compulsory *katharevousa* ('purist') instead of the demotic which had been gradually replacing it. Above all the junta sought to exercise its benevolent despotism through the appointed Commissioners and appointed committees to run the Student Unions, which were expected to concentrate on harmless, non-political activities. The whole system was formalized in tightly restrictive terms under the 1968 Constitution.

That Constitution, however, included an article authorizing freedom of association, which was initially suspended but brought into operation by decree in April 1969.[2] The students naturally assumed that they would then be free to form their own Unions with elected officers. The junta had anticipated this reaction at the end of 1968 by appointing committees with three years' tenure, so that there could be no question of a change before the end of 1971. In the meantime the Commissioners, who were invariably retired senior officers, chiefly from the Army, could ensure discipline and report to the junta on the conduct and attitudes of both teachers and students.

Individually, students continued to rebel. Their gestures were courageous but forlorn. Alexander Panagoulis, who had tried to assassinate Papadopoulos, had been a student at the Athens Polytechnic before his military service. A still more tragic example was Costa Yiorgakis, a Greek student in Italy, who committed suicide in September 1969 in the same manner as Jan Palach a year earlier in Prague, by setting fire to himself in a public square. Panagoulis and Yiorgakis were examples of the crusading commitment of young Greeks to freedom. But their actions did not amount to organized resistance: rather they drew attention to the lack of it. Resistance was still effectively crushed by the security system.

For three years the system succeeded at least in imposing a sullen acquiescence, but even to that mood there were exceptions. As a reflection of Papadopoulos' conflict with Makarios, a number of Cypriot students were deported. In January 1969 eight students were tried for subversion; several more were imprisoned in October for causing bomb explosions; and in May 1971 a large group belonging to the Rhigas Pheraios movement were tried on charges of sedition, though eighteen of them were acquitted. The junta failed to read the signs of unrest correctly. They still believed that their military Commissioners, with their files of data on students, teachers and their families, could keep the world of higher education under control.

Then, at the beginning of 1972, a hesitant agitation began in several institutions. In the Law School of Athens University there was a call for a general meeting to discuss both student elections and a new educational programme. A similar proposal at the Athens Polytechnic was frustrated by the appointed student committee (although its three-year term had already expired). But the University Law School persisted. Its appointed committee was forced to disband, and on 21 March a group of forty-two students applied to the courts for the appointment of a temporary and neutral commission to supervise elections.[3]

The junta promptly intervened again to appoint its own commission for the purpose. But now the student revolt was gathering momentum elsewhere. The University Medical School, the Polytechnic Engineering School and a number of others followed the precedent of applying to the courts. By the spring of 1972 the courts had appointed electoral commissions for most of the schools, fixing a time limit for elections by 10 January 1973. The junta's Commissioners knew well enough who were the ringleaders of these initiatives, so they were summoned by the police to receive 'advice'. But the students refused to be advised.

In October the commissions appointed by the courts declared that the elections were to be completed by the end of 1972. A series of election meetings was held by the students, beginning in Athens on 25 October, and followed by Patras, Salonika and Ioannina before the end of the month. The meetings were not all well organized, and they resulted in some confusion, thanks to the interventions of the junta's Commissioners. Although Kanellopoulos gave the students moral support by criticizing the restrictive conditions under which the elections were held, the junta's Commissioners secured the election of their own nominees in most cases.[4]

The agents of the junta were naturally blamed for the outcome, but probably the students' inexperience also played a part. Their debates tended to overflow from electoral issues to wider ones, such as the content of educational programmes. One student received a suspended prison sentence as a warning. Towards the end of January 1973 the Polytechnic students began to boycott their classes in protest, and to demonstrate in the streets. Clashes with the police became inevitable. Eleven students were arrested, and a few days later about a hundred were called up for military service. The Senate closed the Polytechnic on 24 January.[5]

The junta aggravated the animosity by issuing a decree on 12 February authorizing the Minister of Defence (Papadopoulos himself) to suspend the right of students to have their military service deferred.[6] This time the University Law School was provoked into fresh action. Students occupied the School on 21 February, barricaded themselves inside, and declared that they would not come out until the decree was rescinded; but in fact they came out in less than forty-eight hours. They had discussed their intention in advance with responsible advisers: the politicians Kanellopoulos and Zigdis, and Professors Louros and Pesmazoglou, who promised to support their claims provided that there was no violence. The brief occupation was therefore peaceful, but it made no impact on the junta.[7]

After negotiations with the teaching staff, the students left the Law School on 22 February. It was said that the police promised not to molest them, but broke their promise.[8] The junta showed no inclination to leniency. The call-up for military service continued. The eleven arrested students of the Polytechnic were put on trial, and received suspended sentences. On 2 March Papadopoulos summoned the senior Professors of the Schools concerned, and harangued them on their academic responsibilities.

The whole trouble, he said, had been caused by one retired officer (unnamed), who had been dismissed after participating in the King's coup in 1967, together with 'four other Communist students'. All of them, he said, came from the University of Salonika. In violent and incoherent terms, he told the Professors that they should be ashamed of themselves, and they must regain control of their students.

He also addressed representatives of the Student Unions separately on the same day. To both audiences his message was the same: 'I will not allow anyone to set Greek society ablaze. I am well aware of the headquarters of ex-politicians and certain others who were directing the student agitation, and if necessary I will crush them.'[9] The impact of his outburst was mixed. Some of the senior academics were so appalled that they became unqualified supporters of the students' grievances. Others felt that they had an obligation to support the forces of law and order.

As a result, when the students occupied the Law School again on 20 March, the University Senate agreed that the police should break in and disperse them after six hours' occupation.[10] This time the police handled the students roughly, causing severe casualties. There was now no possibility of compromise between the students and the junta. A cold war between them could break out into violence at any time. The teaching staff were also more inclined than before to support their students, encouraged by another declaration of protest from Kanellopoulos and his political colleagues on 21 March.

The later course of events became known in great detail at the trial, in October 1975, of those responsible for the sack of the Polytechnic. The defendants at that trial included three leaders of the junta – Papadopoulos, Ioannidis and Rouphogalis – and two of Markezinis' Ministers (who were acquitted), as well as many senior officers of the Army and the Police. Although the story was not a simple contrast of black and white, there could be no doubt about the justice of the convictions. The evidence for the prosecution was overwhelming; the evidence for the defence was abjectly feeble, especially when it was confronted with that of Kanellopoulos, Mavros and the Professors at the University and Polytechnic.

Although it was denied at the trial, there was reason to believe that a plan for the use of troops against the students had been drawn up during the summer.[11] The original plan was code-named Themis, after the goddess of law and order, but with an ironic appropriateness it was later changed to Keravnos ('thunderbolt'). For several months, during the heat of the summer vacation, there was an uneasy peace. Then, in July, the Minister of Education resigned and was replaced by a more strong-minded successor. On 25 September another attempt by students to occupy the Law School was fairly easily defeated by the police.[12] There were again demonstrations in the streets, but the decisive clash had yet to come.

Two events in the early autumn, at opposite ends of the world from Greece, had an indirect bearing on local developments. In October a military government in Thailand was forced to resign, largely as a result of student demonstrations in the summer. This lesson was not unheeded by the Greek students. They probably paid less attention to the other event, which was the confirmation in Washington of Dr Henry Kissinger as Secretary of State. He was to prove no friend of the Greeks, apart from the military dictatorship.

The uneasy truce between the students and the junta was ended by a foreseeable occasion in November. The fifth anniversary of the funeral of George Papandreou was commemorated with a demonstration on 4 November, in which many students took part. There were thirty-seven arrests after violent clashes with the police, and seventeen people were sent for trial. Twelve of the seventeen were acquitted on 13 November, and five others received suspended sentences.

As the trial ended, students began assembling in the Polytechnic, and others in various schools of the University. They renewed their demands for elections to the Student Unions, setting a deadline by 4 December. The governing bodies of several Schools closed them to avert further violence, but the Polytechnic remained open with the consent of its Senate. Markezinis' Minister of Education, P. Siphnaios, made a discreet visit to the Polytechnic, but failed to persuade the students to withdraw their demands.

On the 14th Papadopoulos held a meeting with Markezinis, Siphnaios and the Minister of Public Order, P. Therapos.[13] They agreed not to interfere with the movements of the students. Siphnaios then convened a meeting of the Principals of all the Schools of higher education. He told them that he recognized the desirability of student elections, but they could not be held by 4 December. The earliest date he would concede was 15 February next year, presumably because he knew that Markezinis intended to hold the general election on 10 February and wanted the student elections to take place afterwards.[14] The Principal of the Polytechnic, Professor K. Konophagos, objected and supported the students' demand. Siphnaios appeared at first willing to give way. The Senate of the Polytechnic accordingly decided to allow a general assembly of students on that day.[15]

In a state of tense excitement, expecting dramatic events but unsure what they would be, the students were already gathering at the Polytechnic in scores, hundreds, and eventually thousands. Students from the closed Schools at the University joined them in sympathy. The assembly which the governing body had agreed to allow began its proceedings about 10.30 on 14 November, a Wednesday. The forecourt of the Polytechnic was already crowded, not only with students but with other sympathizers. Before long – it is impossible to say when – the crowd included people who were later identified as *provocateurs*. These were not all Communists or anarchists, as the junta maintained; nor were they all agents of the secret services, as left-wing supporters maintained; but there were certainly some of both species. A large crowd also gathered outside the gates of the Polytechnic, which the police belatedly tried to isolate.

Already slogans were being shouted from the forecourt, and written on placards hung from the railings. They began with simple demands, such as 'Bread – Education – Freedom', but they became increasingly aggressive and political. Witnesses at the post-dictatorship trials recorded many of them:

'Tonight Fascism will perish'; 'Workers, peasants and students'; 'Fight, people, they are drinking your blood'; 'You starve, people, because you bow down to them'; 'Popular rule'; 'Down with Papadopoulos'; and so on.[16] It was argued that the more inflammatory slogans were not necessarily produced by left-wing *provocateurs* but also by agents of the junta, in order to create an excuse for military intervention.[17] But the overriding impression was that everyone was taken by surprise as events passed out of control.

At 17.00 on the 14th an official of the Public Prosecutor's office, who alone had power to authorize forcible intervention by the police, called on the crowd outside the Polytechnic to disperse. His call was virtually ignored. An hour later the Chief of the Athens city police summoned Professor Konophagos, the Principal of the Polytechnic, to a meeting in the street. He asked for permission to make a forcible entry in order to disperse the crowd inside. The Principal refused on grounds of academic freedom, but the Police Chief understood him to agree that he would close the Polytechnic on the following day.[18] If so, he was agreeing to something quite beyond his power. From that point onwards there was no possibility of a forcible intervention inside the Polytechnic except on the authority of the Public Prosecutor or, if a state of emergency were declared, on the authority of the government, which meant in practice Papadopoulos himself.

Meanwhile both the students and their professors were separately considering what to do next. The different Schools within the Polytechnic held separate meetings. At 19.00 on the 14th some of the left-wing students took a surprising decision to oppose the occupation. They left the building unhindered by the police, but later returned, again unhindered. The Senate met in a building at a distance from the Polytechnic premises, in order not to become too conspicuous or too closely involved in events. At 21.00 they confirmed the Principal's decision not to allow the police to force their way in. Half an hour later the Minister of Education unexpectedly telephoned the Principal to congratulate him on standing up to the police.[19]

During the night the Polytechnic became not only a hive of activity but the centre of interest for the whole of Athens. Even Pattakos, no longer in office, was seen in the vicinity in his Alfa-Romeo.[20] The students were preparing for a siege, barricading the gates, receiving food from supporters, bringing a short-wave radio-transmitter into operation, and holding night-long sessions of their committees. Since there were so many committees, representing different Schools and discharging different functions, they appointed a central Co-ordinating Committee during the first night. Shortly after 02.00 on Thursday 15 November they issued the first proclamation on their transmitter.[21]

Early that Thursday morning the Senate was again in session, at a different site outside the Polytechnic. The Professors reaffirmed their decision not to authorize a forcible entry by the police.[22] They also decided to send several of their own number into the Polytechnic to make contact with the students. At least four of them separately made their way in, without difficulty, because the police were not yet trying to restrict movement inwards or outwards. At 10.00 the Principal again met the Minister of Education, and told him that there could be no concession on the principle of academic freedom from police intervention. In the afternoon most of the police were consequently withdrawn from the vicinity of the Polytechnic.

The professors who had entered the building held meetings with many groups of students in the Hall of Architecture, and assured them both of their support and of the Senate's refusal to permit a forcible entry. In the atmosphere of feverish excitement it was impossible to foresee what would happen next. One important development was already occurring: organized groups of workers, whom the junta would later denounce, not unreasonably, as Communist-inspired, were moving into the Polytechnic to help the students organize themselves.[23]

About midday a proclamation was issued by a so-called 'Workers' Convention of the Polytechnic'. The proclamation consisted of three clauses, all emphatically socialist in style.[24] In the evening, about 19.00, the Workers' Convention held a joint session with the students' Co-ordinating Committee, after which a joint declaration was issued. The two bodies even held a joint press conference with journalists who were able to enter and leave the Polytechnic unhindered by the police.[25]

There were many other visitors during the night of the 15th. Among them was Kanellopoulos, who arrived in the vicinity about 22.00 with his niece Amalia (Karamanlis' former wife) and her second husband, Dr Megapanos, who drove them in his car.[26] They too noticed the almost total absence of the police, but they did not attempt to enter the Polytechnic. Kanellopoulos' main impression was of the happy excitement of the students inside. He assumed that the police had been called off in order to allow the situation to deteriorate to a point at which the army could intervene justifiably. This was not an unreasonable assumption, for later evidence proved that tanks were already being moved towards the centre of Athens in the early hours of the 16th, long before there was any question of a state of emergency being declared.

During a further session of the Senate on the morning of Friday 16 November, Professor Konophagos was again summoned by telephone to see the Minister of Education. This time Siphnaios adopted a harsher tone than before, reflecting a change of tactics on the part of Papadopoulos.[27] He spoke of foreign-inspired provocation in the Polytechnic, for some reason blaming the French and the Italians; and he hinted at the possible use of force by the authorities.[28] There were reports, he said, of building workers carrying materials into the Polytechnic which could be used not only for barricades but as weapons. There were other reports of extensive damage and sabotage within the Polytechnic, including the issue of fire-arms which were kept under lock and key for use in training. Most of this was found to be quite untrue by Professor Sakellaridis (who later succeeded Konophagos as Principal) when he entered the Polytechnic during that morning. The fire-arms were in fact kept at a separate location, not inside the Polytechnic.[29]

Kanellopoulos also revisited the scene during the morning of the 16th, but again he did not enter the Polytechnic grounds. If he had, he might have found himself become willy-nilly the focus of a real revolution, with unforeseeable consequences. But although he had been for over six years the fount of moral and intellectual resistance to the junta, Kanellopoulos was not a revolutionary. He confined himself to another powerful denunciation of the junta, combined with eloquent support for the students, which was published in the English-language *Athens News*, but nowhere else.[30] For Papadopoulos, it was the writing on the wall.

About midday on the 16th fateful decisions were being taken by the government. Markezinis was holding a meeting in his office to discuss the situation, when he was interrupted by the arrival of Angelis, the Vice-President, who took over the chair.[31] The discussion was at first concerned with a press conference which Markezinis was to hold next day. Then there was another interruption, when Papadopoulos came into the room. He told the meeting at once that drastic action must be taken at the Polytechnic, but he added that there must be no casualties and therefore no use of physical force. Markezinis understood him to be authorizing only the use of tear-gas by the police, but he later concluded that Papadopoulos had already decided on an intervention by the Army.[32]

Papadopoulos left the Prime Minister's office about 13.00, after which there was no further contact between him and Markezinis until the following morning. In the meantime plans for drastic action were going forward. The one definitely identified *provocateur* of the junta, an agent of the KYP, on his own admission entered the Polytechnic about 12.00.[33] There were undoubtedly others, and also plain-clothes men of the ESA mingling with the crowd, as was admitted by a police witness at the trial in 1975.[34] Ioannidis himself, the head of the ESA, was said to have been seen on the spot.[35] The police were now on watch for leading demonstrators on the streets, and no longer displaying a relaxed attitude.

Violent demonstrations were in fact about to begin outside the Polytechnic; and these, unlike the occupation of the building, showed signs of skilful planning and direction. Their target was not the Polytechnic itself. The first crowd of demonstrators, which was halted by the police about 15.30, was in fact marching away from the Polytechnic towards Constitution Square, the centre of Athens. Later another crowd entered the offices of the Nomarcheion (County Council) of Attica, from which the police evicted them. Another crowd again tried to march on Constitution Square, and clashed with police on the way. Another marched on the Ministry of Public Order, which was located at that date in a building a few hundred yards from the Polytechnic, in a parallel street.

Soon after 19.00 the Minister of Public Order, Therapos, was warned at home by telephone of 'large-scale disturbances'.[36] But he knew it would be useless for him to intervene, since the effective controller of the Ministry was its Secretary-General, who was Papadopoulos' younger brother, Constantine, one of the original revolutionary group. By doing nothing, Therapos at least ensured that he could not be convicted of anything at the trial two years later.

The students in the Polytechnic had no responsibility for any of these developments outside. Their own situation was unchanged. During the afternoon of the 16th the Senate once more confirmed its unqualified support for the Principal. At 16.00 the students held another press conference inside the building, during which they received a warning that tear-gas was likely to be used against them. In fact tear-gas began to be fired by the police about 17.00. Many students then took refuge in the Acropole Palace Hotel, just across the street. Curiously enough, at the same time the telephones in the hotel were being used as a command-post by the police. The manager gave remarkable evidence at the Polytechnic trial of the way his hotel became a kind of 'free zone' for both sides.[37] About the same time injured victims of police truncheons began to be carried into the Polytechnic.

Elsewhere in Athens the situation was already much more serious. Firearms were issued to the police guarding the Ministry of Public Order about 18.30. The hostile crowd outside the Ministry was unarmed, except with sticks and stones, but extremely provocative. How and when the order to fire on them was given is, as always in such cases, disputed and uncertain. A police witness later said that the order was given only when the crowd had actually penetrated inside the Ministry building, about 19.30. It was also disputed whether the armed policemen were instructed to fire over the heads of the demonstrators or at their bodies.

Police witnesses at the trial in 1975 almost unanimously claimed that their orders were to fire in the air, not to use unnecessary force, and to avoid casualties.[38] If this was so, then the orders were not meticulously obeyed. Many other witnesses, on the other hand, reported hearing the crude order to 'slug the flesh', meaning to shoot at the demonstrators' bodies.[39] By 20.00, in any case, the Chief of Police could see that the violence was beyond his control.

It had already been decided elsewhere that the army must intervene. Markezinis and his Minister of Public Order, Therapos, had no part in this decision, which was taken on Papadopoulos' authority alone. Evidence that it had been taken was clear when a senior Army officer, Colonel Dertilis, arrived at the Athens Police headquarters as a liaison officer to co-ordinate operations. The hour of his arrival was variously estimated between 17.20 and 18.00.[40] At the latter hour the police moved vehicles into the vicinity of the Polytechnic to carry off any students who were to be arrested. Yet movement in and out of the Polytechnic still remained relatively easy, because there were two subsidiary gates apart from the main gate, and the police were concentrated at the latter. The last visit inside the building by one of the professors took place about 17.30.[41]

The main centre of violence during the evening of Friday the 16th was still at the Ministry of Public Order. A second attack on the building, according to police witnesses, was made by 'anarchists' armed with petrol bombs, as well as sticks and stones, about 21.00.[42] It was implied that the attackers, if not actually students, at least came from the Polytechnic, which was less than a quarter of a mile away. But a witness from the Public Prosecutor's department testified that the students never left the area of the Polytechnic and had nothing to do with the violence elsewhere.[43]

Police witnesses also claimed that shots were fired at about the same time from inside the Polytechnic; but these, if any, were certainly not fired from weapons in the Polytechnic's own armoury, which was under lock and key elsewhere.[44] Victims of bullet wounds were already being carried into local hospitals, but none of them was a policeman. In a final attack by the mob on the Ministry of Public Order, which was repulsed at 22.30, twelve policemen were injured, none of them by fire-arms.[45]

The struggle then moved to its first climax. At 21.30 the available troops were put on alert. At 22.30 the Commandos and Paratroops were ordered to move into the centre of Athens. Others held in readiness included Marines and cadets of the Officers' School. An operational command-post was set up at the Pentagon, which was a mile or so distant from the Polytechnic, across the centre of Athens. It was from that direction that most of the troops had to move towards their target, passing through Constitution Square. Markezinis first heard that tanks were moving from a telephone call by the London *Times* correspondent.[46]

The Chief of Police formally requested military support by telephone at 23.00. Shortly afterwards Papadopoulos ordered the Army to intervene. The students in the Polytechnic learned of the order within a few minutes, through the interception of a police radio message. Since the request for military support had been received only by telephone, the Commander-in-

Chief of the Armed Forces telephoned the Minister of Defence soon after midnight to ask for a request in writing signed by someone in authority. The Minister prudently gave him no satisfaction, presumably calculating that Papadopoulos would not be troubled by such pedantries. But a request signed by the Chief of Police was eventually produced, bearing an obviously fabricated time and date: 23.30 on the 17th (instead of the 16th).[47]

Violence had begun outside the Polytechnic some hours before the troops arrived, though the police denied it. A nurse at one of the central hospitals gave evidence that the wounded began to arrive there at 20.00.[48] These might have come from the Ministry of Public Order rather than the Polytechnic (though the distance between them was small); but a doctor, who heard a broadcast appeal on the Polytechnic radio for medical help and went there about 23.00, found six or seven wounded students in an improvised ward, and heard of three already dead.[49] At the Polytechnic trial over a hundred witnesses came forward to give evidence of wounds they had received from fire-arms, or of those they knew to have been killed or wounded.[50] Allowing for some duplication of evidence, it is clear that at least forty cases of bullet wounds occurred outside the Polytechnic or the Ministry of Public Order before midnight on the 16th – in other words, more than an hour before the army came on to the scene.

Kanellopoulos confirmed that the army took no part in the shooting that night.[51] He made a third visit to the scene about half an hour after midnight, while Mavros also set out with him but took a different route. Mavros' evidence was particularly valuable because he took with him a tape-recorder, which confirmed the innocence of the students' slogans. Their voices were recorded chanting: 'Bread – Education – Freedom!' Then: 'We love the State – we hate the junta!' And finally, when all seemed lost, the strains of the National Anthem.[52]

But the police, according to Kanellopoulos, were in a state of panic. He himself was almost attacked by them, but as soon as the troops arrived their officers set about restraining them. The first tanks were reported in the street leading to the Polytechnic at 01.00 on Saturday 17 November. At about the same time Colonel Dertilis, the Army liaison officer at police headquarters, was told that military units were about to take over responsibility.[53] The arrival of the tanks relieved the Ministry of Public Order at 01.30 from any further damage. By 02.00 three tanks were reported outside the main gate of the Polytechnic. About the same time Constantine Papadopoulos, the Secretary-General of the Ministry of Public Order, was seen in the street outside the Polytechnic. He admitted at his trial in 1975 that he was there in order to provide cover for the use of force, since no one in the Public Prosecutor's office would do so.[54]

A quarter of an hour later, at 02.15, a group of half a dozen students emerged from the Polytechnic to negotiate a peaceful withdrawal. The scene was so chaotic that discrepancies in the accounts of what followed are not surprising.[55] Instead of accepting what was tantamount to a surrender by the students, the officers in charge were said to have imposed impossible terms which made the use of force inevitable. The students asked for half an hour to carry out their evacuation. The officers would allow only ten minutes (or fifteen, by their own account) before they used force. Even while they were arguing, they asked the senior official present from the Public Prosecutor's office to sign a warrant authorizing them to break into the courtyard.[56] He refused, so that in effect only a declaration of a state of emergency could justify the use of force. But the officers were confident that Papadopoulos would protect them, if necessary by issuing a retrospective proclamation of martial law.

Even before the ten minutes' grace had elapsed, a tank was driven against the main gate. One of the professors, who was hurrying to the Polytechnic at that moment, heard the crash as he approached.[57] The officer in charge of the tank swore that it was moving at the minimum possible speed, with its gun traversed to the rear.[58] It was true that the tank was being used only as a bulldozer, not as a weapon. But a photograph showed the tank facing the gate of the Polytechnic with its gun pointing forwards.[59]

The gate was blocked inside by an old Mercedes car, which the tank crushed along with the gate. There were students and a journalist on the pillars supporting the gate, who were thrown to the ground by the impact. The students' radio fell silent at 02.45.[60] Those inside the Polytechnic who were not injured began to rush out through the gap made by the tank. As they reached the street, they were beaten with truncheons or flung into the waiting vehicles. Casualties inside the Polytechnic forecourt were relatively few, because neither troops nor police went in until the evacuation was virtually complete. But casualties outside were heavy.

Exact figures could never be ascertained. Some witnesses said that the soldiers at first tried to restrain the police, but this cannot have been a sustained effort.[61] Others said that the troops, including cadets from the Officers' School, themselves took an enthusiastic part in the violence; and others said that the police tried to restrain the troops.[62] Obviously there were good and bad cases among both forces. The number of arrests was variously estimated between 700 and 1,000; the wounded between 180 and 200; the dead at least twenty-three, but almost certainly more. The injured among the police amounted to less than a dozen, none of them due to fire-arms, and only one really serious.[63] On the other hand, the police fired 24,000 rounds, on the evidence of a police witness.[64]

Mutual accusations continued for months, even years, after the Polytechnic tragedy. The police accused demonstrators of hurling 'Molotov cocktails' (bottles filled with petrol). Civilian witnesses accused the police and army of using 'dum–dum bullets' (soft-nosed, to expand in the wound). Police witnesses spoke of wanton damage by demonstrators to the Polytechnic and Ministry buildings. But later estimates of the damage amounted only to about £10,000 at the Polytechnic and £2,000 at the Ministry.[65] In the case of the Polytechnic, much of this damage was caused not by the students but by the military assault. The professors testified to the great care that the students had taken not to damage property or equipment. The only exception was an irruption into the office of the junta's Commissioner, to destroy his files.

No statistics can be reliable in such a chaotic situation, but in some cases the proportions are striking. The total student body of the Polytechnic was about 4,000, but the number concentrated in it during the siege was conservatively estimated at 5,000. Many students were no doubt absent, but many sympathizers had flocked to join the besieged. Among them were students from the University and elsewhere. Evidence at the trial in 1975 mentioned 'artists, actors, intellectuals and workers', but also 'alien elements'.[66]

In the eyes of the police, the villains of the affair were the workers, whom they described as 'anarchist trouble-makers'.[67] But the Polytechnic teachers and other sympathetic witnesses, who were in a better position to judge, identified the 'alien elements' chiefly as agents of the government: the KYP, the ESA, the Security Service (Asphaleia) and so on. Undoubtedly both kinds of outsiders were present, though in what numbers it is impossible to say.

When it came to assessing the casualties, the breakdown was revealing. One specific figure, compiled from police reports, put the total arrested at 866, including 150 women.[68] Within that total, the number of Polytechnic students was only forty-nine. The remainder consisted of 268 students from elsewhere, seventy-four schoolchildren and 475 workers. There was therefore some justification for the junta's contention that a majority of those involved were not currently students at all. But that would be a very superficial argument for the treatment meted out to them.

No doubt many who rallied to the side of the students were young people of the same generation, perhaps ex-students only a year or two older, now known as 'workers'. As the successor to the Principal of the Polytechnic said in evidence at the trial 'the appearance of the workers was youthful', and they were there 'because their own problems could not be solved without a solution of the political question'.[69] There is also no doubt that, with a minority of callous exceptions, the whole population of Athens was on their side that night.

Papadopoulos' revenge did not end with the sack of the Polytechnic. The last occupants left about 03.30 on Saturday 17 November. Half an hour later the

General in command of the operation received a report that all was quiet. Almost incredibly, the report also said that no shots had been fired.[70] The General went to bed, and did not visit the scene next day.

At 09.30 on the 17th Markezinis was summoned to Papadopoulos' office and asked to approve a proclamation of martial law, which was effectively in operation already.[71] In an act of gratuitous folly, Markezinis agreed. While he was in the office, he heard shots in the distance, but accepted an assurance that they were only blanks or shots in the air. The reality was that the demonstrations had begun again, though at the Polytechnic there was the quietness of desolation and death.

During that Saturday morning the professors braved the demonstrations and the shooting to approach the Polytechnic, where a small crowd was still gathered. They were told that on Papadopoulos' orders no one was allowed to enter the building. It remained closed, under police guard, until the following Thursday, 22 November. Other institutions of higher education were closed throughout Greece, for similar events had occurred, though on a less dramatic scale, at Salonika, Ioannina and Patras.[72]

Meanwhile a number of teachers, including Professor Konophagos, were arrested and their houses were searched. Markezinis intervened, however, to secure the release of some of them. Since they were never charged, it is impossible to say what was their supposed offence: presumably inciting their students to violence, as had earlier been alleged against Professor Pesmazoglou when he was exiled.

The demonstrations continued throughout the 17th, and so did the shooting, which was now the work of the army. At 13.30 on that day Papadopoulos issued a statement blaming the trouble on a conspiracy of former politicians.[73] To add substance to his words, Kanellopoulos, Mavros and Zigdis were placed under house arrest. In the afternoon a high-level meeting took place at the Pentagon, attended by senior police as well as army officers.[74] Not a word seems to have been mentioned at this meeting about civilian casualties. Yet the majority of those who gave evidence at the Polytechnic trial in 1975, some sixty in all, said that they had been wounded during the morning or early afternoon of the 17th: in other words, after the Army had taken over responsibility. But this the Generals did not want to know.

The demonstrations continued for three more days; so did the shooting and the arrests. Five cases of bullet wounds were reported by prosecution witnesses even on the 18th, including two killed. One of the killings was a notorious case of murder by Colonel Dertilis in person. There was also evidence of one man being shot dead on the 19th or 20th. The final death-roll was never exactly established, because many families smuggled the bodies away in order to avoid further harassment.

In 1975, on 10 September, the newspaper *Vima* published the names of forty-three dead. The prosecution referred to twenty-four dead in the charge-sheet when the Polytechnic trial began on 17 October in that year, but an unofficial summary of the trial estimated that the real figure was nearer to eighty.[75] The scale of arrests was equally incalculable, if not more so. Apart from those arrested during the night of the 16th–17th, between five and six thousand more arrests were made on the 18th, and over a thousand on the 19th. But the official figure given by the Security Service was 2,473 between 17 and 29 November.[76]

In the afternoon of Tuesday, 20 November, Papadopoulos convened a meeting at the Pentagon.[77] Markezinis, who arrived shortly before 17.00, said that it was his only visit to the Pentagon, and he had originally been invited on business which had nothing to do with the Polytechnic. He was plainly surprised by the scene in which he found himself. Among the Generals and other senior officers, the only other Minister present was Ephesios, his Minister of Defence. The room in which they met was surrounded with television cameras.

After the Commander-in-Chief had made a formal speech from a written text, Markezinis was called upon to address the meeting and the cameras. He claimed later that it was his duty to stand by the President in his hour of crisis. He committed himself to the rhetorical statement that 'the enemy in our midst shall not pass', or according to his own recollection: 'the enemy of the Nation and the Republic shall not pass'.[78] After the cameras were removed, a debate followed, in the course of which Markezinis strangely congratulated the Army on its 'timely and bloodless intervention'.[79]

Evidently he expected his partnership with Papadopoulos to continue. But he insisted that martial law must not be prolonged beyond the one month sanctioned by the Constitution, after which it could only be renewed with the agreement of the Council of Ministers.[80] Meanwhile the Commander-in-Chief took advantage of a law promulgated by Metaxas in 1940 to dissolve twenty-eight student organizations throughout the country, and to confiscate their assets.[81] Two days later, however, Markezinis announced that a general election would still be held in the near future. He planned to announce the date (10 February 1974) at a press conference on the 25th, which had been postponed from the 17th owing to the crisis at the Polytechnic. Papadopoulos wanted the election postponed till March, and was surprised to find that Markezinis would resign rather than agree.[82]

It remained to placate public opinion abroad, particularly in the United States. The Greek Embassy in Washington issued a statement on 20 November which stressed the material damage done by the 'anarchists', amounting to 'millions of dollars'. It drew attention to the anti-American character of the students' slogans: 'Americans, go home'; 'Greece out of

NATO'; 'No American bases in Greece'; and so on. The statement also quoted a senior official as declaring: 'The anarchists fear the elections.'[83] In other words, it was suggested that the occupation of the Polytechnic had been part of a plot to frustrate the return of democracy.

The truth was that a plot was indeed under way to prevent the elections from taking place, but it had nothing to do with the students or the workers whom the government called 'anarchists'. Papadopoulos and Markezinis were wholly unaware of it, although the latter had received at least one warning that Ioannidis would overthrow them.[84] One member of the government – Therapos, the Minister of Public Order – who perhaps had an inkling of what was to come, had the sense to resign on 23 November. His successor, a General who was sworn in at 11.00 on the 24th, perhaps took the record for the shortest tenure of office in Greek history – less than twenty-four hours.

11 Down a steep place
November 1973–July 1974

According to the most knowledgeable witnesses at the Polytechnic trial in 1975, the tragedy could not have been deliberately provoked by the junta. Ioannidis, who was in the dock, and General Phaidon Gizikis, who was a witness, both pointed out that the violence at the Polytechnic could have been only a hindrance to their plans for the overthrow of Papadopoulos.[1] Papadopoulos himself could have had nothing to gain from provoking the students' revolt. He was clearly taken by surprise and unready to put it down expeditiously, without a reckless abuse of force. The only outcome for himself was that he lost the last shred of public support. It is clear that the revolt, though wholly spontaneous, was quickly exploited by both political extremes. The Communists infiltrated professional agitators, and Ioannidis infiltrated agents of the security services. In the end the students were doomed to be the victims of men more ruthless and crafty than themselves.

The sack of the Polytechnic in 1973, like the sack of the Bastille in 1789, was not the decisive event in the overthrow of the established regime, but it serves equally well as a symbol. Nor was it the event which sealed Papadopoulos' doom, for that was already sealed. The decision that Papadopoulos must go was the Army's reaction to his introduction of the new Constitution in July. The objections of Ioannidis and the senior Generals to the Constitution lay not in the abolition of the monarchy but in other consequences: it elevated Papadopoulos to supreme power; it eliminated the last of his colleagues in the original junta (apart from Ioannidis himself); it established an almost purely civilian government; it held out the prospect of free elections. Two of the Generals who joined Ioannidis in conspiring against him were Khazapis, the Chief of the Defence Staff, and Gizikis, commanding the First Army at Larisa. Both later testified that their decision was taken before the events at the Polytechnic.[2] Gizikis dated it more than two months earlier, Khazapis earlier still.

According to Gizikis, the date on which Papadopoulos was to be removed from office – 25 November – was fixed about a month in advance. It was chosen because of a combination of circumstances: Gizikis was due to make a visit to Ankara on 26 November, together with the Commander-in-Chief, so his presence in Athens on the previous day would not seem abnormal; and President Ceauşescu of Romania was due to visit Athens from 21 to 24 November, so Papadopoulos could be expected to be there on the 25th. The

Polytechnic tragedy caused Ceauşescu's visit to be cancelled, but on 16 November Ioannidis told Gizikis that all was ready and no postponement was necessary. He held his last meeting with his fellow conspirators – all Majors and Colonels, he said later, because he did not trust Generals – on 21 November.[3] Gizikis was to be simply a figurehead.

For a few days life in Athens appeared to be returning to normal. Martial law was gradually relaxed, though not suspended. Universities and Polytechnics were restored to their governing bodies on 23 November. On the next day, a Saturday, freedom of circulation was allowed again in Athens, and military units were withdrawn from the streets. But the tension remained.

Markezinis saw Papadopoulos daily between 21 and 25 November. Neither was conscious of any threat hanging over them. On the 22nd they discussed the American request for an extension of their facilities, including the use of the airport at Elevsis, which Xanthopoulos-Palamas had reported to Markezinis the previous day. Papadopoulos entirely supported Markezinis' intention to refuse the request.[4] On the 23rd they discussed the proposed elections, over which Papadopoulos appeared to accept Markezinis' determination that they should not be postponed beyond 10 February. Markezinis also pointed out that a meeting of the NATO Council was due on 10 December, at which he must inform the allied governments of his own intentions following the expiry of martial law, which under the Constitution would occur automatically after one month. Papadopoulos was in a somewhat depressed mood. He talked of resigning, which Markezinis urged him not to do.[5]

At their last meeting, on 24 November, Markezinis told Papadopoulos and the Vice-President, Angelis, about the warning he had received of Ioannidis' intention to overthrow them. He was astonished by the blind confidence which both men showed in Ioannidis' reliability.[6] On the same day, Papadopoulos' brother Constantine had a meeting with Ioannidis, to discuss the signs of unrest which the prospect of elections was causing in the officer corps. Ioannidis assured him that it was not serious.[7] Constantine Papadopoulos reported accordingly to his brother at a meeting the same afternoon, which was attended also by the Chiefs of Staff and the Minister of Defence. After some discussion, Papadopoulos decided to adjourn the meeting over the weekend. It was his last decision.

The early morning of 25 November closely resembled that of 21 April 1967. The tanks were stationed in central Athens by 03.15; the telecommunications centre was occupied and the telephone system cut off at 03.50; the police headquarters was taken over by Army officers at 04.00. A convoy of armoured vehicles moved southwards to Papadopoulos' residence at Lagonisi. On arrival, an officer handed him a message which read:

At the request of the armed forces, you have submitted your resignation; so have the Vice-President and the Markezinis government. You will follow further developments on the television. Your credit and that of your family will be respected.[8]

It was signed: 'The Revolutionary Committee'. At first, Papadopoulos would not believe that Ioannidis was responsible. When he was convinced he assumed that Ioannidis would make himself Prime Minister; but in this he was mistaken.

At 10.00 it was announced on the radio that 'the President' would shortly address the nation. But the President who appeared on television at 11.15 turned out to be a little-known General called Phaidon Gizikis. He had been sworn in by the Bishop of Ioannina, Serapheim, in place of Archbishop Ieronymos, who was too closely linked with Papadopoulos. Markezinis had meanwhile been woken up by a policeman guarding his apartment, to tell him that he was dismissed.[9]

A new government was sworn in at 17.45 under Androutsopoulos, the nonentity who had for so long faithfully served Papadopoulos. A number of new appointments was also announced in the high command of the Army, in order to remove the Generals particularly associated with Papadopoulos. Three Lieutenant-Generals were new in key posts: G. Bonanos, formerly commanding III Corps in Macedonia, became Commander-in-Chief of the Armed Forces; D. Galatsanos became CGS of the Army; I. Davos became Commander of III Corps. The Chiefs of Staff of the Navy and Air Force, Admiral Arapakis and Air-Marshal Papanikolaou, remained unchanged. The only gesture of dissent against the new order was the curious defection of one officer of the Air Force, who flew his aircraft to Brindisi and sought political asylum.[10]

It was not only a bloodless coup but one which was at first welcomed with relief. Partly this was because it was thought to be a consequence of the Polytechnic tragedy, and therefore an act of redemption for it. Some credence to this optimism was given by the release in December of all those arrested in the attack on the Polytechnic. A number of other gestures were made under Gizikis' authority to appease public opinion. The politicians were released from house arrest. The KYP was placed under the control of the Prime Minister instead of the Ministry of Defence (though in practice Ioannidis was the master of it). The powers of the President were restricted (though Gizikis promoted himself to the rank of full General). Censorship was again abolished (though martial law remained in force). The junta's Commissioners in higher education were removed. Legal action was initiated against the corruption of the former members of the junta. The untrustworthy Archbishop Ieronymos was compelled to resign and replaced by Serapheim of Ioannina. There was again talk of an eventual restoration of democracy, after a course of political reform. There were even hopeful rumours that Karamanlis might return.

In reality this optimism turned out to be false. The public, or at least the press, should have been forewarned by the extraordinary spectacle of Ioannidis himself announcing the abolition of censorship. Only a week was to pass before the offices of *Vradyni* were closed and locked against its editor and staff by the ESA without explanation. It was soon clear that the military dictatorship was not ended but reinvigorated. Many other symptoms became apparent at the same time: martial law was extended indefinitely, the concentration camp on Gioura was reopened, the Constitutional Court was abolished without ever performing any of its functions. All this was not the work of Gizikis, although he obediently signed the decrees, but of Ioannidis, who was now the effective ruler of Greece.

It was widely believed that Ioannidis enjoyed the support of the United States, or at least of the CIA, which was itself an *imperium in imperio*. If the belief were correct, it would have been because Ioannidis was judged to be the most efficient agent available for handling the connected problems which preoccupied the US Administration at the time: that of Greco-Turkish relations and that of Cyprus. Ioannidis knew the problem of Cyprus at first hand from the days of his service there in 1964. He was also cynical enough to be capable of dealing with the Turks uninhibited by Greek nationalism.

There is no evidence from official sources on Ioannidis' relations with the CIA. Speculation about them is based on circumstantial evidence, some of it very striking. A circumstance which attracted particular notice was that in the period of reconstruction after democracy was restored, one of the crimes with which Ioannidis and others were charged was never brought to trial: this was the charge of complicity in the coup against Makarios in July 1974. The trial was suspended by a decree of Karamanlis' government on 7 March 1975, with the agreement of the Opposition leaders, in the interests of 'undistracted confrontation of the problems of Cyprus and the avoidance of a possible disturbance of the country's international relations'.[11] This was generally interpreted to mean that Ioannidis was in a position to produce evidence in court of the complicity of the CIA. For what may be surmised to have been the same reason, President Ford in September 1975 effectively frustrated Congressional investigations into the CIA's role in the same affair.[12]

On the other hand, even if there was a close association between Ioannidis and the CIA in the calamity of July 1974, it does not follow that the CIA had any role in the coup of November 1973 which brought Ioannidis to his dominant position. The myth of the omnipotent CIA dies hard in Greece, but it is nevertheless a myth. It is unlikely that in the extremely delicate circumstances of the eastern Mediterranean in the autumn of 1973 the CIA could have operated without the knowledge and consent of Kissinger, who was now Secretary of State. Yet the fall of Papadopoulos was greeted with such embarrassed confusion by the US Administration as to make any suspicion of complicity absurd.

Like other allied governments, the US Administration was at first uncertain whether to recognize the new Greek regime. A spokesman for the State Department, at a news conference on 26 November, spoke vaguely of 'carrying on day-to-day relationships with this government', and evaded the question of formal recognition.[13] Eventually recognition was tacitly conceded, as it were with a shrug of resignation, by all the major foreign states. It rested in part on the principle of effective control, and in part perhaps on the desperate hope that the new regime might prove better than its predecessor if only because Gizikis started without the infamous reputation of Papadopoulos. But that was to count without Ioannidis.

The US Congress was no less in two minds than the Administration, but it was the opposition to the junta that had the initiative. It happened that during November far-reaching disagreements had occurred between the House and the Senate on the Foreign Assistance Act, as a result of which a Committee of Conference between the two was convened. On 27 November, two days after the fall of Papadopoulos, the Committee agreed on a clause, among other amendments, which would ban economic or military aid to any country 'which practices the internment or imprisonment of that country's citizens for political purposes'.[14] This was intended to replace the Pell Amendment, which the Senate had passed on 25 June, but the House had not.[15] The outcome of the Committee of Conference was an agreed Bill which became law as the Foreign Assistance Act 1974 on 17 December.

Other pressures were emerging in Congress at the same time. On 27 November Don Edwards, a member of the House of Representatives, wrote a letter to Kissinger ironically urging him to adopt 'the novel position of supporting the democratic majority' in Greece, and arguing that 'US silence is tantamount to intervention'.[16] On 5 December the Senate Foreign Relations Committee was briefed in closed session by Rodger Davies.[17] As no report of the meeting was published, it can be assumed that what was said was not generally favourable to the new regime.

Not surprisingly, Senator Pell reintroduced his original amendment on 20 December, in the form of a Bill 'to prohibit all military assistance to Greece until it is determined that Greece is fulfilling its obligations under the North Atlantic Treaty', a phrase which was again defined to include political as well as military obligations.[18] It was stronger and more precise than the clause in the Foreign Assistance Act. The Bill was passed by the Senate on 23 January 1974, but it was overtaken by events on its way to the statute-book.[19]

The Congressional reaction continued in the New Year. On 18 January the House Foreign Affairs Committee appointed a special study mission to Greece under Don Fraser, which published a severely critical report on 22 February.[20] The report included, as an Appendix, an equally damning report on *The Situation in Greece* from the Parliamentary Assembly of the Council of Europe, dated 11 January. On 19 February the House Committee once more vented its disapproval on the State Department officials, Arthur Hartman and Rodger Davies, at a joint meeting of its Subcommittees on Europe and on the Near East and South Asia.[21]

Five weeks later the House Subcommittee on Europe heard evidence from Zigdis, the former Deputy of the Centre Union and one of the junta's victims. He testified that 'the net result of the dictatorial government in Greece has been the weakening of the Greek armed establishment'; and he emphasized 'the danger of disintegration of the armed forces'.[22] This was a real danger, which the Administration ignored at its peril. Unfortunately Ambassador Tasca, whom the Subcommittee heard on the same day, sought to reassure the Subcommittee with his customary apologia.

In Europe also there were growing pressures against the Greek regime, if not much effective action. The Council of Europe's adverse report on *The Situation in Greece* was neither the first nor the last example. The NATO Ministerial Council was also becoming impatient. At Brussels in December 1973, the Danish and Norwegian Foreign Ministers expressed regret that the Greeks were still deprived of their democratic rights; and at Ottawa in June 1974 a new voice was added to those of the Dutch and Scandinavian Foreign Ministers. The Portuguese dictatorship had fallen two months earlier. The new Foreign Minister, Dr Mario Soares, expressed amazement to his colleagues that 'regimes could continue to be accepted which respected neither the rights of men nor the rules of democracy which the Atlantic Alliance held sacred'.[23]

But all these were mere words. Only the US Administration had any power to act against the dictatorship in Greece. Its response, though hesitant, was not entirely negative. It was willing to continue negotiating the sale of military aircraft to Greece, on the ground that these were necessary for external defence and of little use for internal repression; but in March 1974 it suspended a plan to station an aircraft-carrier in Greek waters. This was no more than a symbolic gesture, but it led Senator Pell to welcome the interruption of 'expanding military ties' with Greece.

The pressure for legislative action to bind the Administration still continued. On 10 April a Bill was introduced in the House similar to Senator Pell's, intended to terminate military assistance to Greece.[24] It was not destined to make progress, however, for both the Greek dictatorship and the Nixon Administration were moving towards their almost simultaneous extinction. But the activity of Congress was not wasted. One initiative at this date had an important sequel.

On 11 July the House Subcommittee on Foreign Operations and Government Information began hearings on the Freedom of Information Act Security Classification Amendments.[25] By mere coincidence, these hearings coincided with the major crisis which was about to erupt in the eastern Mediterranean. They were the first step in a process which eventually imposed a closer constitutional control over the CIA. In the sequel, a Select Committee on Intelligence was set up by the House in 1975, and a Standing Senate Committee on Intelligence Activities in 1976. These committees could not themselves do more than monitor the activities of the CIA, but their existence obliged the Administration to control them. The tragedy of July 1974 at least promoted these innovations.

Turkey and Cyprus were inevitably at the centre of the reconstructed junta's concern during its eight months in office. Nor was this solely on account of American interest, important though that also was. A new Turkish government, formed in January 1974, posed a new threat. The Prime Minister was Bülent Ecevit, who had studied Greek and was once a student of Henry Kissinger's at Harvard. He had won a general election three months earlier but, as he had not an overall majority, much bargaining was needed before he could form a coalition government.

Ecevit's name was little known in Greece, but it was soon to become familiar. On 1 February, presenting his government to Parliament, Ecevit spoke in favour of a federal solution to the Cyprus problem. This was also thought to be favoured by Kissinger, but it was repugnant to the Greek Cypriots. A few days earlier, however, the scene in Cyprus had undergone a major change. On 27 January, General Grivas died.

As a conciliatory gesture, President Makarios at once released a hundred of Grivas' supporters from gaol, and offered an amnesty to any others who would surrender within five days. But there was little response to the amnesty, and the prospect of reconciliation was quickly dissipated. Grivas' successor in command of EOKA-B was a less aggressive officer from mainland Greece, Major Karousos, who was said to be an opponent of the military dictatorship. Within three weeks, however, he was forced to flee from the island in danger of his life. On arrival in Rhodes, he was arrested and sent to Athens, where he was held in custody by the National Military Security (ESA), under Ioannidis' personal command.

During the same month it was alleged, on the authority of the President of the Cypriot National Assembly, Glavkos Clerides, that a notorious supporter of Grivas, Nikos Sampson, had recently visited Athens to meet a visiting American who had previously been head of the CIA station in

Nicosia.[26] Sampson was a former hero of EOKA, who had been condemned to death for murder under British rule but later reprieved and finally released on independence. Makarios could have been in no doubt that he was plotting mischief.

Another new factor in Greco-Turkish relations also emerged during February 1974. It became known that an American company, which had been exploring the Aegean seabed since 1972, had found oil 'in commercial quantities' off the island of Thasos. Hitherto the Turks had not challenged Greek control over Aegean waters, in accordance with the international law of the sea. But now the Ecevit government began to repudiate the notion of the Aegean as a 'Greek lake'. The long-lasting conflict which followed embraced not only the control of territorial waters and the seabed, but also the air-space above the Aegean.

The Greek government, which essentially meant Ioannidis, now faced harassing problems on many sides. Yet another was added in March 1974, when a Labour government returned to power in Britain. One of the earliest decisions of the new Foreign Secretary, James Callaghan, was to cancel a visit to Greece by the Royal Navy, as a mark of disapproval. George Mavros courageously published a statement supporting Callaghan's decision. He was at once arrested and deported to Gioura, where he was held for two months. The Greek government then made its own gesture of independence by withdrawing from a NATO exercise in the Aegean, as a protest against Turkish violations of Greek air-space.

Greco-Turkish relations steadily deteriorated. On 27 March Ecevit repeated his view that only a federal solution was possible to the Cyprus problem. Clerides, who had been engaged for six years in intermittent talks on communal problems with Denktash, broke them off. Makarios was more worried about his relations with Athens. On 7 April he publicly blamed the Greek government for renewed outbreaks of violence. Later in the month he revoked the amnesty offered to Grivas' followers, and again outlawed EOKA-B. He also insisted that he himself, and not the Greek government, must be responsible for choosing the officers of the National Guard. Ioannidis was by then convinced that Makarios must be eliminated.

Whether or not Ioannidis' determination was backed by the US government (or at least by the CIA), there is no reason to suppose that the Americans would have regretted the elimination of Makarios. He was regarded as pro-Soviet and pro-Arab. He was naturally disliked by the Israelis, whose interests were paramount in Washington. It was alleged in August, by the German magazine *Der Spiegel*, that the Israeli government had for some time been pressing the US government to remove Makarios from the scene. It was also alleged that Ioannidis had secret contacts with the Israelis through his Jewish brother-in-law.[27] Whatever the truth of these allegations, it was clear that Makarios was a perennially troublesome factor in Greco-Turkish relations, which were critical for wider reasons in American eyes.

The US Administration offered to mediate between its quarrelling allies. A meeting was arranged at the end of May 1974 between Greek and Turkish Generals, but the multiple causes of dispute could not be settled at that level. On 19 June, during a meeting of the NATO Council in Ottawa, the Greek and Turkish Foreign Ministers (S. Tetenes and Professor Günes) had an amicable discussion which resulted in a draft agreement on procedure for resolving the disputes. The plan was announced in a statement on the 20th, but on the next day Tetenes received a telegram from Androutsopoulos, presumably not sent on his own initiative, ordering him to repudiate it. Tetenes hurried home and warned Androutsopoulos that this decision left no alternative but the use of force. He therefore proposed to resign immediately after the meeting of NATO Prime Ministers in Brussels on 26 June.

In a statement published over a year later, Tetenes explained that there was another reason why he preferred not to remain in office.[28] Makarios was demanding the removal of all the Greek mainland officers from the National Guard forthwith. He would allow no exceptions, nor even a withdrawal by stages. Tetenes concluded that Makarios was 'deliberately aiming at a clash with the National Centre'. Xanthopoulos-Palamas, his predecessor, called it 'Makarios' passion for walking on the edge of a precipice'.[29]

Tension in the Aegean was also rapidly growing. A Turkish survey-ship was exploring the Aegean seabed for oil during May, trespassing in waters hitherto recognized as Greek. The Greek government was reported to be considering a unilateral extension of its territorial waters, as other countries had done, but did not actually carry it out. At the same time it was negotiating new contracts to buy arms from France and the USA, though these could not have been delivered in time to strengthen Greece in an immediate conflict.

Ioannidis saw the need for drastic action – what Papadopoulos would presumably have called 'surgery' – but he did not see the Turks as the primary enemy. The primary enemy for him was Makarios. Hostility between the two men came into the open in June and early July 1974. Ioannidis was said to have made representations to Washington in mid-June, through his contact in the CIA, insisting that 'something must be done about Makarios'.[30] Another CIA officer, a Greek–American, was reported to have had a meeting with Ioannidis about this time, but the report was officially denied.[31] It was even suspected that Ioannidis had a secret agreement with the Turks about what was to be done; but this was pure speculation.

On 26 June, however, a spokesman for Makarios declared bitterly that 'the leadership of EOKA-B is in Athens'.[32] He went on: 'We can say that the leaders of EOKA-B in Athens are the agents of the revolutionary military regime.' This was on the same day as the NATO summit in Brussels, at which the Greek and Turkish Prime Ministers, Androutsopoulos and Ecevit, were both present, but apparently never exchanged a word on Cyprus or their other disagreements. Tetenes, the Greek Foreign Minister, took this as the last straw, and submitted his resignation on 1 July.

There was now a general expectation that the tension could only end in an eruption of violence. Awareness of the crisis was becoming more urgent in the US Administration. It should have been strengthened, and perhaps was, after Kissinger visited Cyprus on 7 May (though on other business, to meet the Soviet Foreign Minister, Gromyko, on the Middle East crisis).[33] During the second half of June Ambassador Tasca was instructed to give Ioannidis a direct warning not to attempt any action against Makarios. He evaded the instruction on the ground that Ioannidis was only a subordinate officer. He contented himself with delivering the warning to Androutsopoulos and the Greek Foreign Ministry, leaving it to the General commanding JUSMAGG to convey it to the Chiefs of Staff.[34] Naturally the warning had no influence on Ioannidis, even if it ever reached him. It was pointless to make representations to men who, even if nominally Ioannidis' superiors, were in reality his underlings.

The evidence on Ioannidis' machinations during the crucial months is purely circumstantial, but nothing is unbelievable about him. It is clear that throughout the crisis he was confident that there would be no violent reaction by the Turks. Makarios was equally convinced that Ioannidis would not attempt drastic action against himself, because the Turks would be the beneficiaries. He was so certain of his own security that he spent a week in May away from Cyprus, on a visit to Communist China.

In Athens Averoff, who saw the threat more clearly than most, was sending warnings in all directions: to Makarios, to Gizikis, and to Karamanlis.[35] The onset of the crisis was signalled on 2 July by three resignations from the Ministry of Foreign Affairs. The most important of the three was not Tetenes, the Minister, but Angelos Vlachos, the Secretary-General. Vlachos knew Cyprus well, having served there as Consul-General during British rule, and he correctly suspected what Ioannidis was plotting. Although Tetenes was replaced as Foreign Minister by K. Kypraios, the Minister of Industry (who also retained his previous post), the effective control of foreign policy remained in Ioannidis' hands.

On the same day that the three resignations were announced, two more decisive events took place. A formal letter of complaint was addressed by Makarios to Gizikis; and a high-level meeting was held in the office of the Commander-in-Chief, General Bonanos, in the Pentagon. The two events were connected, for Makarios' complaint to Gizikis was precisely about the conspiracy which was being brought to a head on that day at the meeting in the Pentagon. The meeting was attended by Gizikis, Androutsopoulos, Ioannidis and Bonanos alone. It was probably the first time Gizikis and Androutsopoulos heard about the plot against Makarios.

Makarios' letter to Gizikis, though written the same day, was not delivered until several days later, but its existence was reported in the press on 3 July.[36] Copies were taken by Makarios' private secretary to Karamanlis in Paris and to Constantine, who was in England. Karamanlis told the emissary that unless Makarios could 'guard his back against the probable reaction of Ioannidis', both Cyprus and he himself were threatened with catastrophe. Constantine brought the letter to the attention of British Ministers, who were concerned as parties to the 1960 Treaty of Guarantee of the Republic of Cyprus.[37]

The letter began with an expression of regret that it was necessary to bring to the President's attention numerous unfriendly acts for which the Greek government was responsible.[38] The matters of complaint included the return of Grivas to the island in 1971, promoted by 'certain circles' in Athens; the creation of the illegal EOKA-B, supposedly to fight for *enosis* but in fact to conduct a reign of terror against Makarios; the supply of arms to EOKA-B through Greek officers of the National Guard; the dissemination of propaganda against the Cypriot government and Makarios personally; the support of pro-Grivas newspapers with finance from Athens and material from the KYP; the encouragement of the dissident bishops to demand Makarios' resignation; the direct control of EOKA-B from Athens after Grivas' death; the selection, on orders from Athens, of Cypriot officers unacceptable to Makarios for the National Guard; and other grievances.

Summarizing his message, Makarios wrote that 'more than once before now I have sensed, and sometimes almost felt, an invisible hand reaching out from Athens and seeking to terminate my earthly existence'. As evidence, he enclosed with his letter a copy of an incriminating document dated 14 May, which was apparently a letter from the joint commander of EOKA-B to Ioannidis, under the pseudonym 'Kadmos'.[39]

Makarios concluded with two demands: that the Greek government should withdraw all mainland officers from the National Guard, replacing them with about a hundred others whose role would be confined to reorganization, instruction and advice; and secondly, that it should order EOKA-B to cease its subversive activities. He reminded Gizikis that he was not a local functionary but 'the elected leader of a large section of Hellenism'; and he demanded appropriate treatment by the 'National Centre', which he acknowledged to be in Athens. No reply to his letter was ever received.

After the high-level meeting in Bonanos' office on 2 July, three senior officers from the National Guard, all mainland Greeks, were summoned to be told by

Ioannidis on the same day that their force was to be used to overthrow Makarios.[40] The date of the operation was to be Monday 15 July. The three officers were uneasy, but Ioannidis assured them that there was no risk. They remained in Athens a few days longer to complete the operational plans, and returned to Cyprus between 6 and 9 July. One of them was said to be carrying a draft proclamation, to be issued by Makarios' presumed successor in the Presidency.[41.]

On 5 July Makarios told a press conference that he did not believe in rumours of an impending coup against him. But this was the same day on which his letter was delivered to Gizikis, and on which also a Cypriot newspaper, known to be close to Makarios, published details of the alleged plot against him by 'certain military circles' in collaboration with the National Guard and EOKA-B.[42] Evidently Makarios hoped to scare off Ioannidis by giving his conspiracy the maximum publicity.

The strangest thing about this most public of conspiracies was that both Makarios and Ioannidis displayed the utmost calm about it. Not surprisingly, there were suspicions of what the Greeks call a *skinothesia*, a charade. There was an assumption that the Americans were the stage-managers, and the Turks were to play a carefully controlled part. Even if military action was to be taken, it was not expected to lead to war. But this was wishful thinking. The calm of both Makarios and Ioannidis was due to fatal errors of judgement: Makarios misjudged Ioannidis, and Ioannidis misjudged the Turks.

On the day after Makarios' press conference, his letter to Gizikis was published in the press. The intention was no doubt to reinforce his indirect warning to Ioannidis. But as Karamanlis had foreseen, Ioannidis was not to be scared off. A series of further meetings was convened, not merely to complete the planning but also to involve others in complicity. According to one uncorroborated account, the Chiefs of Staff of all three services were first involved at a meeting under Gizikis' chairmanship on 8 July, with Bonanos and Ioannidis also present, but no officers from Cyprus.[43] A meeting of the Council of Ministers was reported to have discussed Makarios' letter on 11 July, but it is uncertain how much they were told.[44] One further meeting was held on 13 July, two days before the coup, in Bonanos' office.

This time Ioannidis was not present, presumably because the decision in principle had already been taken and all that remained was to settle operational details. Gizikis was in the chair. Others present included the Commander-in-Chief (Bonanos), the three Chiefs of Staff (Galatsanos, Papanikolaou, Arapakis) and their deputies, the Commander of the Cypriot National Guard (Denisis) and other officers from Cyprus. According to press reports, the Prime Minister and the Ministers of Foreign Affairs and Defence were also present.[45]

Ostensibly the purpose was to reach conclusions on Makarios' letter to

Gizikis. But after a perfunctory discussion the meeting was adjourned until Monday 15 July. The Chief of the Naval Staff assumed that the real object of the adjournment was to detain the officers of the National Guard in Athens over the weekend, since they might be unreliable.[46] It could also have been to give Makarios a false sense of security.

Meanwhile Makarios appeared perfectly cool. On 12 July he received the new US Ambassador to Cyprus, Rodger Davies, formerly the Deputy Assistant Secretary of State, who was to be assassinated only a few weeks later. On 13 July Makarios told a British journalist that he had had no reply to his letter to Gizikis. Later that day the Greek Ambassador in Nicosia told Makarios that the Greek government had met that morning to discuss his letter, with the Commander of the National Guard in attendance. The discussion was to be resumed on the 15th, and it was suggested that Makarios might like to attend. It was not strictly true that the Council of Ministers had discussed the letter; but in any case Makarios declined to go to Athens, and retired to his country house in the Troodos mountains for the weekend.

Bonanos reconvened the meeting with the Chiefs of Staff in the Pentagon at 08.00 on Monday 15 July. It has not been confirmed exactly who was present, but the purpose of the meeting was not in doubt. There was no further discussion of Makarios' letter to Gizikis. Bonanos simply informed his colleagues that the coup had taken place in Nicosia and Makarios was 'probably dead'.[47] But he overestimated the success of his planning. In fact the action had scarcely begun, and its outcome was to be far different from what he imagined.

The armoured vehicles of the National Guard began to move about 08.10 that morning. Makarios was in his car on the way back from Troodos to the presidential palace. His first appointment on arrival was to receive a party of Greek schoolchildren from Cairo. About 08.25, while one of the children was making a speech to him, the first shots were fired at the palace. Soon after 08.30 a separate attack was launched against Makarios' Reserve Corps. Another unit of the National Guard occupied the radio station. By 11.00 the radio station began broadcasting that Makarios was dead. In the early afternoon it announced that Nikos Sampson, the hero of EOKA, had assumed the presidency in his place.

But in fact, by a miracle, Makarios had escaped. His adventures on the run were fantastic and sometimes hilarious. His escape route was by way of the Troodos mountains, the monastery of Kykko (where he had once been a novice monk), the village of Ano Panayia (his birthplace), the coastal town of Paphos (where a unit of UNFICYP was stationed), and thence in a British helicopter to Akrotiri (one of the sovereign bases). From Akrotiri he was flown next day to Malta, and from Malta to London on the 17th. Ioannidis' plot to eliminate him had failed. On the day after the coup Ioannidis made a telephone call to Sampson with a demand which became notorious. Using Makarios' family name, he urged Sampson: 'Nikolaki, I want Mouskos' head – you'll get it for me, eh, Nikolaki?'[48] But Sampson also failed.

When Makarios arrived in London on 17 July, the Turkish Prime Minister was already there, to demand joint action under the 1960 Treaty of Guarantee. Since the British government was unwilling to co-operate, Turkey was entitled to take unilateral action, within certain limits. One limitation was that the action must have 'the sole aim of re-establishing the state of affairs created by the present Treaty'.[49] Another limitation lay in the legal opinion given to the Secretary-General of the United Nations by his advisers in 1960, that action by armed force would be contrary to the UN Charter.[50] But Ecevit regarded these limitations as impracticable in the circumstances.

The Turks had been planning armed intervention in Cyprus for some years. It had been narrowly averted in 1963–4, and again in November 1967. In 1974 there were to be no restraints. The imminent threat of a Turkish invasion at last galvanized the United Nations into action. The Security Council was summoned to meet on 18 July. Late on the 17th Kissinger sent his Assistant Secretary, Joseph Sisco, to London and thence to Athens and Ankara on a desperate mission to avert the outbreak of war. Sisco was joined by Robert Ellsworth from the Department of Defence.

Neither Kissinger nor President Nixon had much regard for Makarios. Nixon called him the 'Mediterranean Castro', and Kissinger saw him as an enemy of Israel. He was undeniably a stumbling block in relations with Turkey. Thinking that he was politically finished in any case, Kissinger was on the brink of formally recognizing Sampson (whom he later called 'an unsavoury adventurer').[51] Others thought otherwise: officials of the State Department argued that US support for Makarios might help to undermine the junta; and the Secretary for Defence, James Schlesinger, advocated a gesture of 'conspicuous dissociation' from the Greek government. But Kissinger rejected both proposals, and extracted from consultations with Congressional leaders what he called 'the unanimous advice that we should not get involved at all'.[52]

His negative attitude towards Makarios found little support in the Security Council on 18 July. The British representative proposed, with general agreement, to adjourn until Makarios arrived from London. He arrived the same evening, and made an eloquent speech to the Security Council next day, accusing the Greek government of aggression against Cyprus.[53] Kissinger could no longer treat him as 'politically finished'. But even when he felt obliged to receive Makarios, he was careful to address him as Archbishop and not as President.

Meanwhile Sisco had been shuttling energetically across the Aegean, making two visits each to Athens and Ankara on the 19th. By that date Ecevit was himself back in Ankara. Having returned empty-handed from London, and finding that Sisco brought no concessions from Athens, he ordered the long-planned invasion of Cyprus to start that night. The Turks always insisted, however, that their action was not an invasion but simply an implementation of the Treaty of Guarantee.

Ioannidis remained strangely complacent throughout the crisis, even when he learned that Turkish ships had been seen embarking troops and equipment in the south coast ports during the 18th. He saw no reason even to meet Sisco, who had to force him to join a conference with Androutsopoulos on the 19th.[54] He assured his colleagues that there was no cause for alarm: the Turks were only holding exercises and making a show of strength. The only explanation of his complacency which Makarios could offer, when he was interviewed in 1975, was that Ioannidis wanted the Turks to land in Cyprus in order to justify a Greek landing there as well, the outcome of which would have been 'double *enosis*', or partition.[55] But the flaw in that theory is that Ioannidis made no plans for such a Greek operation until too late.

His fantasies were exploded at 21.15 on 19 July, when six ships were detected approaching Cyprus by coastal radar-stations controlled by Greek officers, who immediately reported the movement to Athens. By 02.00 on the 20th a further eleven ships were detected. The movements of both groups were anxiously followed, until the first landings began at 05.00. Everyone who saw Ioannidis during the 20th was convinced that he had been taken by surprise. He was reported to have shouted angrily at Sisco on the 20th: 'You've fooled us!' It has been suggested that Papanikolaou and Arapakis invented this story.[56] Their supposed reasoning was that if the Americans could be incriminated in the plot, their own participation was also justified. But there is no real reason to doubt that the story was true.

Ioannidis' accusation against the Americans was made at a conference in the early morning of 20 July, in General Bonanos' office. Those present on the American side were Sisco, Tasca, Ellsworth and an interpreter from the Embassy; on the Greek side, Ioannidis, Bonanos and the Chiefs of Staff, but no Ministers. Ioannidis had shed all pretence of calm, and announced bluntly Greece's intention of declaring war. No one seems to have remarked on the irregularity of such a decision being made, in the absence of any member of the government, by a Brigadier whose official function was merely internal security. Ioannidis then stormed out of the room, to convene a council of war at 08.30.

The reaction of the western allies to this crisis was unheroic. Even though war appeared probable between two members of NATO, Dr Luns, the Secretary-General, made no effort to initiate any kind of intervention. The

British government, which had the aircraft-carrier *Hermes* and other units of the Mediterranean fleet in the vicinity of Cyprus, as well as aircraft and troops on the island, confined their role to rescuing residents and holiday-makers from the north coast. The US government sent aircraft to Cyprus for the same purpose; and even this action was criticized in the Senate, on the technical ground that the President failed to account for his action to Congress within forty-eight hours, as required by the recently enacted War Powers Resolution of 1973.[57] No thought seems to have been given to the possibility of interposing an allied force between Turkey, Greece and Cyprus, to prevent or halt hostilities.

Ioannidis' council of war on the morning of 20 July was naturally for Greeks only. It was attended by the same group of officers as the earlier meeting with the Americans, and also by the President, the Prime Minister, and the Ministers of Foreign Affairs, Defence and Public Order. Again Ioannidis dictated the proceedings. He insisted on immediate mobilization with a view to declaring war on Turkey. A communiqué was published at 11.00, and the decree of mobilization was signed that afternoon by Gizikis, who issued an address to the nation at 15.00.[58]

It was soon evident that in the case of the Army, whose efficiency had been undermined by seven years of purges, the mobilization was a fiasco. In any case the Turkish forces were vastly superior, and had the advantage of close proximity to Cyprus. The Chiefs of Staff, meeting separately the same afternoon, agreed that war was impossible. Bonanos reported accordingly to Ioannidis. He nevertheless insisted that there must be an armed intervention, although the Security Council had passed a resolution that day calling for a cease-fire.

The only action taken on the 20th was the despatch by Arapakis of two submarines to Cyprus, but they were later recalled.[59] The Chiefs of Staff agreed in private that defence policy could not be left any longer in Ioannidis' hands. On the 21st they communicated their views to Bonanos, who agreed. The same afternoon the four of them collectively told Gizikis that operations against the Turkish forces were simply impossible. Gizikis summoned Ioannidis to a meeting with them in the evening. Against their advice, Ioannidis nevertheless insisted that some military action must be undertaken, even if it were only a gesture of despair.

A unit of Commandos was ordered to fly to Cyprus in fifteen transport aircraft during the night of 21–22 July, with the object of seizing Nicosia airport. Of the fifteen aircraft four were destroyed and eleven returned without succeeding in landing.[60] This was the only engagement of Greek mainland forces during the Turkish invasion, though the officers and men serving with the National Guard also suffered casualties. Far heavier were the

Cypriot casualties of EOKA-B, whose men fought the Turks desperately but in vain.

During the afternoon of the 21st, and before the Commando operation was launched, Sisco flew back to Athens from another visit to Ankara, to press for agreement on the cease-fire demanded by the UN Security Council. Ioannidis was unmoved. The Chiefs of Staff realized that they would have to take the initiative themselves to avert war, since Ioannidis would not and the nominal government was impotent. Because Arapakis was the only one fluent in English, the onus fell on him.[61]

Sisco telephoned him during the night of 21–22 July, soon after midnight, imploring him to ensure that the Greek forces would respect the Security Council's resolution. The Admiral telephoned in succession to Bonanos, Androutsopoulos and Kypraios, all of whom refused to take the responsibility. Arapakis then decided to act on his own, without attempting to contact Ioannidis. He telephoned Sisco and told him that he was ready to order a cease-fire.

Sisco asked him if he spoke for the government. With heroic untruthfulness, Arapakis replied that he did. He even claimed to speak for Ioannidis, telling himself that 'national interest comes first'. It was a repetition, in more honourable circumstances, of the words which Pattakos had used to Spandidakis on 21 April 1967.

Sisco, who had another line open to Kissinger in Washington, now acted as intermediary between the Admiral and the Secretary of State. Kissinger, according to his memoirs, had already secured the Turks' agreement to a cease-fire, so he was able to reassure Arapakis on this point.[62] Arapakis pressed Kissinger that the cease-fire should be announced first by the US government, once the time was settled. He did so in order to make sure that both the Americans and the Turks were committed. Kissinger reluctantly agreed because, as he put it at a news conference on the 22nd, the Greeks and the Turks had 'no great confidence' in each other.[63]

Kissinger's news conference on 22 July supplemented Arapakis' account on a number of points. He explained that he had been in contact by telephone not only with the Greeks and the Turks but also with the British, French and West German Foreign Ministers, because in his view the crisis was an issue affecting all NATO and western Europe. He even added, rather curiously, that he had involved the French Foreign Minister in his capacity as Chairman of the EEC Council of Ministers, although none of the contending parties was a member of the EEC. He explained how the tasks had been shared between himself and Callaghan: he had concentrated on securing the cease-fire, and Callaghan on organizing negotiations under the 1960 Treaty of Guarantee of Cyprus.

Once the cease-fire was agreed in principle, the timing had to be settled.

Kissinger and Arapakis both claimed responsibility for choosing the hour of 14.00 GMT. Arapakis' account was the more circumstantial. He proposed, by his own account, that the announcement should be made in Washington at 04.00 GMT on the 22nd. It would be made simultaneously in Athens and Ankara at 07.00 GMT, and take effect at 14.00 GMT. Almost as an afterthought, Arapakis recalled that a meeting of the Council of Ministers was to be held in Athens at 08.00 (06.00 GMT), so that they would have the opportunity to agree with what he had arranged. Once the timetable was settled, he again rang Kypraios to tell him the news. Everything then went according to plan, except that the announcement in Athens was slightly delayed, no doubt because the Council of Ministers wanted to have its say before bowing to the inevitable. By 14.00 GMT it was certain, at least for the time being, that war had been averted.

At his news conference on 22 July Kissinger showed his intense relief that the crisis had apparently been overcome. He also showed other things. His attitude towards Makarios had somewhat changed. In reply to a question, he said that Makarios' return to power 'is certainly not excluded'.[64] He also made what amounted to an indirect denial of complicity in precipitating the recent events in Cyprus. When he was asked if those events had taken him by surprise, he said that he had read many articles explaining 'why we were taken by surprise by the coup in Cyprus', and pointed out that 'Makarios also was taken by surprise'.[65] The word 'also' amounted to a disclaimer of prior knowledge on his own part.

But before making that disclaimer, he made the point that if he denied prior knowledge, the press would call it an 'intelligence failure', and if he claimed prior knowledge, 'you will say other things'.[66] This was a valid point, for there was widespread suspicion at the time of US intervention in other countries (for example Chile, less than a year earlier). Kissinger's words might justifiably divert suspicion from himself, but not necessarily from the CIA.

Kissinger continued to deny, either directly or by implication, any personal complicity on a number of occasions. At another news conference on 19 August, while expressing sympathy with the Greek Cypriots, he said that 'it is important to remember that the original dislocations were not of our own making'.[67] A less explicit but more considered denial came in an interview with James Reston on 5 and 6 October (published in the *New York Times* on 13 October).

In this interview he indulged in a philosophical speculation about the proper attitude of a powerful democracy towards unpopular dictatorships, with special reference to the recently overthrown governments of Portugal and Greece. 'One of the troubles of western societies,' he mused, 'is that they are basically satisfied with the *status quo*, so that ... the tendency is not to change.' He went on to criticize this as 'a mistaken conception', and to regret that because 'we really lack a philosophy for how to shape a new political evolution', the result was that 'one tends to leave well enough alone'.[68]

Kissinger's enemies would regard these words as a brazen deception. Even those less suspicious of him would doubt whether his words could be regarded as exculpating the CIA as well as himself. They would also doubt whether the notorious independence of the CIA could extend to risky operations behind the back of an exceptionally strong Secretary of State. These matters were never publicly examined because what was known in Athens as 'the Cyprus File' was to remain closed, at least for the foreseeable future. A definitive verdict is therefore not yet possible.

It is widely believed in Greece, however, that allied collusion in the tragedy of July 1974 was not limited to the CIA's encouragement of the attack on Makarios. The Americans were further accused of helping to guide and even control the Turkish invasion of Cyprus. It was alleged that the US military attaché in Nicosia directed the Turkish advance on the airport, although it was defended by a Canadian unit of UNFICYP.[69] British complicity was also alleged, for helicopters with Turkish markings were said to have been seen taking off from HMS *Hermes* while she was off the north coast of the island.[70] It can only be doubted whether even the opening of the Cyprus file would reveal firm evidence of such extremes of collusion.

As an interim verdict, it may be thought reasonable to believe that a member of the CIA may possibly have dropped indiscreet hints to Ioannidis, without authority. So far as Kissinger is concerned, it seems probable that he was so preoccupied with other problems in the first half of 1974 – at first with his 'shuttle diplomacy' between Egypt and Israel, and later with the final stages of the 'Watergate scandal', leading to President Nixon's resignation – that he gave too little attention to Greece and Cyprus until it was too late. It is interesting that his memoirs do not mention Cyprus as one of his problems until the crisis broke. But he certainly ought to have been aware of it earlier.

12 Yesterday's men
1974–81

In Athens there remained the unfinished business of eliminating the military dictatorship. Monday 22 July was a day of many rumours.[1] One rumour said that a group of 250 officers of III Corps in Macedonia had issued a statement demanding the resignation of the government and the return of the King. The story was broadcast by *Deutsche Welle* from West Germany, but its authenticity is highly doubtful. Another rumour said that General Davos, commanding III Corps, was moving on Athens with his armoured units to arrest Ioannidis. A third said that the government had already fallen. This appears to have originated accidentally from Kissinger, who had been surprised to find himself negotiating over the telephone with an Admiral instead of Ioannidis or Androutsopoulos. Kissinger had also mentioned at his news conference on the 22nd a rumour that 'there may be a coup in Greece at this moment', but he added that the report was 'very sketchy' and there was 'no official word'.[2] The hard fact was that Ioannidis was still in power.

President Gizikis at last intervened personally. At 20.00 on 22 July he convened a meeting in his office, attended by Androutsopoulos, Kypraios, Bonanos and the three Chiefs of Staff. The first business for discussion was an invitation from Callaghan, the British Foreign Secretary, to a tripartite conference in Geneva under the 1960 Treaty of Guarantee of Cyprus. The invitation was accepted without argument. But during the meeting news arrived that the cease-fire was breaking down and that Nicosia was about to fall to the Turks. After a confused discussion, Gizikis asked Kypraios to telephone the US Ambassador and demand an intervention by the Secretary of State. Kypraios did so, speaking to Tasca in imperfect English, of which Air-Marshal Papanikolaou was convinced that not a word had been understood. His opinion was disputed by Ioannidis, who knew even less English, but supported by Admiral Arapakis, whose English was fluent.[3]

Arapakis made an addition to this account in his record of those days. He was convinced that Tasca had refused Kypraios' request. Kypraios then asked that Sisco should come to the telephone and speak to Androutsopoulos. But Sisco had left Athens to return to the United States, and was in fact already airborne. On Kypraios' insistence, a message was transmitted to him through the American base at Athens airport, and his aircraft was recalled. Sisco then spoke to Androutsopoulos from the American base, and reassured him that the Turks would not attack Nicosia. Still, the atmosphere of desperate confusion remained.

The Chiefs of Staff, despite their resolution on the day before, had not planned in detail how to remove Ioannidis. But conversations between them on other matters during 21 and 22 July, during which nothing specific was said, had created a tacit understanding without a conscious plan. The decisive opportunity arose on the morning of the 23rd. It was perhaps also the final opportunity, for if it were missed, Ioannidis, who still commanded a residual loyalty in some regular units of the Army as well as the ESA, was capable of precipitating a further catastrophe. It is not surprising that there were different recollections of the course of events among those who took part in them.

Admiral Arapakis recalled that he was the first to arrive in General Bonanos' office on the morning of the 23rd.[4] He spoke to Bonanos of the humiliating situation created by the existing regime, and reminded him of their earlier agreement that Ioannidis must go. Bonanos promptly invited Air-Marshal Papanikolaou and General Galatsanos to join them, which they did at 08.00. All four confirmed their agreement on the removal of Ioannidis. Bonanos then went to report accordingly to President Gizikis. The others awaited the President's summons. Arapakis used the interval to make sure that his senior subordinates supported him.

Gizikis' summons came at 09.15. In the meantime a meeting of the Council of Ministers was due to begin at 08.30. But as soon as Androutsopoulos arrived for the meeting, he adjourned it and left to await a summons to the President's office. In angry frustration, the remaining Ministers continued their futile discussions until 09.30. Then they dispersed, having settled nothing, for the last time.[5]

At the meeting of the service chiefs in Gizikis' office, as Arapakis later recalled, all four of them agreed that 'the government of the country must be returned to the political leaders'. Gizikis then offered his resignation, as also did Galatsanos. But Arapakis insisted that the chiefs of the armed services had a duty to act in unison and not to renounce their responsibilities. Bonanos and Papanikolaou supported him. Consequently the resignations were withdrawn, and Ioannidis was summoned to hear their decision.

Ioannidis replied that he disagreed with them, but since they were unanimous against him, he would not resist. 'I will withdraw,' he said; and added with mock subservience: 'I request two days' leave from the head of the Army.' The meeting first extracted from him a promise that he would enforce obedience on all officers who still looked to him for orders. Gizikis then requested him to inform Androutsopoulos that 'his government was under resignation'.[6]

Air-Marshal Papanikolaou's recollection was slightly different. He recalled that at the beginning of the meeting in Gizikis' office 'nothing specific was proposed by anyone'. Then Ioannidis walked in, apparently uninvited, and took a seat. Although the discussion continued, there was still no specific proposal until Papanikolaou took the initiative. After describing the disastrous state of affairs which Ioannidis had caused, he concluded: 'We unanimously request that you leave us.'

There was no dissent, but perhaps there was surprise as well as relief when Ioannidis stood up, put on his cap, expressed his contrary opinion, and started to leave the room. Gizikis would not let him go, however, until he had first guaranteed the obedience of his military following. Ioannidis did so, and then went to Androutsopoulos' office to tell him that they were both dismissed.[7] In fact, however, Ioannidis himself retained command of the ESA, at least nominally, for a dangerous interval of several weeks.

Despite disagreements on points of detail, which continue through the record of that dramatic day, the broad outline of events is not in doubt. As soon as Ioannidis had left the meeting, Gizikis told his staff to telephone the principal political leaders and invite them to a conference. There was difficulty in finding the telephone numbers of some of the politicians – ironically, Ioannidis was perhaps the one man who could have supplied them instantly, since he had them all under surveillance – but by 11.00 most of the calls had been made. Those invited were Kanellopoulos, Markezinis, Athanasiadis-Novas and Stephanopoulos, as former Prime Ministers; Mavros, Averoff and Garouphalias, as former senior Ministers; and Xenophon Zolotas, a former Governor of the Bank of Greece, as well as a former Minister.[8]

They arrived at the President's office between 13.00 and 14.00. Shortly before the latter hour, the conference began under Gizikis' chairmanship. In a neighbouring room Archbishop Serapheim waited with two other priests, ready to swear in a new government. In another room were the four chiefs of the armed forces, who were almost immediately invited, by general consent, to join the meeting. Androutsopoulos and his Council of Ministers were simply ignored, also by general consent. Nobody bothered to mention them, or knew where they were.

The dictatorship had lasted seven years, three months and two days; or, in the words of one of its journalist–historians, '2,650 days and nights of conspiracy'.[9] It had brought disaster on Cyprus; it had demoralized the armed forces and police; it had disgraced the reputation of Greece abroad; it had created suspicion and hostility between the Greek people and their allies, especially the United States. It had also completely failed to achieve any of the objectives which it declared on coming into power. There were probably, for example, more Greeks who called themselves Communists in 1974 than in 1967.

The one area of apparent success in the early days of the junta, which was the national economy, was also a scene of devastation by the end. In 1974 Greece was burdened with the highest rate of inflation in Europe (almost thirty-two per cent) and an increase in the public debt of almost 200 per cent over 1967.[10] The most favoured sectors of public expenditure were those which all dictatorships find advantageous: the purchase of foreign arms, and the provision of telecommunications (including television, the chosen instrument of Big Brother).[11] It was typical of the moral climate of the dictatorship that the chief beneficiaries were men like Tom Pappas.

Such were the Augean stables which confronted the political leaders who met in Gizikis' office in the early afternoon of 23 July. No minutes were recorded of their discussions, which lasted three and a half hours in the first instance.[12] From the disjointed accounts of individual participants, it is impossible to be sure in what order subjects were raised or names put forward. The following account is therefore to some extent conjectural.

Gizikis introduced the discussion with a statement which not only took credit to the armed forces for the overthrow of the dictatorship, but also clearly indicated that they expected to have a continuing influence. He proposed that the Ministries of Defence, Public Order, and the Interior should be allotted to 'persons enjoying the confidence of the armed forces'. Mavros was the first to utter the devastatingly mild reply: 'You must be joking, Mr President!' Gizikis hastily withdrew his proposal, and emphasized that the service chiefs had no wish to interfere.[13]

That naturally raised the question: what about Ioannidis? The politicians were assured by the service chiefs that Ioannidis had given his word of honour not to oppose whatever was decided by them, and he would certainly keep it. Admiral Arapakis noted silently that although the statement was reassuring to the politicians, it was not strictly true. Nor would any prudent man trust Ioannidis' honour.

The meeting then went on to discuss the formation of a civilian government. There was some sterile theorizing about its presumptive character: should it be 'all-embracing' (*oikoumeniki*), 'political', 'service', 'transitional'? Markezinis showed that experience had taught him nothing by proposing as Prime Minister Xanthopoulos-Palamas, who had been invited to the meeting but was absent in Corfu. It was an absurd notion that a man who had never held elective political office should become Prime Minister at one of the most desperate crises in Greek history. But his name seems to have been rejected chiefly because he was thought to be hostile to Makarios, which he did not deny.[14]

After this suggestion had been crushed by Mavros and Averoff, the latter next put forward the name which might have been expected to be in the forefront of everybody's mind: Karamanlis.[15] The Generals may indeed have had him in mind, but feared him because he was the strongest candidate available. It was said that Bonanos, who had also learned nothing from experience, wanted Garouphalias as Prime Minister.[16] Gizikis, with an equal lack of judgement, tried to have the name of Karamanlis ruled out of consideration because he had been out of the country for over ten years, and in any case time was too short to locate him. A government must be sworn in on the instant.

The next name to be proposed was that of Kanellopoulos. It would have been a just reward for his exemplary conduct during the dictatorship; it could be claimed that he had been, and still was, the only legitimate Prime Minister since April 1967. But was he a sufficiently strong man to confront the crisis? Averoff, for one, doubted it. Nevertheless, Kanellopoulos' name was one that could not be opposed, least of all in his own presence. It was quickly agreed that he should form the new government.

Since it seemed logical that the government should be a coalition of the two largest parties, ERE and the Centre Union, it was equally quickly agreed that Mavros, as the leader of the latter, should be Deputy Prime Minister. The matter would have been settled without more ado, and the two men would have taken the oath of office at once, had not Mavros asked for an adjournment so that he could consult his colleagues in the Centre Union. Much to Gizikis' annoyance, it was agreed to adjourn the conference soon after 17.30, and to reassemble three hours later.[17]

Gizikis had some justification for his impatience, because a large and excited crowd had gathered outside the former Parliament building where the conference was taking place. Moreover, Ioannidis had disappeared, and no one could tell what mischief he was plotting. Averoff, who stayed in the building during the adjournment, went to a neighbouring room for a glass of water, and there found two officers, evidently still loyal to Ioannidis, who engaged him in conversation. They made it plain that the Army would continue to insist on Gizikis' condition, putting it in a more extreme form: the Ministries of Defence, Public Order, and the Interior must be held by serving officers.[18]

Much disquieted, Averoff returned to the President's office, where he found the service chiefs still with Gizikis. He promptly renewed, more urgently than before, his argument in favour of Karamanlis as Prime Minister. Arapakis supported him. According to Arapakis' own account (which was written for Karamanlis' eyes), it was he himself who pressed Averoff to rejoin them in Gizikis' office 'in order to continue jointly our effort to secure Karamanlis' return', whereas Averoff was hesitant because of what had already been agreed at the conference.[19] It is unnecessary to dispute the greater share of the credit. In any case, under the pressure from the two of them, first Bonanos and then Gizikis were compelled to agree. Averoff was made responsible for contacting Karamanlis, which he succeeded in doing, after several fruitless calls, through a relative living in Paris.

Karamanlis was brought to the telephone to speak to Gizikis. He was reluctant to make an immediate decision; he said he would return to Athens on the following day, and then decide. But the service chiefs insisted that the critical situation would not allow even twenty-four hours' delay. Gizikis offered to send an aircraft to Paris for him, but the French President, Giscard d'Estaing, who had been closely following events, offered his own aircraft, which Karamanlis accepted.[20]

Before leaving Paris, Karamanlis telephoned to Constantine in London. Constantine wanted to accompany him, but Karamanlis demurred and said he would communicate with him in a few days' time. There was no guarantee of the King's early return, though the King thought that it could be taken for granted. In this he was to be disappointed.

When Kanellopoulos and Mavros returned to the President's office at 20.30, they learned that the matter had already been decided behind their backs, and that Karamanlis was on his way. With characteristic generosity, Kanellopoulos told Gizikis that he was glad of the solution.[21] He recognized that Karamanlis was a stronger man than himself, and that he would have the support of the great majority of the population. This was important, because Ioannidis' followers were still in two minds about accepting civilian rule.

There was a momentary fear that the Marines, who had been devoted tools of the junta, would oppose the change by force. There were even fears of a riot among the large crowd outside the Parliament building. But when an announcement was made to the crowd at 22.30 that Karamanlis was on his way, the outburst of enthusiasm in response left no doubt that any opposition was doomed.

Probably no one in Athens slept that night. Motor horns sounded an uninterrupted paean. Most of the population seemed to be at the airport when the Caravelle carrying Karamanlis landed at 02.00. The nightmare of the longest period of unconstitutional government in Greek history was over, but the anxiety was not. There followed what were justly called, in an authoritative account, 'the seventy critical days'.[22]

When Karamanlis arrived in Gizikis' office, he still refused to take office until two conditions were satisfied: first, that the politicians should whole-heartedly support his efforts, and secondly, that the Army should return to its barracks and to its proper duties.[23] Both assurances were immediately given. But the first could not be regarded as binding either Andreas Papandreou, who was still absent in America, or the extreme left, which had not been represented at the conference.

The second assurance was also not wholly persuasive. Part of the officer corps was still in a contumacious mood; many of the younger officers remained loyal to Ioannidis, under whom they had been trained in the Officer Cadets' School; and a menacingly large proportion of the Army was concentrated in the vicinity of Athens. Averoff, who was appointed Minister of Defence, described the government as 'the prisoner of the Army'.[24] In the Pentagon he was at first treated almost as contemptuously as his predecessors. Even Ioannidis once marched into his office uninvited, and had to be peremptorily ordered out. It was not until 26 August that Ioannidis was even compulsorily retired; and he still remained at liberty for a time.

Much was left unsettled for the time being, in a mood of euphoria. The government formed by Karamanlis in the last week of July was immensely popular, not merely because it was not the junta but because it included able and attractive personalities. There were professional men as well as politicians in it; and several of the politicians – Averoff, Mavros, Mangakis, Pesmazoglou – had suffered persecution and imprisonment under the junta. But one criticism was heard from the first. Although it was a coalition, the left was hardly represented in it. Neither Papandreou nor EDA nor either of the Communist Parties was included. Papandreou had virtually excluded himself by his antagonism to the monarchy, whose future Karamanlis wished to leave at least as an open question; and also by his hostility to the EEC, of which Karamanlis hoped that Greece would become a full member. Besides, Papandreou had not yet returned to Greece. The leaders of EDA and the Communists, however, were available in Greece; and they were initially much less intransigent than Papandreou. Although the Communists were technically outlaws still, Karamanlis did not intend that they should remain so.

But Karamanlis could not bring himself to admit representatives of the extreme left even to a government of national unity. He had an extremely delicate task to carry out in circumstances of great uncertainty. He judged it to be essential that he should be supported by colleagues of unquestionable loyalty, some of whom might well have refused to serve in a government which included the extreme left. His coalition was therefore limited to the old-established parties, together with a number of eminent personalities from outside politics. There was also, however, one even more eminent absentee: Kanellopoulos, who did not wish to serve as a Minister again after the abrupt reversal of fate on 23 July.

Two striking facts illustrate the uncertainty of Karamanlis' position in the early days. Although he had accommodation in the Hotel Grande Bretagne, he did not dare sleep there for several weeks. He repaired every night to a yacht anchored in Phaliron Bay, with a naval vessel standing by. Nor did he at first dare to proceed against the ringleaders of the junta. A general amnesty was announced one month after his return which would, as drafted, whether intentionally or not, have covered the Colonels and their accomplices.

It was only after a courageous lawyer instituted a private prosecution against Papadopoulos and fourteen others on 9 September, that the government acted.[25] At the beginning of October a decree was issued to the effect that political offences were not covered by any amnesty. On 23 October, in conditions of great secrecy, the leading Colonels were arrested at night, on the orders of the Public Prosecutor and under the personal supervision of Averoff. They were held in isolation on the island of Kea to await trial. Even after that, Ioannidis was still left at liberty until the New Year.

There were compelling reasons for moving so cautiously. The government's control could not be secure until the Army had been drastically purged; but it was not easy to purge the Army while war with Turkey still seemed imminent. Yet a beginning had to be made. Karamanlis ordered the Commander-in-Chief to disperse the military units in Attica to the north-eastern frontier area, where they were needed in case of hostilities. He overcame the resistance of the Army commanders to this order – not, as Greek legend had it, by exclaiming: 'Either me or the tanks!' – but by threatening to call a mass demonstration against the high command in the centre of Athens.[26] A few days later, again in complete secrecy, the Supreme Council of National Defence met under Karamanlis' chairmanship, to enforce the retirement of the Commander-in-Chief (Bonanos), the Chief of the General Staff of the Army (Galatsanos), and eight other Generals.

The demoralization of the armed forces under Papadopoulos, Angelis, Ioannidis and their immediate subordinates was such that nothing could be done to help the Greek Cypriots against the Turkish invasion, unless there were determined support from the western allies. This was not forthcoming, partly because the allies were inclined to regard all the Greeks as tarred with the same brush, however unjustly, and partly because many of them regarded Turkey as a more important member of the alliance than Greece.

The tripartite conference at Geneva, convened by Callaghan under the 1960 Treaty of Guarantee, met in two equally abortive stages, one at the end of July and the other in early August. It failed to diminish the Turkish pressure on Cyprus. The cease-fire of 22 July was briefly broken ten days later. Then, on 14 August, a more vigorous Turkish advance began. It continued until it had reached its final objective, known as the Attila Line, on 16 August. This gave the Turks control over some forty per cent of the island. Only then did a new cease-fire become effective and lasting.

Soon afterwards, the Greek Cypriots' hostility to the United States was brutally signalized by the assassination of the new Ambassador, Rodger Davies, on 19 August. Twelve days later, when Karamanlis addressed his first mass meeting in Salonika, he was confronted with banners bearing the slogan: 'Kissinger to Nuremberg!' He remarked at this time that he was the only friend the United States had in Greece, and he dared not admit it. A year later, on 23 November 1975, vengeance was again carried to the point of murder. The victim was the new head of the CIA station in Athens, who had not been involved in any of the earlier events.

Karamanlis did not deceive himself about the future of Greece in the western alliance. He knew that eventually his government would have to make its peace with the US Administration. He knew, too, that it was impossible for Greece to fight a single-handed war against Turkey, either in Cyprus or in the Aegean or on the north-east frontier. But he had to take precautions against the worst contingency. He had also to respond to Greek public opinion, which demanded an assertion of independence against the feeble reactions of the allies. These were the reasons why he withdrew the Greek forces from NATO command, and reopened the question of US defence facilities in Greece. As a matter of dignity, he also rebuffed a pressing invitation from Kissinger to go to Washington for a meeting with President Ford, who had succeeded Nixon on 9 August.[27] For the same reason his Foreign Minister, George Mavros, refused an invitation to London.

By the beginning of October 1974 a precarious stability had been achieved at home and abroad. Open hostilities in Cyprus had ended; war with Turkey had been averted. The first legal steps against the ex-dictators and their fellow conspirators had been taken. An electoral law had been approved, and a programme for a referendum on the constitution had been published. Both the election and the referendum were to take place before the end of the year. Greece and the world recognized that at last a legitimate and competent government was in control. The seventy critical days were over.

Apart from the criminal charges against the Colonels and their accomplices, including high treason, not the least of the stains on their character was a total failure to comprehend the legacy of corruption and demoralization which they left behind them. At all the trials which took place in 1975–6 – for conspiracy, for illegal actions in office, for torture, for the murders at the Polytechnic, for perversion of justice, for destroying evidence of their crimes – there was one common characteristic of the accused: a complete lack of contrition. The arrogance of Papadopoulos and Ioannidis in particular was breathtaking.

Three of the accused, Papadopoulos, Makarezos and Pattakos, were sentenced to death for high treason. That Ioannidis received no death sentence was a mark of the objectivity of Greek justice. But in practice it made no difference, since all the death sentences were commuted to life imprisonment, on the recommendation of Karamanlis' government, and Ioannidis had earned more than one life sentence on his own account. The only criticism made of the trials was on the ground of leniency.

None of the civilian Ministers who had served the junta – more than a hundred in all – was convicted of any offence. Some of the officers of the Army and Police who were put on trial were acquitted; others, after conviction, were acquitted on appeal; and some of the sentences, even on those convicted of torture, were reduced on appeal.[28] There was also a drastic purge of officers and officials in the public service. The purge went deep into local government and the judiciary as well as the Ministries. But many Greeks thought that it was not drastic enough. A special ground of complaint was the fact that those guilty of the plot against Makarios – apart from Sampson, who was sentenced to twenty years' imprisonment in Nicosia – escaped prosecution altogether. Yet theirs was perhaps the most serious crime of all, since it had nearly precipitated a major war.

It was Karamanlis' decision that the prosecution of Ioannidis and others for the attempt against Makarios should not proceed. On 7 March 1975 it was announced that the prosecution was to be suspended in order not to distract attention from the solution of Cyprus' current problems, and to avoid 'a possible disturbance of the country's international relations'. The three major party leaders then in opposition – Mavros, Papandreou and Iliou – had been consulted and agreed; but all three emphasized that they had agreed not to a complete withdrawal of the prosecution, only to a postponement until a more appropriate time.[29] Later they all demanded that the 'Cyprus File' should be opened, though Papandreou failed to take any steps to open it even when he became Prime Minister himself in 1981.

Karamanlis' example of discretion in this matter was followed by President Ford a few months later. Both the Senate and the House of Representatives had Select Committees on Intelligence, which were engaged in investigating the CIA's activities at public hearings during 1975. The House Committee, under the chairmanship of Otis G. Pike, was about to consider the case of Cyprus on 12 September, when the President issued an order that it should be 'cut off from all classified documents'. The ostensible reason for his decision was that the Committee had broken an undertaking not to publish a particular passage (amounting to four words in all) from a document relating to the Israeli–Egyptian conflict in October 1973.[30] But it was suspected that the real reason was anxiety about possible revelations of the CIA's role in the attack on Makarios. The Committee nevertheless continued its hearings, and received testimony from officials of the State Department (including Tasca, who was no longer *en poste* in Athens). Their testimony at least made one thing clear: that no advance warning of the Turkish invasion of Cyprus had been received from the CIA.[31]

At the same time the Senate Committee on Intelligence, under the chairmanship of Frank Church, was also debarred from access to classified documents relating to Cyprus. The result of this suppression of evidence was that speculation in Athens ranged far and wide.[32] It was generally assumed as certain that the CIA had been implicated with Ioannidis. There was an inclination to acquit the State Department of complicity, but not Kissinger personally. Kissinger, it was supposed, contemplated the elimination of Makarios, followed by a token landing of the Turks in northern Cyprus, a token intervention of the Greeks in the south, and partition of the island. He was therefore discomfited by the survival of Makarios and the scale of the Turkish invasion. But naturally there is no warrant for these speculations in Kissinger's memoirs.

Although Makarios was able to return to Cyprus in December 1974, and to resume his dual role as Archbishop and President until his death in August 1977, his island and people had suffered irreparable damage. The Turks had gained almost everything they wanted from the criminal folly of Ioannidis. Cyprus was to remain indefinitely divided into a Turkish North and a Greek South – a division which Denktash, the Turkish Cypriot leader, tried to formalize by a unilateral declaration of independence in 1983. Although the US Administration temporarily cut off military supplies to Turkey, over the objections of Kissinger and the Chiefs of Staff, the Turks were able to force a reversal of the embargo eventually by cutting off the Americans' access to their own defence facilities in Turkey.

By the end of 1978, US relations with Turkey were back to normal; but not so with Greece. Greco-Turkish relations remained tense, over disputes under, above and on the surface of the Aegean, as well as over Cyprus. Since the Greeks believed that US policy unduly favoured Turkey, their relations with the United States also remained tense. After withdrawing Greek forces from NATO command, Karamanlis drastically reduced the facilities available to the United States in Greece, and terminated the agreement for homeporting of the 6th Fleet. But he could not do more without encouraging the US Administration to confer still greater favours on Turkey at the expense of Greece.

Karamanlis next faced the daunting task of restoring constitutional government at home and Greece's reputation abroad. In this task he at least had the asset of being known to be indispensable. His political experience was unique, his international reputation higher than that of any Greek since Venizelos. But although no one else could have achieved what he did, the success and even the survival of his government were at first uncertain. The remnants of the junta still hoped to recover power; the danger of war with Turkey remained real; the Army was not wholly reliable; each of the domestic problems was exceedingly intractable, yet all of them had to be solved at once. Karamanlis' eventual success served to obscure the fact that the initial odds were heavily against him.

By the end of 1974 Greece had an elected Parliament, in which even the

Communists were legitimately represented. Karamanlis was again an elected Prime Minister; Mavros was leader of the official Opposition; and Papandreou led a small party of Socialists (PASOK) which was destined, seven years later, to win an overall majority. The constitutional future of Greece had been settled in December 1974 by a plebiscite, which chose a republic in place of the monarchy by a majority of about two to one.

In February 1975 the government frustrated a clumsy attempt at another military coup – sponsored, it seemed, by Ioannidis from his prison cell. A new constitution, mainly devised by Karamanlis, was voted by Parliament in June, after contentious debates and the abstention of the opposition from the final vote. By the end of 1975 Karamanlis was able to declare that the purge of the public services was complete. Most of the trials of the junta and its accomplices were concluded, and the rest were approaching their verdicts.

The next two years could be claimed to have restored domestic normality in Greece. In 1977 Karamanlis won another general election, though with a much reduced majority; and Papandreou succeeded Mavros as leader of the official Opposition. Karamanlis remained in office as Prime Minister until he was elected President in 1980. A year after that Greek democracy passed another test, when the next election resulted in a decisive victory for PASOK, and Papandreou became the head of Greece's first Socialist government.

It could not easily be forgotten that the military coup of 1967 had been precipitated by the expectation of just such a result under Papandreou's father. But unlike the election of May 1967, which never took place, the election of October 1981 resulted in a peaceful transition of power. Karamanlis, as President of the Republic, handled the transition with exemplary tact. His unquestioned pre-eminence was generally recognized as the nation's guarantee that democracy could work, and that no further 'deviation' in any direction was likely to occur.

The self-appointed heroes of the junta were now forgotten men, though the voice of Papadopoulos was still occasionally heard even from prison. Their legacy was almost entirely liquidated, but it left one characteristic relic. The Greek habit of believing that whatever befalls them is always due to foreign intrigue, never to themselves, was still operative. Since 1967, the CIA has been cast in the role of permanent villain. Even after the fall of the junta, no event could be regarded as purely accidental – not even, for example, the motor accidents which killed Alexander Panagoulis in 1976 or Henry Tasca in 1979.

Karamanlis saw it as one of the primary aims of his last years in office to cure his people of the delusion that Greece is the centre of the earth, the chief object of every country's foreign policy, and the perennial victim of foreign conspiracies. He declared his aim of converting the Greeks into a mature European nation. That was in part the object of his determination to bring Greece into full membership of the European Economic Community, which he achieved, as President, at the beginning of 1981. For him this was primarily a political rather than an economic objective, which is one reason why Papandreou, a professional economist, was opposed to it. Although Papandreou, as Prime Minister, gave up any thought of secession from the EEC, Karamanlis for his part later confessed that he had been disappointed in his aim of 'Europeanizing the Greeks'. The seven years of retrogression imposed by the junta had been too heavy a burden.

Nevertheless the decade which followed the fall of the junta was marked by considerable success. Greece's international standing was greatly improved. Much of the improvement was symbolic, but none the less important: there was, for example, the immediate readmission of Greece to the Council of Europe; and Karamanlis enjoyed a personal success at many international gatherings. He restored friendly relations not only with allied and neutral countries in the west, but also with the Soviet bloc, with the Middle East, and as far afield as southern Asia and the Far East.

The outstanding problems which Karamanlis had to leave to his successors were those of defence and of relations with the United States and Turkey. But he left them at least in progress towards solution. The full reintegration of Greece into NATO was achieved a few months after Karamanlis moved up to the Presidency. Agreement on US defence facilities was reached under Papandreou's government, after years of hard bargaining. The Greco-Turkish dispute on the control of air-space over the Aegean was eventually settled in Greece's favour, but disagreements over Cyprus and over the continental shelf under the Aegean remained intractable. Public opinion in both Greece and Turkey was so sensitive that these problems were likely to remain unsolved for many years. They were the legacy not of Karamanlis but of history, aggravated by the military dictatorship.

Meanwhile the former Colonels remained in gaol. Karamanlis had declared from the first that life sentences would mean imprisonment for life, without remission. Since their capacity for future mischief was negligible after ten years' imprisonment, it would not have mattered much if they were eventually to be released, though one or two of their subordinates who were released became the victims of private vengeance. Many leading politicians, including Mavros and Papandreou, considered that the sentences of death on the three ringleaders should have been carried out. Perhaps, for their own good as well as their country's, it was best to leave them where they were.

Note on sources

Official records relating to the military dictatorship remain closed, with few exceptions, at any rate in the capitals where they might be most useful (Athens, London and Washington). Among the exceptions are various *pièces justificatives* published by the governments concerned and documents revealed during the post-dictatorship trials; together with occasional leaks and the products of diligent enquiries by journalists, Congressmen and parliamentarians. The sources of such material are indicated in the References; but those officially published are indicated in the Bibliography as: I – Official, Parliamentary and Congressional Publications.

Other published material can be divided into two further categories, separated chronologically by the fall of the dictatorship in July 1974 (known in Greek as the *metapolitevsis* or 'change of political system'). There are fairly sharp differences of character between these two categories, apart from their dates.

During the dictatorship books about it, mostly hostile, were published in many languages: Greek, English, French, Italian, German, Dutch, Scandinavian and no doubt others. After the fall of the dictatorship, however, little more was published in any language except Greek. Propaganda both for and against the dictatorship naturally dried up. The field was then free for more serious investigation of the causes and history of the aberration from democracy.

I have used works published during the dictatorship only where they contribute directly to knowledge of what actually happened between 1967 and 1974, particularly if they are personal reminiscences of participants. Those written by Greek victims of the junta and their foreign sympathizers are listed in the Bibliography as: II (a) – Contemporary Witnesses.

Another class of contemporary works consists of propaganda in defence of the junta, either by its own Greek supporters or by a minority of foreign writers who thought that a case could be made for it. This group is listed as: II (b) – Contemporary Apologists.

There was also a limited class of serious attempts by historians and sociologists, during the dictatorship, to explain its character and origins, so far as the evidence then available permitted. This group is listed as: II (c) – Contemporary Investigations.

Finally there are the works published after the *metapolitevsis*, which attempt a more definitive account of the dictatorship. Since foreign interest in the junta sharply declined as soon as it fell, these are mostly works written in Greek or by Greeks in other languages. This group is listed as: III – Post-dictatorship.

All the works listed in the Bibliography are cited in the text simply by the author's name, where that is known. Official publications are cited by their titles. References are also given in the text to other sources (principally Parliamentary and Congressional Records, and newspapers), which it is unnecessary to include in the Bibliography.

Since the series of trials of the junta all have the same editor, they are distinguished for convenience as follows:

> Trials/A = Trials of the principal accused;
> Trials/B = The Polytechnic trial;
> Trials/C = Trials of the torturers.

Each series consists of several volumes, but the pages are numbered consecutively from beginning to end of each series. It is therefore unnecessary to distinguish the volume numbers in the references. Thus, volume III of Trials/B runs from page 981 to page 1447; so, since there is no possibility of confusion with another volume in that series, a page in that volume is cited simply as, e.g.: Trials/B, p. 1269.

The following abbreviations are used in the References and Bibliography:

CRH	Congressional Record (House of Representatives)
CRS	Congressional Record (Senate)
EAACG	European–Atlantic Action Committee on Greece
HASC	House Armed Services Committee
HC Deb.	House of Commons Debates
HFAC	House Foreign Affairs Committee
HFAC	House Foreign Affairs Committee (later HIRC House International Relations Committee
HMSO	Her Majesty's Stationery Office
SASC	Senate Armed Services Committee
SDB	State Department Bulletin
SFRC	Senate Foreign Relations Committee

References

1 Men of tomorrow

1 Woodhouse, pp. 145–6.
2 A. Papandreou, p. 97.
3 Text, with Turkish reply, in SFRC, Hearings before Subcommittee on US Security Agreements and Commitments Abroad, part 7, 9 June 1970, pp. 1848–54.
4 A. Papandreou, pp. 104–5.
5 Grigoriadis, I p. 18.
6 Text in Grigoriadis, III pp. 53–6.
7 A. Vlachos, p. 294.
8 A. Papandreou, p. 107.
9 Stern, pp. 92–3.
10 Kakaounakis, I p. 103.
11 Kakaounakis, I pp. 44, 125.
12 Trials/C, pp. 1188–244.
13 Kanellopoulos, pp. 29–30.
14 Grigoriadis, II p. 16, quoting Papaterpos in *Vima*, 25 May 1975.
15 Kanellopoulos, pp. 38–9.
16 A. Papandreou, p. 6.
17 A. Papandreou, pp. 189–93. The most prominent 'disaffected member' of the junta was Colonel D. Stamatelopoulos, but he was not 'living abroad' in 1969.
18 Grigoriadis, I p. 21.
19 Grigoriadis, I pp. 15, 20, quoting Garouphalias in *Acropolis*, 22 September 1974.
20 A. Papandreou, p. 115.
21 A. Papandreou, p. 120.
22 Text of the correspondence in Trials/A, pp. 1727–36; extracts in A. Papandreou, pp. 126–43.
23 Grigoriadis, I p. 25.
24 Grigoriadis, I p. 27.
25 N. Kranidiotis, in *Hellenic Review of International Relations*, 2, II, 1981–2, pp. 454–5.
26 Mayes, pp. 183–4.
27 Rousseas, pp. 227–68, gives the investigators' report on the accused politicians, in an imperfect English translation; extracts in A. Papandreou, pp. 156–7. Kakaounakis, I pp. 64–5, gives the investigators' report on the accused officers.
28 Woodhouse, pp. 180–1.
29 Grigoriadis, II pp. 10–13. Kanellopoulos revealed the details, apart from Papandreou's unilateral undertaking, in 1975: Trials/A, p. 69; Kanellopoulos, pp. 98–102.
30 Differing accounts of this episode are given in Kanellopoulos, pp. 137–9; A. Papandreou, pp. 179–80.
31 A. Papandreou, p. 164; Trials/A, p. 486.
32 A. Papandreou, p. 188.
33 Kanellopoulos, pp. 158, 179–80.
34 A. Papandreou, pp. 178–9.
35 Woodhouse, p. 180.
36 Grigoriadis, II pp. 22–3.
37 Woodhouse, p. 183.

2 Coup d'état or revolution?

1 Rousseas, p. 57, for example. Grigoriadis, II p. 23, dismisses the allegation.
2 Grigoriadis, I pp. 26, 47.
3 Grigoriadis, I pp. 24–5; Kakaounakis, I p. 77.
4 Grigoriadis, I p. 50; Kakaounakis, I pp. 80–1; Trials/A, pp. 324–48.
5 Trials/A, pp. 1075–6.
6 Trials/A, pp. 1050, 1063; Grigoriadis, I pp. 59–60; II p. 19. The latter's account derives substantially from interviews with Pattakos, parts of which were submitted in evidence to

the court in 1975: Trials/A, pp. 1275–300.

7 Trials/A, p. 1019 (Spandidakis); p. 1071 (Angelis); p. 1063 (Zoitakis).

8 Trials/A, p. 227.

9 Trials/A, pp. 878–84.

10 Trials/A, p. 346.

11 Trials/A, p. 1280.

12 Trials/A, pp. 1009–10.

13 Trials/A, p. 1077.

14 Trials/A, p. 218 (Papadatos): p. 1010 (Spandidakis).

15 Trials/A, p. 1044.

16 Trials/A, p. 185.

17 Trials/A, p. 232.

18 Trials/A, p. 218.

19 Trials/A, pp. 185–6.

20 Trials/A, p. 1057; supplemented by private information.

21 Trials/A, p. 186.

22 Trials/A, p. 1057.

23 Trials/A, pp. 1010–11.

24 Trials/A, pp. 1028–9.

25 Trials/A, pp. 1275–300; Grigoriadis, I pp. 55–62.

26 Trials/B, pp. 1266–7.

27 Grigoriadis, III p. 343, quoting interview with Senator Thomas Eagleton in *Acropolis*, 22 August 1975.

28 Kakaounakis, I p. 105.

29 Grigoriadis, I pp. 53–4.

30 Kakaounakis, I p. 204.

31 Grigoriadis, I pp. 57–9. The earliest version of the story was given to C. S. Sulzberger, of the *New York Times*, on 28 September 1969, by the retired Chief of the General Staff, Solon Ghikas, but published only five years later, in *Vima*, 4 August 1974.

32 Trials/A, p. 1063.

33 Trials/A, p. 1065.

34 Grigoriadis, I pp. 59–60.

35 Trials/A, p. 1045.

36 Kakaounakis, I pp. 98–100.

37 Grigoriadis, I p. 60.

38 Kakaounakis, I p. 185.

39 Grigoriadis, II p. 26.

40 H. Vlachos, pp. 41–2.

41 A. Papandreou, p. 189.

42 The following account is based on Grigoriadis, I pp. 63–99.

43 Grigoriadis, I p. 66.

44 Grigoriadis, I p. 83; Spandidakis' version of Pattakos' words was slightly different: Trials/A, p. 1014.

45 Trials/A, p. 502.

46 Grigoriadis, I pp. 79–80.

47 Trials/A, pp. 157–68; Grigoriadis, II pp. 21–2.

48 Trials/A, pp. 85, 428–9, 456–76, 1014.

49 Trials/A, p. 172.

50 Text in Grigoriadis, I pp. 85–6.

51 Trials/A, p. 1014.

52 Trials/A, p. 1015.

53 Trials/A, pp. 106–10.

54 Grigoriadis, I p. 87.

55 The King's version was given to C. S. Sulzberger, of the *New York Times*, on 3 May 1967, and published in *Vima* on 4 August 1974; Kanellopoulos' version in a letter to *Vima*, published on 6 August 1974. Grigoriadis, I pp. 88–93, gives extracts from both accounts.

56 Grigoriadis, I p. 93.

57 Stern, pp. 11–13 and 18–19, summarizes the evidence, which is inconclusive.

58 A. Papandreou, p. 192.

59 Text in Stern, p. 43.

60 Stern, pp. 37–9.

61 Stern, pp. 49–50.

62 A. Papandreou, pp. 192–3.

63 Katris, p. 40.

64 H. Vlachos, p. 32.

65 French translation in *Le Monde*, 22 April 1967; reprinted in Sartre, pp. 235–6.

66 Grigoriadis, I pp. 97–8.

67 Grigoriadis, I pp. 103–4.

68 Woodhouse, pp. 184–5.

69 R. Clogg, in Clogg and Yannopoulos, pp. 36–54.

70 *Vima*, 29 August 1971.

71 Yiorgalas, p. 5.

3 Resistance and reaction

1 Grigoriadis, I p. 108.

2 R. Clogg, in Clogg and Yannopoulos, pp. 38–9.
3 Grigoriadis, I pp. 109–10.
4 Grigoriadis, I p. 366, quotes the first use of the phrase on 29 March 1968.
5 Grigoriadis, I pp. 126–7.
6 Grigoriadis, I p. 113, quoting Mrs Vlachos' statement on 25 April 1967.
7 G. Yannopoulos, in Clogg and Yannopoulos, pp. 178–84, where more than twenty organizations were listed.
8 Text in Grigoriadis, I pp. 224–6.
9 R. Clogg, in Clogg and Yannopoulos, pp. 42–5.
10 Text in Grigoriadis, II pp. 213–14.
11 Text in SDB, 56, pp. 750–1; and in A. Papandreou, pp. 200–1.
12 Text in Grigoriadis, I pp. 334–5.
13 SFRC, Hearings before Subcommittee on US Security Agreements and Commitments Abroad, part 7, 9 June 1970, pp. 1841–2.
14 The Times, 5 May 1969.
15 Grigoriadis, I p. 133.
16 Grigoriadis, I p. 134.
17 N. Kranidiotis, in Hellenic Review of International Relations, 2, II, 1981–2, pp. 454–6; Grigoriadis, I pp. 136–8.
18 SDB, 57, p. 859.
19 Tsakalotos, pp. 233–5.
20 A. Papandreou, p. 217.
21 Woodhouse, pp. 185–9.
22 Text in A. Papandreou, pp. 219–24.
23 Grigoriadis, I p. 156.
24 Text in Grigoriadis, I pp. 160–1.
25 Text in Grigoriadis, I pp. 165–7.
26 Stern, p. 55.
27 Text in Grigoriadis, I p. 160.
28 Grigoriadis, I pp. 182–3.
29 Grigoriadis, I pp. 187–9.
30 Grigoriadis, I pp. 193–4.
31 Xanthopoulos-Palamas, p. 208.

4 The monstrous regiment

1 A. Papandreou, pp. 240–56.
2 J. Pesmazoglou, in Clogg and Yannopoulos, p. 77.
3 A. Papandreou, p. 246.
4 Grigoriadis, I p. 292.
5 Statement of the aims of PAK in A. Papandreou, pp. 322–4.
6 Text in Grigoriadis, I. pp. 231–2.
7 H. Vlachos, in Clogg and Yannopoulos, p. 65; Grigoriadis, I pp. 360–2.
8 HC Deb. 5s. vol. 762, col. 1662, 11 April 1968.
9 Extracts in A. Papandreou, pp. 270–3, 280–5, 290–4; and in Grigoriadis, I pp. 327–8.
10 HC Deb. 5s. vol. 767, col. 241, 25 June 1968.
11 HC Deb. 5s. vol. 767, col. 1500, 3 July 1968.
12 A. Papandreou, pp. 304–7.
13 Grigoriadis, I p. 246.
14 SDB, 58, p. 610.
15 Grigoriadis, I p. 241.
16 Grigoriadis, I pp. 243–52.
17 Kakaounakis, I pp. 276–7.
18 Grigoriadis, I pp. 234–6, and partial facsimile on pp. 237–8.
19 Kakaounakis, I pp. 268–9.
20 Kakaounakis, I p. 270.
21 Analyses of the Constitution in Grigoriadis, I pp. 217–21, and in Demichel, pp. 189–202.
22 A. Papandreou, pp. 274–8.
23 Demichel, p. 200.
24 Grigoriadis, II pp. 75–86.
25 Trials/C, pp. 322–9, and passim.
26 Grigoriadis, II pp. 321–2.
27 Grigoriadis, I pp. 328–32.
28 SFRC, Hearings before Subcommittee on US Security Agreements and Commitments Abroad, part 7, 9 June 1970, p. 1845.
29 Grigoriadis, I pp. 363–4; Woodhouse, p. 190.
30 Analysis of the 15-year plan in Nikolakos, pp. 167–9.
31 J. Pesmazoglou, in Clogg and Yannopoulos, pp. 98–9.
32 J. Pesmazoglou, in Clogg and Yannopoulos, pp. 75–96.
33 Grigoriadis, III pp. 315–20.
34 R. Clogg, in Clogg and Yannopoulos, p. 54.

35 R. Clogg, in Clogg and Yannopoulos, pp. 41–2.
36 Grigoriadis, II pp. 88–101.
37 Grigoriadis, I pp. 316–22.
38 Grigoriadis, I p. 358.

5 Onward, Christian soldiers!

1 Grigoriadis, II p. 50.
2 Woodhouse, pp. 190–1.
3 M. Goldbloom, in Clogg and Yannopoulos, pp. 246–7.
4 SDB, 60, p. 573.
5 Stern, p. 59.
6 Woodhouse, p. 191.
7 Woodhouse, p. 192.
8 R. Roufos, in Clogg and Yannopoulos, p. 159.
9 Information from Peter Thompson (Secretary, EAACG).
10 HC Deb. 5s. vol. 793, col. 1139, 16 December 1969.
11 Text in Grigoriadis, II pp. 92–6.
12 H. Vlachos, in Clogg and Yannopoulos, p. 67.
13 Text in Grigoriadis, II pp. 50–2.
14 Panayiotakos, pp. 305–6.
15 Grigoriadis, II p. 52.
16 Woodhouse, pp. 192–3; text in Grigoriadis, II pp. 53–5.
17 Stern, p. 62.
18 SFRC, Report on Foreign Assistance Act of 1969, 10 December 1969.
19 CRS, vol. 115, part 29, p. 38717, 12 December 1969.
20 For names in both categories, see Stern, pp. 139–40.
21 The effect of the separation of powers on US policy towards Greece is examined by John Brademas in *Hellenic Review of International Relations*, 2, II, 1981–2, pp. 355–66.
22 Grigoriadis, II p. 45.
23 Grigoriadis, II pp. 74–5.
24 Grigoriadis, II p. 45.
25 Grigoriadis, II p. 58.
26 Grigoriadis, II pp. 59–61.

6 A new era

1 Summary in Woodhouse, p. 194.
2 Grigoriadis, II pp. 115–16.

3 Grigoriadis, II pp. 124–5.
4 H. Vlachos, in Clogg and Yannopoulos, pp. 70–1.
5 Grigoriadis, II pp. 146–9.
6 HC Deb. 5s. vol. 793, col. 1139, 11 December 1969.
7 Grigoriadis, II p. 159.
8 Grigoriadis, II p. 295.
9 HFAC, Hearings on Foreign Military Sales Act, pp. 43–75, 17 February 1970.
10 HFAC, Hearings on Foreign Assistance and Related Agencies Appropriations for 1971, part 1, pp. 303–550; part 2, pp. 560–75.
11 SFRC, Hearings on US Security Agreements and Commitments Abroad, part 7, 9–11 June 1970, pp. 1769–880.
12 SFRC, ibid., 9 June 1970, p. 1782.
13 CRS, vol. 116, part 16, pp. 21995–22016, 29 June 1970.
14 Grigoriadis, II pp. 161–2.
15 Text in Grigoriadis, II pp. 165–6; also in Kakaounakis, I pp. 328–31.
16 Text in Grigoriadis, II p. 164.
17 Grigoriadis, II p. 167.
18 SDB, 63, p. 413.
19 SDB, 62, p. 678.
20 Stern, p. 68.
21 SDB, 63, p. 413.
22 SDB, 63, p. 688.
23 SASC, *Naval Vessel Loans*, pp. 1–37, 20 August 1970; Senate Report 91–1349, 19 November 1970.
24 Grigoriadis, II pp. 334–6.
25 Grigoriadis, II p. 336.
26 Grigoriadis, II p. 169.
27 Grigoriadis, II pp. 170–1.

7 The American commitment

1 Extracts in Grigoriadis, II p. 300.
2 Both versions, with correspondence, in CRS, vol. 117, part 25, pp. 32615–17, 21 September 1971.
3 SFRC, *Greece, February 1971*; Staff Report, 4 March 1971.
4 SDB, 64, p. 295.
5 SDB, 64, p. 447.

6 M. Goldbloom, in Clogg and Yannopoulos, pp. 251–2.
7 Grigoriadis, II p. 175.
8 Grigoriadis, II p. 176.
9 Xanthopoulos-Palamas, pp. 280–1.
10 HFAC, Hearings on Foreign Assistance and Related Agencies Appropriations for 1972, part 1, pp. 1–245,
24–25 March 1971; Hearings on
Foreign Assistance Act of 1971, part
3, pp. 515–53, 2 June 1971.
11 HFAC, Greece, Spain and Southern
NATO Strategy; Hearings before
Subcommittee on Europe, 12 July–15
September 1971; extracts in SDB, 65,
pp. 161–3.
12 SDB, 65, p. 205.
13 CRH, vol. 117, part 22, pp.
29110–11, and p. 29137, 3 August
1971.
14 SFRC, Foreign Assistance Legislation, FY 72, pp. 216–29.
15 CRS, vol. 117, part 29, p. 38283,
29 October 1971.
16 SDB, 66, p. 577.
17 Grigoriadis, II p. 186.
18 Trials/C, pp. 153–66.
19 Information from Peter Thompson
(Secretary, EAACG).
20 Grigoriadis, II p. 128; text in
Panayiotakos, pp. 345–6.
21 Grigoriadis, II p. 129; text in
Panayiotakos, pp. 347–9.
22 Text in Panayiotakos, pp. 326–7.
23 Text in Panayiotakos, pp. 328–30.
See also Mayes, p. 215; Kranidiotis in
Hellenic Review of International Relations, 2, II, 1981–2, p. 458.
24 Grigoriadis, II pp. 180–2.
25 Grigoriadis, II p. 185.

8 Towards a home port

1 R. Roufos, in Clogg and Yannopoulos, p. 159; The Times, 16
November 1971.
2 Information from Peter Thompson
(Secretary, EAACG).
3 Kranidiotis, in Hellenic Review of
International Relations, 2, II, 1981–2,
p. 458; text in Panayiotakos, pp.

355–6; also in Grigoriadis, II pp.
132–3.
4 Panayiotakos, pp. 358–61.
5 Grigoriadis, II p. 133; Mayes, p. 217;
Panayiotakos, p. 362.
6 Grigoriadis, II pp. 134–6.
7 Panayiotakos, pp. 150–1, 422–6.
8 Panayiotakos, pp. 363–4; Grigoriadis, II pp. 138–9.
9 Markezinis, pp. 80–2.
10 Grigoriadis, II pp. 200–1.
11 Xanthopoulos-Palamas, pp. 284–5.
12 HASC, Hearings before Special
Subcommittee on NATO Commitments, pp. 13430–44, 12 January
1972.
13 HFAC, Political and Strategic Implications of Homeporting in Greece; Hearings before Subcommittee on Europe
and Subcommittee on the Near East,
7 March–18 April 1972.
14 SDB, 66, pp. 549–51.
15 SFRC, Hearings on Department of
State Appropriations Authorization,
pp. 181–201, 9 March 1972; HFAC,
Hearings on Foreign Assistance Act
of 1972, part 1, pp. 85–102, 20 March
1972.
16 HFAC, Report No. 92–1273, on
H.R. 16029, to amend the Foreign
Assistance Act of 1961 and for other
purposes, 1 August 1972.
17 CRH, E. 5598–9, 22 May 1972.
18 HFAC, Delinquent International Debts
owed by Selected Countries, pp. 113–38,
5 December 1972.
19 Grigoriadis, II p. 191.
20 Grigoriadis, II pp. 177–8.
21 Grigoriadis, II pp. 304–6.
22 Grigoriadis, II p. 155.
23 Xanthopoulos-Palamas, p. 283.
24 HFAC, Decision to Homeport in Greece;
Report of Subcommittees on Europe
and the Near East, with minority and
additional views, 31 December 1972.

9 Turn of the tide

1 New York Times, 9 January 1973.
2 Grigoriadis, III pp. 67–8.

3 Text in Grigoriadis, II pp. 221–3.
4 Text in Grigoriadis, II pp. 217–19.
5 Text in Grigoriadis, II pp. 219–21.
6 Text in Grigoriadis, II pp. 224–9.
7 Woodhouse, p. 198.
8 Trials/C, pp. 264–83.
9 Grigoriadis, II p. 230.
10 Grigoriadis, II p. 262.
11 EAACG Bulletin No. 7, 3 July 1973, p. 5.
12 CRS, vol. 119, part 17, pp. 21146–51, 25 June 1973.
13 HFAC, *Implementation of Homeporting in Greece*; Hearings before the Sub-committee on Europe, 16–30 July 1973; preface by Chairman, pp. v–vii; evidence of Admiral Zumwalt, 19 July, pp. 51–112; evidence of Rodger Davies, 30 July, pp. 113–49.
14 SDB, 69, pp. 56, 346.
15 Grigoriadis, III pp. 14–15.
16 Texts of the two decrees in Grigoriadis, III pp. 15–16.
17 Grigoriadis, III pp. 15–16.
18 Grigoriadis. III pp. 18–20.
19 Markezinis, pp. 175–211.
20 Markezinis, pp. 263–8.
21 Text in Grigoriadis, III pp. 26–7; partial facsimile, p. 29.
22 Markezinis, pp. 326–37.
23 Grigoriadis, III pp. 57–63; Panayiotakos, p. 335.
24 Text in Grigoriadis, III pp. 53–6.
25 Grigoriadis, III pp. 64–5; text in Panayiotakos, pp. 336–8.
26 Grigoriadis, III pp. 65–6.
27 Grigoriadis, III p. 45.
28 Kissinger, pp. 708–9.
29 Grigoriadis, III p. 47.
30 Markezinis, pp. 463–8.
31 SDB, 70, pp. 279–84.
32 Markezinis, pp. 329–33.
33 Trials/B, p. 186.

10 The students' revolt

1 Trials/B, p. 1251.
2 Grigoriadis, II p. 43.
3 Trials/B, p. 15.
4 Trials/B, pp. 17–18; Kavvadias, p. 16.
5 Trials/B, pp. 21–2; Kavvadias, pp. 18–20.
6 Trials/B, p. 22; Kavvadias, p. 21.
7 Grigoriadis, II pp. 214–15.
8 Trials/B, pp. 454–5.
9 Grigoriadis, II p. 215.
10 Text of the Senate's request to the police in Grigoriadis, II p. 317; also in Kavvadias, pp. 24–6.
11 Kakaounakis, II pp. 26–7; denial by General Khazapis in Trials/B, p. 209.
12 Kavvadias, p. 29.
13 Markezinis, p. 415.
14 Markezinis, pp. 387, 391.
15 Trials/B, p. 34; Kavvadias, pp. 32–4; Kakaounakis, II p. 15; Grigoriadis, III p. 75. It is impossible to reconcile the dates and times given by the various sources. I have relied in the main on the reports of the Polytechnic trial (Trials/B), supplemented by other sources where the evidence given in court is incomplete.
16 Trials/B, pp. 285, 428, 437, 837, 1043–4.
17 Trials/B, pp. 405–6, 1204.
18 Trials/B, pp. 34, 1199.
19 Trials/B, p. 380.
20 Trials/B, p. 318.
21 Trials/B, pp. 272–4.
22 Trials/B, p. 404; Markezinis, p. 422.
23 Kavvadias, p. 35.
24 Trials/B, p. 313.
25 Trials/B, pp. 272–3.
26 Trials/B, pp. 959–60. Kanellopoulos at first mistakenly dated this visit to the previous night: Trials/B, pp. 205–7.
27 Markezinis, p. 416.
28 Trials/B, pp. 393–4.
29 Trials/B, p. 440.
30 Trials/B, p. 962.
31 Markezinis, pp. 417–18.
32 Trials/B, p. 192; Markezinis, p. 418.
33 Trials/B, p. 1217.
34 Trials/B, p. 752.
35 Grigoriadis, III p. 117.
36 Trials/B, p. 200.
37 Trials/B, pp. 1067–8.
38 Trials/B, pp. 1107, 1112, 1116, 1154, 1158, 1160, 1180.

39 Trials/B, pp. 715, 724, 943, 1080, 1176.
40 Trials/B, pp. 1121, 1223.
41 Trials/B, p. 405.
42 Trials/B, p. 343.
43 Trials/B, p. 401.
44 Trials/B, pp. 433, 440.
45 Trials/B, p. 647.
46 Markezinis, p. 424.
47 Trials/B, p. 1094; text and facsimile in Kakaounakis, II pp. 35–7.
48 Trials/B, p. 1138.
49 Trials/B, p. 464.
50 Trials/B, pp. 585–957, 1074–100.
51 Trials/B, p. 962.
52 Trials/B, pp. 1043–5.
53 Trials/B, p. 1223.
54 Trials/B, p. 1167.
55 Trials/B, pp. 37, 279, 408, 461, 499, 604, 965, 1161–5; Grigoriadis, III pp. 101–5.
56 Trials/B, p. 398.
57 Trials/B, p. 405.
58 Trials/B, p. 1165.
59 Kavvadias, p. 131; and other publications.
60 Text of the final broadcasts in Kavvadias, pp. 145–83.
61 Trials/B, p. 962.
62 Trials/B, p. 699.
63 Trials/B, pp. 351–4.
64 Trials/B, p. 756.
65 Trials/B, pp. 357–9.
66 Trials/B, p. 405.
67 Trials/B, p. 338.
68 Trials/B, p. 1014; Grigoriadis, III p. 105.
69 Trials/B, p. 437.
70 Trials/B, p. 1227.
71 Trials/B, pp. 192–5; Markezinis, pp. 426–8.
72 Markezinis, p. 426; Kavvadias, pp. 74–82.
73 Grigoriadis, III pp. 109–10.
74 Trials/B, pp. 1129, 1231.
75 Trials/B, frontispiece (page unnumbered).
76 Trials/A, p. 978.
77 Trials/B, p. 194; Markezinis, pp. 443, 450–8; Grigoriadis, III pp. 110–11.
78 Trials/B, p. 1312; Markezinis, p. 452; Grigoriadis, III p. 112.
79 Markezinis, p. 454.
80 Trials/B, p. 193; Markezinis, p. 455.
81 Grigoriadis, III p. 119.
82 Trials/B, pp. 196–7; Markezinis, pp. 479–81.
83 Information from Peter Thompson (Secretary, EAACG).
84 Markezinis, p. 473.

11 Down a steep place

1 Trials/B, pp. 1238–42 (Ioannidis); p. 202 (Gizikis); Grigoriadis, III pp. 114–15.
2 Trials/B, p. 202 (Gizikis); p. 209 (Khazapis).
3 Trials/B, pp. 203–4; Markezinis, p. 394; Kakaounakis, II pp. 91, 101–2.
4 Markezinis, pp. 465–6.
5 Markezinis, pp. 474–82.
6 Markezinis, pp. 486–7.
7 Grigoriadis, III p. 126.
8 Kakaounakis, II p. 48.
9 Markezinis, p. 490.
10 Grigoriadis, III p. 128.
11 Vima, 8 March 1975.
12 New York Times, 12 September 1975.
13 New York Times, 27 November 1973.
14 House Report 93–664, 27 November 1973.
15 CRS, vol. 119, part 17, pp. 21146–51, 25 June 1973.
16 Information from Peter Thompson (Secretary, EAACG).
17 SFRC, Subcommittee on European Affairs, 5 December 1973.
18 Senate Report 93–622, Restrictions on Military Assistance to Greece, 20 December 1973.
19 CRS, vol. 120, part 1, p. 513, 23 January 1974.
20 HFAC, Controlling Damage: US Policy Options for Greece; Report of a study mission to Greece, 18–21 January 1974.
21 HFAC, US–Europe Relations and the 1973 Middle East War; Joint Hearings before the Subcommittee on Europe and the Subcommittee on the Near

East and South Asia, 1 November 1973–19 February 1974, pp. 30–59. See also SDB, 70, pp. 279–84.

22 HFAC, *Testimony of John Zighdis on American Policy towards Greece*; Hearing before Subcommittee on Europe, 27 March 1974.

23 EAACG Bulletin No. 9, 6 July 1974.

24 CRH, vol. 120, part 8, pp. 10667–71, 10 April 1974.

25 House Report 12004, 7 July–1 August 1974.

26 Stern, p. 95.

27 Grigoriadis, III pp. 257–8.

28 Panayiotakos, pp. 371–4.

29 Xanthopoulos-Palamas, p. 207.

30 Mayes, p. 239.

31 Stern, p. 95.

32 Grigoriadis, III p. 160.

33 Kissinger, pp. 1063–5.

34 Stern, pp. 100–1.

35 Grigoriadis, III p. 178.

36 Markezinis, pp. 546–7.

37 Woodhouse, p. 205.

38 Text in Grigoriadis, III pp. 169–73; English summary in Mayes, pp. 234–5.

39 Text in Kakaounakis, II pp. 260–6.

40 Grigoriadis, III p. 168; Kakaounakis, II p. 257. Grigoriadis mentions only the second meeting, at which the attendance was exclusively military.

41 Kakaounakis, II p. 268.

42 Mayes, p. 236.

43 Theodorakopoulos, p. 33.

44 Markezinis, p. 548.

45 Grigoriadis, III p. 177; Kakaounakis, II p. 270; Markezinis, p. 549. There are discrepancies between the sources on this meeting. Grigoriadis has Bonanos (not Gizikis) in the chair. He and Kakaounakis disagree with Markezinis in omitting the presence of Ministers. Grigoriadis further disagrees with Theodorakopoulos (n. 43) in stating that this was the first time the Chiefs of the Navy and Air Force Staffs learned of the plot against Makarios. The discrepancies cannot be reconciled, but it seems likely that there were two meetings on this day (as on 2 July), one including Ministers and one limited to service chiefs.

46 Grigoriadis, III p. 177.

47 Grigoriadis, III p. 182.

48 Mayes, p. 243.

49 *Cyprus* (Cmnd 1093, HMSO, London, July 1960), p. 87.

50 See D. S. Constantopoulos, in *Hellenic Review of International Relations*, 2, II, 1981–2, pp. 485–530, for a study of the legal aspects of the crisis over Cyprus.

51 Kissinger, p. 1190.

52 Kissinger, p. 1191.

53 English text in Panayiotakos, pp. 385–91.

54 Kakaounakis, II p. 294.

55 Grigoriadis, III p. 246.

56 Kakaounakis, II p. 302.

57 CRS, vol. 120, part 20, pp. 25915 17.

58 Grigoriadis, III p. 222.

59 Kakaounakis, II p. 329.

60 Grigoriadis, III pp. 237–8.

61 For Arapakis' personal account, see Grigoriadis, III pp. 239–42.

62 Kissinger, p. 1192.

63 SDB, 71, p. 258.

64 SDB, 71, p. 259.

65 SDB, 71, p. 261.

66 SDB, 71, p. 260.

67 SDB, 71, p. 356.

68 SDB, 71, p. 630.

69 Kakaounakis, II pp. 340–1.

70 Kakaounakis, II p. 334.

12 Yesterday's men

1 Grigoriadis, III pp. 260–2.

2 SDB, 71, p. 258.

3 Grigoriadis, III pp. 262–4.

4 Grigoriadis, III pp. 265–6.

5 Grigoriadis, III pp. 267–8.

6 Grigoriadis, III p. 266.

7 Grigoriadis, III pp. 264–5.

8 Markezinis, p. 561.

9 Title of Kakaounakis' book.

10 Grigoriadis, III pp. 303, 333.

11 Grigoriadis, III pp. 320–2.

12 Markezinis, pp. 561–2.

13 Grigoriadis, III p. 275.
14 Markezinis, pp. 562, 567; Xantho-poulos-Palamas, pp. 179–80; Grigori-adis, III pp. 278–81.
15 Grigoriadis, III pp. 278–9, 282–3.
16 Markezinis, p. 567.
17 Grigoriadis, III pp. 275–8; Mar-kezinis, pp. 569–70.
18 Grigoriadis, III pp. 283–4.
19 Grigoriadis, III pp. 285–6.
20 Markezinis, pp. 571–4.
21 Grigoriadis, III pp. 287–8.
22 Title of Stavros Psycharis' book, based on information from Karaman-lis and Averoff.
23 Woodhouse, p. 213.
24 Psycharis, p. 111.
25 Trials/A, pp. 1431–3.
26 Woodhouse, p. 216.
27 Woodhouse, p. 218.
28 For the trials of the torturers, see Trials/C, pp. 89–773 (Army and Military Police); pp. 777–1182 (Polytechnic cases); pp. 1188–244 (Navy); pp. 1251–557 (Security Ser-vice).
29 Woodhouse, pp. 233–4.
30 House Select Committee on Intelli-gence Agencies and Activities; Pro-ceedings, part 4, 9 September–11 November 1975; Appendix, pp. 1507–10.
31 House Select Committee on Intelli-gence Agencies and Activities; Pro-ceedings, part 2, 11 September–31 October 1975.
32 For examples, see Grigoriadis, III pp. 251–7; Kakaounakis, II pp. 334–41.

Bibliography

I – Official, Parliamentary and Congressional publications
Council of Europe: *The Greek Case*; Report of the European Commission on Human Rights (4 vols., Strasbourg 1969)
Council of Europe: *The Situation in Greece*; Report of the Committee on European Non-Member Countries (Strasbourg 1974)
Greece, Royal Ministry of Foreign Affairs: *The Greek Case before the Commission on Human Rights of the Council of Europe* (Athens 1970)
HFAC: *Greece, Spain and Southern NATO Strategy* (Washington 1971)
HFAC: *Political and Strategic Implications of Homeporting in Greece* (Washington 1972)
HFAC: *Delinquent International Debts owed by Selected Countries* (Washington 1972)
HFAC: *Decision to Homeport in Greece* (Washington 1972)
HFAC: *Implementation of Homeporting in Greece* (Washington 1973)
HFAC: *Controlling Damage: US Policy Options for Greece* (Washington 1974)
HFAC: *US–Europe Relations and the 1973 Middle East War* (Washington 1974)
HIRC: *Cyprus 1974* (Washington 1974)
HMSO: *Cyprus* (Cmnd 1093, London 1960)
HMSO: *Report from the Select Committee on Cyprus* (London 1960)
SASC: *Naval Vessel Loans* (Washington 1970)
SFRC: *Greece, February 1971*; Staff Report (Washington 1971)
SFRC: *Restrictions on Military Assistance to Greece* (Washington 1973)

II (a) – Contemporary witnesses
Amalia Fleming, *A Piece of Truth* (London 1972)
Panayiotis Kanellopoulos, *Istorika dokimia* (Athens 1975)
Yiannis Katris, *Eyewitness in Greece: the Colonels Come to Power* (St Louis, Missouri 1971)
George A. Mangakis, *Elevtheria agapi mou* (Frankfurt-am-Main 1971)
Melina Mercouri, *I Was Born Greek* (London 1971)
A. Minis, *111 meres stin ESA* (Athens 1973)
Andreas Papandreou, *Democracy at Gunpoint: The Greek Front* (New York 1970)
Margaret Papandreou, *Nightmare in Athens* (New Jersey 1970)
I. S. Pesmazoglou, *Agonistika* (2 vols., Athens 1974, 1981)

George Rallis, *I Alitheia gia tous Ellines politikous* (Athens 1971)
Stephen Rousseas, *The Death of a Democracy: Greece and the American Conscience* (New York 1967)
George Seferis, *The Land within a Wall* (Montreal 1969)
M. Theodorakis, *Journals of Resistance* (London 1973)
Th. Tsakalotos, *I machi ton oligon* (Athens 1971)
Helen Vlachos, *House Arrest* (London 1971)

II (b) – Contemporary apologists
David Holden, *Greece without Columns* (London 1972)
G. Papadopoulos, *To Pistevo mas* (7 vols., Athens 1968–72)
Th. Papakonstantinou, *Politiki Agogi* (Athens 1970)
G. Yiorgalas, *I Ideologia tis Epanastaseos* (Athens 1971)
Kenneth Young, *The Greek Passion* (London 1969)

II (c) – Contemporary investigations
Athènes-presse libre: *Le Livre noir de la dictature en Grèce* (Paris 1969)
Mario Cervi, *Dove va la Grecia?* (Milan 1968)
Richard Clogg and George Yannopoulos (eds.), *Greece under Military Rule* (London 1972)
André and Francine Demichel, *Les dictatures européennes* (Paris 1973)
Jean Meynaud, *Rapport sur l'abolition de la démocratie en Grèce* (Montreal 1967)
J-P. Sartre (ed.), *Aujourd'hui la Grèce* (Paris 1969)
Philip Williams, *Athens under the Spartans* (London 1967)

III – Post-dictatorship
Oriana Fallaci, *A Man* (London 1982)
Solon Grigoriadis, *Istoria tis Diktatorias* (3 vols., Athens 1975)
Christopher Hitchens, *Cyprus* (London 1984)
N. Kakaounakis, *2650 meronychta synomosias* (2 vols., Athens 1976)
Ph. Kavvadias, *Edo Polytechneio ... Edo Polytechneio ...* (Athens 1974)
Henry Kissinger, *Years of Upheaval* (London 1982)
Ch. Korizis, *To avtarchiko kathestos 1967–1974* (Athens 1975)
Sp. Markezinis, *Anamniseis 1972–1974* (Athens 1979)
Stanley Mayes, *Makarios: A Biography* (London 1981)
Marios Nikolakos, *Antistasi kai antipolitevsi 1967–1974* (Athens 1975)
K. P. Panayiotakos, *Stin proti grammi amynis* (Athens 1979)
Stavros P. Psycharis, *Oi 70 krisimes imeres* (Athens 1976)
P. Rodakis, *Oi dikes tis khountas*:
   Trials/A: *I diki ton protaition* (4 vols., Athens 1975)
   Trials/B: *I diki tou Polytechneiou* (5 vols., Athens 1976)
   Trials/C: *Ai dikes ton vasaniston tis eptaetias* (3 vols., Athens 1976)

BIBLIOGRAPHY

Laurence Stern, *The Wrong Horse: The Politics of Intervention and the Failure of American Diplomacy* (New York 1977)

T. Theodorakopoulos, *The Greek Upheaval: Kings, Demagogues and Bayonets* (London 1976)

A. Vlachos, *Deka chronia tou Kypriakou* (Athens 1980)

C. M. Woodhouse, *Karamanlis: the Restorer of Greek Democracy* (Oxford 1982)

Ch. Xanthopoulos-Palamas, *Diplomatiko triptyeho* (Athens 1979)

187

Index

Acheson, Dean 4–5, 7
AEM ix, 38
Agnew, Spyro 57, 63, 94–6, 100
AHEPA 39
Ambatielos, Tony 1
Amnesty International 51, 62
Androutsopoulos, A. 48, 90, 144, 150–53, 156–8, 161–3
Angelis, O. x, 8, 16–18, 30, 45–8, 54
  Commander-in-Chief 60, 82, 102, 168
  Vice-President 120–21, 133, 143
  deposed 144
Anne-Marie, Queen 39, 44–5, 48
Anthimos, Bishop 5, 53, 75, 102
Antonakos, Air-Marshal 8, 19, 24, 30, 43, 45–6
Arapakis, Admiral 144, 153–4, 156–9, 161–5
Areopagus 26, 56
Arnaoutis, Major 24, 26
Aslanidis, C. 8, 21–2, 98, 119, 121
Asphaleia (Security Service) 38, 65, 138
ASPIDA ix, 5–6, 8, 10, 12–13, 33
Athanasiadis-Novas, G. x, 11, 163
Averoff-Tositsa, E. x, 35, 44, 55, 58, 91–2, 117–18, 120, 125, 151, 163–8

BBC 91
Bitsios, D. x, 13, 15, 24
Bonanos, General 144, 151–4, 156–7, 161–3, 165, 168
Brademas, John 93
Brillakis, A. x, 24, 36, 51, 125
Brosio, M. 52

Çağlayangil 41
Callaghan, James 149, 158, 161, 168
Carrington, Lord 83, 109
Castro, Fidel 155
Ceauşescu, President 142–3
Centre Union (EK) 2–4, 6–7, 11, 14, 51, 53, 58, 66, 96, 110, 147, 165

Chapman, Ann 100–1
Chrysostomos, Archbishop 27, 34
Church, Senator Frank 170
CIA 6–7, 9–10, 20, 23, 27–8, 94, 145–6, 148–50, 159–60, 169–72
Clerides, G. x, 53, 148–9
Colossus of Rhodes 60
Commission of Human Rights 39, 52, 57, 69, 76, 78
Constantine II, King x, 10–19, 23–31, 34–5, 39, 42, 43–8, 54
  in exile 49–50, 56–7, 63, 66, 69–70, 83, 85, 94–5, 112, 115–18, 128, 152, 161, 166
  deposed 117–19, 172
Council of Europe 39–40, 51–2, 56–7, 63, 67–72, 76, 78, 102, 147, 173
Council of State 14, 56, 65

DA ix, 38, 51, 65, 76, 90, 104
Davies, Rodger 80, 85, 92–3, 106, 119, 124, 146–7, 154, 168
Davos, General 144, 161
Dedes, Admiral 30, 43, 46–7
Defenders of Freedom 90
De Freitas, Sir Geoffrey 52
De Gaulle, President 1–2, 62
Demirel, S. x, 41
Denisis, General 153
Denktash, R. x, 4, 42, 53, 149, 171
Dertilis, Colonel 135–6, 139
Dimou, Tassos 38
Dovas, General 43–4
Drakopoulos, Ch. 96

EAACG ix, 91–2
EAM ix, 11
EAN ix, 113
Ecevit, Bülent x, 148–9, 151, 155–6
EDA ix, 2, 23, 33, 38, 57, 167
EDKA ix, 37
Edwards, Don 146

EEC ix, 40, 59, 113, 122, 158, 167, 173
EENA ix, 9
Eisenhower, President 63
EK *see* Centre Union
Elizabeth, Queen 2, 114
Ellsworth, Robert 155–6
Engolphopoulos, Admiral 19, 24, 30
EOKA ix, 4–5, 75, 149, 154–5
EOKA-B 75, 101–2, 114–15, 122–3,
    148–50, 152–3, 158
Ephesios, N. 122, 140
EPOK ix, 115–16
ERE ix, 2–3, 12–13, 24, 96, 110, 165
Erselman, Brigadier 43, 46–7
ESA ix, 21, 38, 54, 98, 112, 122, 133, 138,
    148, 162–3

Federation of Industry 59
Fleming, Lady (Amalia) x, 77–8, 95–6,
    100, 105, 121
Ford, President 145, 169–70
Fourth of August 61
Fraser, Donald 107, 147
Frederika, Queen x, 1–2, 26, 45, 60
Free Greeks 90
Fulbright, Senator 80, 87

Gaddafi, Colonel 22, 70, 84
Galatsanos, General 144, 153–4, 156–9,
    161–3, 168
Garouphalias, P. x, 10–11, 116, 165
George II, King 29
Ghikas, Solon 43, 70
Giscard d'Estaing, President 166
Gizikis, General 142–6, 151–4, 157,
    161–6
Glezos, M. 37, 91, 105
Goodpaster, General 92
Greene, Sir Hugh 91, 93
Grivas, General x, 4–7, 12, 42, 98, 101–3,
    114–15, 122–4, 148–9, 152
Gromyko, A. 151
GSEE (General Federation of Trade
    Unions) 35
Günes, Professor 150

Hartke, Senator 80
Hartman, A. 124, 147
Hays, Wayne 94, 105, 119
Heath, Edward 113–14

Hermes Plan 75–6
Hill-Norton, Sir Peter 114
Hitler 61
Humphrey, Senator 89

Iakovos, Archbishop 74
IDEA ix, 7–9
Ieronymos, Archbishop 27, 34, 42, 45,
    48, 51, 115, 144–5
Iliou, I. x, 10, 23, 33, 125, 170
International Press Institute 40
International Red Cross 62
Ioannidis, D. xi
    career and intrigues 7–9, 21–3
    in control of security 50, 54–5, 98, 103,
        122–3, 125, 133, 141–6, 148–58,
        161–3, 165–8, 170–71
    tried and sentenced 129, 169, 172–3
Iordanidis, General 65, 76

Johnson, President 4, 35, 42
JUSMAGG ix, 6–7, 20, 23, 28, 151

Kanellopoulos, Amalia (later Karaman-
    lis, Megapanos) 3, 132
Kanellopoulos, Panayiotis xi, 9
    Leader of Opposition 3, 12–14
    Prime Minister 14–15, 19, 23–4, 26–7,
        29
    resistance to dictatorship 33–6, 38, 43,
        58, 66–7, 70, 76, 87, 93–5, 119, 121,
        125, 139
    support for students 128–9, 132–3, 136
    post-dictatorship 163, 165–7
Karamanlis, Constantine xi
    Prime Minister (1955–63) 1–2, 6, 9,
        11, 30, 43
    living abroad (1963–74) 1–3, 12–13,
        15, 31, 43–4, 48–9, 56, 58, 63, 66–7,
        74, 78, 91, 94, 98, 117–21, 145,
        151–3, 164–6
    condemnation of dictatorship 44, 67,
        70–1, 116–17, 119
    return to office 114, 145, 166–73
Karayiorgas, Professor 65, 76
Kardamakis, General 9
Karousos, Major 148
KET ix, 21, 23
Khazapis, General 142

Kissinger, Henry 111, 123, 129, 146, 148, 151, 155, 158–61, 168–9, 171

KKE ix, 3, 19, 30, 33, 35–8, 46–7, 55, 77, 79, 87, 91, 96, 125, 130–32, 138, 142, 163, 167, 172

KKE (Interior) 36–7, 51, 58, 96, 167, 172

KNE ix, 58

Knox, John 49

Koliyiannis, K. 36–7

Kollias, Constantine xi, 13, 26–7, 29–31, 33, 41, 44–5, 48

Kollias, General 17–19, 43–8

Konophagos, Professor 130–33, 139

Konophaos, Admiral 117

Konstantopoulos, S. 37

Küchük, F. xi, 4

KYP ix, 6–7, 9, 11, 38, 133, 138, 144, 152

Kypraios, K. 151, 153, 157–9, 161

Kyprianou, Sp. xi, 97, 102

Ladas, I. 8, 21–2, 32, 41, 50, 54–5, 61, 82, 98, 119

Laird, Melvin 64, 80, 84, 92

Lambrakis, G. 2, 88, 100

Laskaris, General 17, 21

Liarakos, General 43, 45, 47–8

Livanos, D. 24

LOK (Commandos) ix, 21, 135

Louros, Professor 128

Lowenstein, J. 88–9

Luns, Dr 52, 118, 156

McGovern, Senator 107

Makarezos, N. xi
  career and intrigues 8, 11, 16, 20–23, 30
  seizure of power 23–7
  in office 44, 50, 55, 58–9, 98, 102–3, 114–15, 121
  tried and sentenced 169, 172–3

Makarios III, Archbishop xi
  President of Cyprus 4–7, 53, 96–7, 102–3, 114–15, 122–5, 148, 155, 159, 164, 170–71
  relations with General Grivas 6–7, 12, 98, 101–3, 114–15, 122–5, 148, 152
  relations with junta 41–2, 53–4, 57–8, 75–6, 81, 83, 96–7, 101–3, 114–15, 122–4, 127, 145, 148–56, 160

Manettas, General 17–18, 43, 45–6

Mangakis, G. A. xi, 38, 76, 104–5, 109, 114, 167

Mangakis, G. B. 38

Markezinis, Sp. xi, 3
  Prime Minister 119–22, 124–5, 130, 133, 135, 139–41, 143–4, 163–4

Mary, Queen of Scots 49

Mavros, George 44, 51, 66–7, 70, 93–5, 119, 125, 129, 136, 139, 149, 163–7, 169–70, 172–3

Mavroyenis, G. 57

Megapanos: see Kanellopoulos, Amalia

Mercouri, Melina xi, 38, 121

Metaxas, General 6, 29, 32, 61, 91, 99, 140

Metternich, Count 111

Mexis, A. 8, 41

Minis, Tasso 95

Mintoff, Dom 96

Mitsotakis, Costa 23, 121, 125

Moose, R. 88–9

Moustaklis, Major 113, 116–17

MSI (Italian Social Movement) 61

Mussolini 32, 44

Nasser, President 9, 22, 61, 70, 84

National Guard (Cyprus) 5, 42, 75–6, 101–2, 122–3, 149–50, 152–4, 157

National Resistance Council 90–91

NATO 5, 12, 39–42, 52, 61–2, 67–9, 76, 78, 80, 83–4, 87–8, 92, 96, 105, 109, 114, 116, 118, 140–41, 143, 146–7, 149–51, 156, 158, 171, 173

Nikolopoulos, General xi, 9

Nixon, President 63, 66, 70, 74–5, 84–5, 89, 94, 106–9, 111–12, 118–19, 123, 147, 155, 160

North Atlantic Assembly 40, 69, 92, 109

OECD (Organization for Economic Co-operation and Development) 62

Oikonomou-Gouras, P. 31, 41–2

Olivier, Laurence 114

Onassis, A. 77

Operation Thunderbolt (Keravnos, formerly Themis) 129

Opropoulos, D. 8, 30, 43, 50

PAK ix, 51, 90, 105

Palach, Jan 127

PAM ix, 38, 51, 90
Panagoulis, A. 53–5, 57, 75, 95, 100, 120, 127, 172
Panagoulis, G. 54
Panayiotakos, K. 68, 102
Panouryias, General 12, 16–17
Papadatos, General 17–18, 23–4
Papadongonas, Commander 117
Papadopoulos, Constantine 134, 136, 144
Papadopoulos, George xi
  career and intrigues 7–12, 16–17, 20–22, 30
  seizure of power 23–7, 33–5, 41, 53
  ideology 31–2, 35, 37, 54, 60–61, 72, 77, 86, 89–90, 96, 109, 115–16, 150
  Prime Minister 48–50, 53–6, 58, 60–65, 72, 76–9, 81–6, 89–91, 96–9, 100–18
  other offices 48, 81, 98, 104, 108, 121, 128
  dissension with colleagues 20, 22, 54–5, 60–61, 77, 79, 81–2, 85, 98–9, 103–4, 109–10, 112–13, 115, 119, 121–2, 125, 142–3
  Regent 103–4
  President 118 seq.
  relations with USA 49, 67, 74–7, 79–80, 82–5, 87–9, 92–4, 96, 100, 105–8, 111–12, 119, 124, 140–41, 146, 163
  relations with Cyprus 53, 57–8, 75–6, 81, 83, 97–8, 101–3, 114–15, 123–5, 127
  attitude to students 107–8, 113, 125–42
  deposition 142–6
  tried and sentenced 129, 142, 169, 172–3
Papagos, Field-Marshal xi, 2
Papakonstantinou, Th. 37
Papaligouras, P. xi, 19, 23
Papandandreou, Andreas xi
  Minister 4–7, 10, 13–14
  in opposition 23, 27–8
  under arrest 33–4, 37, 43, 50, 54, 64
  living abroad 9, 22, 50–51, 53, 56, 58, 63, 66–7, 93, 105, 119, 121, 125, 166–7
  return to politics 170, 172–3

Papandreou, George xi
  Prime Minister 5–7, 9–11
  in opposition 13–14, 28, 172
  under dictatorship 23, 33–4, 43–4, 51
  death and funeral 58, 66, 130
Papandreou, Margaret 6, 50, 93
Papanikolaou, Air-Marshal 144, 153, 156–7, 161–3
Papaspyrou, D. 79, 93, 106
Papaterpos, A. 8–9, 12, 33
Pappas, Commander 116–18
Pappas, Tom 31, 63, 77, 89, 94, 164
Paraskevopoulos, I. xii, 13–14
Partsalidis, D. 37, 96
PASOK (Panhellenic Socialist Party) 172
Pattakos, S. xii
  career and intrigues 9, 11–12, 16–17, 19–22
  seizure of power 23–7
  ideology 31, 50, 55, 61, 82, 85, 110, 115, 122
  in office 34, 48, 50, 54–5, 63–4, 72, 79, 81–2, 84–5, 90, 95, 98, 102–4, 110
  dismissed 121–2, 131
  tried and sentenced 169, 173
Paul, King xii, 1–3, 10
Pell, Senator 71, 118–19, 146–7
Pericles Plan 9, 12
Peridis, General 43–5, 47
Pesmazoglou, Professor John (Ioannis) xii, 40, 50, 105, 107, 128, 139, 167
Pike, Otis 170
Pipinelis, P. xii, 2, 81
  Foreign Minister 43, 48, 54, 63, 68–9, 72–3
'Pledge of the Nation' 60
Plevris, K. 61
Pranger, Robert 80
Progressive Party 3, 119
Prometheus Plan 12, 21, 25

Rallis, George xii, 23–5, 76, 106, 119
Rauti, P. 61
Reserve Corps (Tactical Reserve Police, Cyprus) 101–2, 115, 122–3, 154
Revolutionary Council 20, 22, 31, 55, 77, 79, 82, 113
Rhigas Pheraios 58, 126–7
Richardson, Elliot 64

Rogers, William 63, 70–71, 83, 88, 106, 120

Rosenthal, Benjamin 92

Rouphogalis, M. 8, 21, 82, 129

Royal National Foundation 60

Rozakis, Admiral 24, 47–8, 117

Rush, Kenneth 120

Rusk, Dean 39, 49

Sadat, Anwar 84

Sakellaridis, Professor 133, 138

Sampson, N. 148–9, 154–5, 170

Schlesinger, James 155

Sepheris, George 67, 78

Serapheim, Archbishop 144–5, 163

Servan-Schreiber, J. 77–8

Siphnaios, P. 130–32

Sisco, Joseph 88, 106, 155–6, 158, 161

Soares, Mario 147

Spandidakis, General xii, 11–12, 16–21, 23–7, 30, 41–2, 48

Spanidis, Admiral 24

Stamatelopoulos, D. 21–22, 27, 77, 79, 81, 85, 110

Stans, Maurice 89

Stasinopoulos, M. xii, 14, 65

Steiakakis, Major 22

Stephanopoulos, S. xii, 11–13, 41, 66, 125, 163

Tactical Reserve Police, Cyprus: see Reserve Corps

Talbot, Phillips 23–4, 27–9, 40, 45–6, 63, 71

Tasca, Henry 71, 74, 79–80, 83, 93–4, 105–6, 147, 151, 156, 161, 170, 172

Tetenes, S. 150–51

Theodorakis, M. xii, 24, 35, 37–8, 50, 56, 77–8, 88, 105

Therapos, P. 122, 130, 134–6, 141

Totomis, P. 31

Tsakalotos, General 43

Tsaroukhas, G. 57

Tsatsos, Constantine xii

Tsirimokos, I. xii, 11–12

Tsouderos, Virginia 105

UNFICYP ix, 4–5, 102, 154, 160

United Nations 4, 42, 102, 124, 155, 157–8

Vance, Cyrus 42

Van der Stoel, Max 52, 56, 63, 118

Venizelos, E. 171

Vidalis, Brigadier 25, 30, 43, 47, 66, 95, 106, 121

Vlachos, Angelos 151

Vlachos, Helen xii, 16, 29, 36, 93, 121

Wilson, Harold 52, 69, 113

World Council of Churches 51

Xanthopoulos-Palamas, Ch. xii, 39, 49, 63, 92, 97, 104, 108, 111, 122–4, 143, 150, 164

Yiorgakis, C. 127

Yiorgalas, G. 31, 37, 79, 82

Yiorkatzis, P. 5, 42–3, 53–4, 57, 75–6

Zagorianakos, General 120, 136, 140

Zigdis, I. xii, 76, 93, 119, 128, 139, 147

Zoitakis, G. xii, 16, 18–19, 21–23, 25, 30, 46

Regent 48, 102–3

Zolotas, Xenophon xii, 163

Zumwalt, Admiral 106, 111, 119